PRESCRIPTIVE MODELS OF ORGANIZATIONS

STUDIES IN THE MANAGEMENT SCIENCES

Editor in Chief

MARTIN K. STARR

Volume 5

NORTH-HOLLAND PUBLISHING COMPANY — AMSTERDAM · NEW YORK · OXFORD

PRESCRIPTIVE MODELS OF ORGANIZATIONS

Edited by

PAUL C. NYSTROM

and

WILLIAM H. STARBUCK

1977

NORTH-HOLLAND PUBLISHING COMPANY — AMSTERDAM · NEW YORK · OXFORD

658.4
P 933

© *North-Holland Publishing Company - 1977*

This North-Holland/TIMS series is a continuation of the Professional Series in the Management Sciences, edited by Martin K. Starr

North-Holland ISBN for this volume: 0 7204 05734

Reprinted from TIMS Studies in the Management Sciences, Volume 5

Published by:

NORTH-HOLLAND PUBLISHING COMPANY
AMSTERDAM · NEW YORK · OXFORD

Sole distributors for the U.S.A. and Canada:

ELSEVIER NORTH-HOLLAND, INC.
52 VANDERBILT AVENUE
NEW YORK, NY 10017

Printed in The Netherlands

CONTENTS

North-Holland/TIMS Studies in the Management Sciences 5 (1977) 1—5
© North—Holland Publishing Company

WHY PRESCRIPTION IS PRESCRIBED

PAUL C. NYSTROM and WILLIAM H. STARBUCK

University of Wisconsin, Milwaukee

This special issue prescribes how organizations should be designed. The articles set forth general philosophical orientations toward design processes, specify properties organizations should have, describe tools for diagnosing organizations' defects, and tell how to bring about desired changes within organizations.

The published articles are the best of forty-seven that were submitted in a competition sponsored by TIMS's College on Organization. The College solicited manuscripts by means of notices published in eighteen journals and professional newsletters; then the submitted manuscripts were evaluated by the 118 referees listed just before this article. All of the published articles went through extensive revisions before they were accepted for publication and again afterward. Because the manuscript competition was widely advertised, because manuscripts were submitted and evaluated by well-known researchers and practitioners, and because the published articles were carefully edited and revised, it is likely that this special issue typifies the best that contemporary management scientists can contribute to organizational design. That is, the faults and virtues a reader sees in these articles probably inhere in the methods, ethics, and social structures of today's management science.

This special issue is one of several projects through which TIMS members are striving to reorient the study of organizations. In the fall of 1974, the University of Pittsburgh sponsored a conference on the management of organization design. Ralph Kilmann, Louis Pondy, and Dennis Slevin have assembled the papers from that Pittsburgh conference into a two-volume anthology [7]. *Management Science* has regularly published articles on organizational design, and in May 1975 the journal established a department of interactive behavior and organizational design; under Arie Lewin's leadership, this department is explicitly soliciting manuscripts that prescribe organizational characteristics. Workshops on radical approaches to organizational design were sponsored by the College on Organization at the University of Illinois in 1975 and at Duke University in 1976. Finally, Paul Nystrom and William Starbuck are editing a three-volume *Handbook of Organizational Design* [11] that includes many TIMS members among its 107 authors.

Motives for emphasizing prescription vary from person to person, of course [12]. Most people hope to improve what organizations do and how they do it, by making organizations more efficient, more humane, more rational, more useful to society, more submissive to top managers, more democratic, or whatever. The design criteria span the full range of purposes for which human beings form organizations. However, design criteria make for treacherous ground. Many authors find it difficult to articulate their criteria: although they can readily say what properties an organization should embody, they avoid explaining why certain properties are desirable. Either these authors are unsure what values they hold, or they are embarrassed to state their values overtly. Such obscurities are nurtured by the unrealistic principle that scientists ought not inject personal values into their work [8,9], and the practical consequences are opposite to what scientists are supposed to be trying to achieve. For one thing, covert values violate the principle that scientists ought to communicate honestly and forthrightly. For another thing, statements of the form "An organization should be x" appear to come from opinionated and high-handed sources, whereas statements of the form "In order to achieve y, an organization should be x" do not.

When authors do explicate their design criteria, a reader can commonly observe an author endorsing contradictory criteria at different points in a single article. Such contradictions may arise from a reader's own oversimplification of the design problem: an effective organization incorporates checks and balances to prevent excessive emphasis on any single criterion [5]. But contradictions may also arise because authors have not thought through the logical relations among interdependent design components. Although this is often a deficiency for which the authors are at fault, it is not always such. Because organizations are so complex and embody so many unknown contingencies, there are cases in which the only practical method for discovering logical contradictions is by actually trying to create an organization that matches a design.

Discovery of unseen contradictions is one of several reasons why prescription can facilitate the study of organizations [14, pp. 1101–1103]. Nearly all of the purely descriptive studies confound situations that are logically impossible with situations that happen not to have occurred because they are inefficient, foolish, untraditional, or unthought of. To see what is not possible, an observer must be surprised by unexpected failures and then find out the reasons for failure; and compared to passive observers, the people who try actively to change situations encounter unexpected failures more often and have stronger motives for diagnosing why failures occur.

Prescription can contribute greatly to a science which sees organizations as flexible, adaptive systems. For organizations to fit effectively into their environments, they must move into environments in which their existing reaction patterns will succeed, they must learn appropriate reaction patterns, or they must remodel their environments to accommodate what they can already do [10]. Understanding organizational adaptation depends upon distinguishing among and comprehending the alternative adaptive mechanisms — the previously established reaction patterns, the processes that preserve old reaction patterns and create new ones, and the long-run strategies for discovering or inventing appropriate environments.

Little about adaptation can be learned through naturally occurring events.

Because nearly all naturally occurring events are composed of routine, programmatic reactions by both organizations and their environments, long-run strategies, stabilizing processes, and innovative processes are immersed in the inexplicable noise. Moreover, naturally occurring events allow organizations to intermingle the diverse adaptive mechanisms in uncontrolled, but nonrandom, mixtures that can only be unscrambled by observers who understand the mixtures' origins. New insights about adaptive mechanisms come primarily from observing events which abruptly surprise organizations or which disrupt organizations' usual reaction patterns. As spontaneous occurrences, such events have to be unusual: the ones that happen most frequently generate the least information, and the most informative ones happen least often. But events need not arise spontaneously. They can be engineered, and they can be engineered so as to reveal scientifically useful information while they are yielding immediate benefits [1,2,13].

Of course, the engineering of events requires prediction: successful prescriptive scientists must convince other people that their theories are sufficiently complete and effective to predict rather accurately how their prescriptions will alter the trajectories of future events. Consequently, it appears that greater emphasis on prescription will lead to greater emphasis on predictive accuracy. Emphasis on predictive accuracy will, in turn, underline the costs of using erroneous theories and will multiply the incentives to discriminate better hypotheses from worse ones. Since proposed theories can take into account the known empirical regularities, serious theoretical proposals rarely contradict any important regularities, and all theories postdict almost equally well; the differences between theories do not come into sharp relief until after prediction replaces postdiction.

Organizations also explicate the values of forecasted and realized consequences. This encourages the prescribing scientists to make their own values explicit and to discuss their design criteria forthrightly, and it also fosters the development of more innovative theories. As Gordon and Marquis inferred from their study of medical sociology:

Given a research environment that allows freedom of choice, many scientists choose safe rather than dangerous but original research paths. If the resistances to innovation are not overcome, the effect of facilitating conditions such as freedom obviously is reduced . . . .

We believe that the visibility of research consequences, in addition to aiding in the location of relevant problems, is one of the more important factors in overcoming the resistance to innovation. For instance, in an organizational setting where the owner of an organization or his representative can accurately evaluate the findings of a project in terms of organizational goals, he can encourage the researcher who shows high probability of solving such problems. Also he can reward the researcher in relation to the extent to which the researcher aids in problem solution. As a consequence, the researcher is motivated to seek solutions to difficult but "relevant problems" in preference to less relevant but easier problems. In seeking a solution to the difficult problems the researcher at times must abandon traditional methods and thinking. This would appear to be as true for the academic as for the non-academic researcher. Kuhn, for instance, has observed that "the novel theory seems a direct response to crises."

On the other hand, where it is difficult for an administrator to relate the results of research to the attainment of organizational goals, the difference between the competent and the better solution becomes blurred . . . . As a consequence, the constraint toward seeking the best solution is reduced, and extra impetus to go beyond competent but traditional research methods is lacking [4, pp. 198–199].

Thus, organizational design is another domain in which progress originates in the collisions between cultures. The different social functions performed by managers and management scientists are supported by encouraging the two groups to coalesce into separate subcultures that reinforce their distinctive values, expertise, and artistry. But neither subculture is complete in itself: each focuses on part of reality and misses part, and the two subcultures complement one another. Interactions with managers can help management scientists achieve greater understanding of organizations; and management scientists can help managers design more effective organizations, for organizations are rarely managed in ways that scientific studies imply they should be.

It may well be, however, that science's benefits from interaction with practice will exceed the benefits to practice from interaction with science. Disillusionment is growing over the traditional injunction that one ought to understand problem contexts thoroughly before one tries to solve problems. The disillusionment stems partly from impatience over slow rates of scientific progress; problem contexts change faster than scientists learn to understand them. One outcome is that data often contribute little to prescriptive studies, because data describe how things are, not how they ought to be. Disillusionment also arises from a suspicion that being able to solve problems well depends hardly at all on being able to define problems well.

Organizations and individuals apparently generate solutions to problems by means of processes that act quite independently of the processes that perceive and label problems [3,6,15,16], and this is probably as it should be. Problems are usually misperceived, and even when problems are perceived fairly accurately, their oversimplified characterizations uncouple what is said from what is perceived. Effective solution attempts nearly always combine multiple direct attacks on problems' separable components, and these attempted solutions modify the original problems by producing undesirable as well as desirable effects, some effects being unanticipated ones. So attempted solutions themselves turn into components of the problem contexts, and successful solutions are ultimately invented through iterative sequences of experiments in which progress depends upon observing and reacting to intermediate effects. Yet while experiments are being run, the technological and social environments evolve and create new problems and new potential solutions that render past problems and past solution attempts obsolete.

Thus, the articles in this special issue can be interpreted as proposing experiments for organizations to try. Because organizations running these experiments will obtain effects that no one really predicts in advance, and because undesirable effects can be attacked through supplementary experiments, the benefits from experimenting will depend strongly on whether the actual effects are accurately observed and used as bases for further experiments. An effective organization is not an end state to be achieved, but an evolutionary process to be kept active.

References

[1] Box, George E.P. and Draper, Norman R., Evolutionary Operation, Wiley, New York, N.Y., 1969.

[2] Campbell, Donald T., "Reforms as Experiments," American Psychologist, Vol. 24 (April 1969), pp. 409–429.

[3] Cohen, Michael D., March, James G. and Olsen, Johan P., "A Garbage Can Model of Organizational Choice," Administrative Science Quarterly, Vol. 17 (March 1972), pp. 1–25.

[4] Gordon, Gerald and Marquis, Sue, "Freedom, Visibility of Consequences, and Scientific Innovation," American Journal of Sociology, Vol. 72 (September 1966), pp. 195–202.

[5] Hedberg, Bo L.T., Nystrom, Paul C. and Starbuck, William H., "Camping on Seesaws: Prescriptions for a Self-Designing Organization," Administrative Science Quarterly, Vol. 21 (March 1976), pp. 41–65.

[6] Hewitt, John P. and Hall, Peter M., "Social Problems, Problematic Situations, and Quasi-Theories," American Sociological Review, Vol. 38 (June 1973), pp. 367–374.

[7] Kilmann, Ralph H., Pondy, Louis R. and Slevin, Dennis P., eds., The Management of Organization Design, Vols. I and II, Elsevier North-Holland, New York, N.Y., 1976.

[8] Merton, Robert K., "Behavior Patterns of Scientists," American Scientist, Vol. 57 (Spring 1969), pp. 1–23.

[9] Mitroff, Ian I. and Mason, Richard O., "On Evaluating the Scientific Contribution of the Apollo Moon Missions via Information Theory: A Study of the Scientist-Scientist Relationship," Management Science, Vol. 20 (August 1974), pp. 1501–1513.

[10] Nystrom, Paul C., Hedberg, Bo L.T. and Starbuck, William H., "Interacting Processes as Organization Designs," in The Management of Organization Design, Vol. I: Strategies and Implementation, Ralph H. Kilmann, Louis R. Pondy, and Dennis P. Slevin (eds.), Elsevier North-Holland, New York, N.Y., 1976, pp. 209–230.

[11] Nystrom, Paul C. and Starbuck, William H., eds., Handbook of Organizational Design, Elsevier North-Holland, New York, N.Y., forthcoming.

[12] Starbuck, William H., "The Current State of Organization Theory," in Contemporary Management, Joseph W. McGuire (ed.), Prentice-Hall, Englewood Cliffs, N.J., 1974, pp. 123–139.

[13] Starbuck, William H., "Systems Optimization with Unknown Criteria," Proceedings of the 1974 International Conference on Systems, Man and Cybernetics, Institute of Electrical and Electronics Engineers, New York, N.Y., 1974, pp. 67–76.

[14] Starbuck, William H., "Organizations and Their Environments," in Handbook of Industrial and Organizational Psychology, Marvin D. Dunnette (ed.), Rand McNally, Chicago, Ill., 1976, pp. 1069–1123.

[15] Starbuck, William H. and Hedberg, Bo L.T., "Saving an Organization from a Stagnating Environment," in Strategy + Structure = Performance: The Strategic Planning Imperative, Hans B. Thorelli (ed.), Indiana University Press, Bloomington, Ind., 1977, forthcoming.

[16] Watzlawick, Paul, Weakland, John and Fisch, Richard, Change: Principles of Problem Formation and Problem Resolution, Norton, New York, N.Y., 1974.

North-Holland/TIMS Studies in the Management Sciences 5 (1977) 7–23

MANAGING TURBULENCE *

LES METCALFE and WILL McQUILLAN †

London Graduate School of Business Studies

Guiding large-scale social systems through crises that threaten the integrity and survival of the organizations composing them is the main challenge advanced societies confront. A general approach to managing turbulence is derived from a study of the British National Economic Development Office's involvement with problems arising on large industrial construction sites. This article examines the formation of a group, as an interpersonal model, representing an inter-organizational system and discusses its role in designing a framework of institutions for macro organizational management.

The principal problem of social organization facing advanced societies is guiding large-scale social systems through radical transformations of their objectives and structure [7]. In pluralistic societies, this problem becomes one of redesigning complex networks of formally autonomous, but interdependent, organizations. The need to give more attention to these problems is exemplified by the breakdown of government in New York City, the commercial collapse of Rolls Royce and Lockheed, and the crisis in the British banking system. In these and other cases, organizations have either been unaware of the extent of their dependence on an institutional framework their own decisions were undermining, or have been unable to mobilize sufficient support to effect significant institutional change.

Redesigning pluralistic systems requires extensive, coordinated action, redefining the roles and relationships of the various organizations around a shared definition of the tasks, opportunities and problems facing them. Recent British industrial experience shows that attempting to impose change unilaterally is counterproductive in contexts where many groups have the leverage to frustrate or veto policies

* Received May 1975; revised February 1976, April 1976.

† The research on which this article is based is a comparative study of Economic Development Committees, financed by the Social Science Research Council. We are grateful for the cooperation of the National Economic Development Office, and especially the help of Alan Reddrop, Michael Beales and Tom Schaeffer in connection with the investigation of the Large Industrial Construction Sites Working Party. We wish to acknowledge the assistance of Prithpal Singh, now of the Indian Institute of Technology, New Delhi, in data analysis; we also thank our colleagues at the London Business School, Professor David Chambers and Dr. Dennis Bumstead, the anonymous referees and, finally, Professors Paul Nystrom and William Starbuck for their editorial advice. This is a revised version of a paper presented at the conference on Interorganizational Decision-Making and Public Policy, International Institute of Management, West Berlin, June 1975.

they see as contrary to their interests. In managing structural discontinuity, a delicate balance must be struck between maintaining the impetus for change and being responsive to the fears and anxieties of the groups involved, because the failure of efforts to make systemic changes renders it more difficult to create the climate of mutual trust and tolerance necessary to persuade these groups to give up entrenched positions.

The absence of an overall authority structure to resolve conflicts means that the stability of pluralistic systems depends on the outcome of multilateral bargaining among the leaders of organizations. This method of making collective decisions depends on the capacity and willingness of organizations to participate in working out courses of action that meet the different needs of several groups. Unfortunately, there is no guarantee that the investments in technical expertise and political commitment necessary to sustain a collective decision-making process will be made. Interorganizational networks are, therefore, continually faced with the threat of dispersion and disintegration as organizations pursue their sectional interests [5]. Limits are set on the process of disintegration if most organizations, most of the time, play reasonably clearly defined and widely accepted roles, but when major changes occur, pluralistic systems are poorly equipped to recognize them. Information about what is happening is fragmented; different organizations perceive different things to be important and cannot agree on a mutually acceptable pattern of structural change [22]. Pluralistic systems drift into crises and respond ineffectively to them. When the component organizations belatedly recognize the seriousness of the problems confronting them, they react defensively, seeking to preserve the existing structures of relationships [9].

Organizational interdependence and environmental turbulence

Managing structural discontinuities becomes more difficult and more important as the level of interdependence among sets of organizations increases, transforming the causal texture of the environment from disturbed reactive to turbulent [8]. A disturbed reactive environment is analogous to an oligopolistic market situation. The competitive operations of the component organizations interact to create a precarious, but temporarily predictable, pattern of environmental constraints. As organizational interdependence increases, linking together larger numbers of culturally and functionally diverse organizations, individual units become increasingly vulnerable to the unpredictable interaction of external events. The environmental parameters of organizational behavior change too rapidly for the rational evaluation of alternative courses of action. As the environment becomes turbulent, vicious circles are set up between organizations and their environments; recurrent crises generate uncertainty and conflict which exacerbate misunderstanding and mistrust and lead to the progressive breakdown of interorganizational relations.

Turbulence, in other words, exhibits the structure of the classic problem of public policy, a situation in which what is individually rational is collectively irrational [2]. In turbulent conditions, attempts by individual organizations to adapt are invariably defeated because the consequences of their own actions feed back in unpredictable and contradictory ways. In a disturbed reactive environment it may be rational in the short run for an individual business to buy its way out of temporary difficulties, or for a trade union to press its demands forcefully when its bargaining position is strong. But in turbulent conditions the collective effect of panic reactions and power tactics is to nullify any immediate gains and further undermine the stability of the whole system.

The question arises whether it is possible to manage pluralistic systems of this level of complexity. It has been argued elsewhere that it is possible to do so, but only if processes of macro organizational management are instituted [14]. This term is deliberately used to suggest an analogy with macro economic management. Macro organizational management involves the creation of a framework of institutions to deal with the systemic implications of interorganizational conflicts — problems beyond the capacity of individual organizations. The function of these institutions is to mediate the integrative planning processes needed to steer an otherwise ungovernable system. By coordinating efforts at the system level to redefine the direction and redesign the structure of the organizational network as a whole, they regulate the environment of organizations operating at the micro level and reduce the uncertainty they face to manageable proportions.

It is much easier for a pluralistic society to slide into turbulence than to struggle out of it. However, the purpose of this paper is to analyze just such a process, the creation of macro management capabilities in a turbulent industrial environment. The aim is to abstract from a specific case guidelines for designing the evolution of interorganizational systems facing major structural changes [13,16]. To provide a background for analyzing the process of managing turbulence, the broader research project is outlined.

Research aims and methods

The research project is a comparative study of the behavior and effectiveness of Economic Development Committees in the United Kingdom. Economic Development Committees are organizations set up under the aegis of the National Economic Development Council. The National Economic Development Council, familiarly known as Neddy, is the national forum for consultation on economic matters between government, management and unions. Economic Development Committees, or Little Neddies, are responsible for examining the economic performance of specific industries, identifying obstacles to growth and seeking agreement among the management, trade union and government bodies concerned with their industries on ways of promoting economic development. Both the National Economic Development Council and the Economic Development Committees are aided in their work by the professional staff of the National Economic Development Office, which is publicly financed, but formally independent of the government.

Economic Development Committees provide an unusually favorable setting for studying interorganizational relations. They are established on a voluntary basis by coopting individuals from the leadership of management, unions and government organizations, and are concerned with facilitating tripartite cooperation. Since they are nonexecutive bodies, operating through influence, they depend heavily for their effectiveness on gaining the trust and support of the organizations they serve. They can be characterized as network organizations because they are concerned with integrating the activities of the networks of organizations in which they are located [1].

The research has proceeded in two stages. The first stage was a cross-sectional study of the relations between twenty Economic Development Committees and their organization sets. The second stage, employing measures of organization set structure developed in the cross-sectional study [15], was a more detailed examination of the interorganizational networks in different industries. Its purpose was to assess the effectiveness of Economic Development Committees in contributing to the capacity of industries to steer their own development. Four industries were selected from the twenty already investigated: agriculture, hotels and catering, mechanical engineering, and wool textiles. In addition, a decision was taken to investigate the work of the Large Industrial Construction Sites Working Party, because it was confronting a very difficult set of problems in managing the emergence and institutionalization of a new industry. It is the work of this body that is analyzed below.

A variety of data sources was used in preparing this article. Documentary sources, including background papers, minutes and research reports of the Large Sites Working Party were initially useful, as were observations of a meeting of the Working Party itself and of one of several conferences arranged to inform practitioners, from all sides, of its recommendations. However, the most valuable data were tape-recorded interviews with members of the Working Party and the National Economic Development Office staff.

Large industrial construction

Large industrial construction accounts for about ten percent of fixed capital investment in the United Kingdom. It encompasses the construction of conventional and nuclear power stations, oil refineries, chemical plants, steel works, smelters and, in recent years, oil rigs for drilling operations in the North Sea. At any one time there are about forty to fifty sites of various kinds in operation, each of them representing expenditures of many millions of pounds.

In common with other forms of construction activity, the organization of large industrial construction relies on craft administration [24]. Craft systems are designed to meet situations with marked variations in the combination of activities needed to perform specific tasks. They are appropriate when a high rate of social reconstruction is needed to adapt human resources flexibly to new tasks. As Stinchcombe [25] has argued, craft systems based on contracts for particular tasks, rather than continuous employment contracts, provide a means of minimizing fixed overhead costs, especially administrative costs.

The growth of interdependence

The emergence of turbulence in the large sites context was due to the interaction over time of two groups of factors: the accentuation of certain characteristic features of craft administration systems and a new element, the growing interdependence of organizations in ostensibly different industries.

Large industrial construction primarily serves the power and process industries. Quantitatively, both the number and size of plants have increased over time. In the early fifties, the oil companies began building refineries near markets instead of near sources of supply. The late fifties saw a surge in chemical and petrochemical plant construction, followed in the sixties by steel works and aluminium smelters. North Sea oil rigs are the most recent activities to be added to the large sites system. Throughout the post-war period, the size of plants of each type has increased substantially. Power stations, for example, increased in size more than tenfold in the space of fifteen years. An important consequence of increased plant size was a lengthening of the period of construction activity and, hence, of employment on particular sites. The size of individual plants grew against a background of large fluctuations of activity typical of capital goods industries, accentuated in the British context by government mismanagement of the economy.

Associated with these quantitative increases and fluctuations were important qualitative changes. One, implicit in the discussion above, was the increasing diversity of plants under construction. Another related factor was the increasing technical sophistication of new plants. New technologies in the process industries and in nuclear power plants created difficulties in moving between design and construction. In themselves, increasing size and number of plants, fluctuating workloads and uncertainty arising in the design stage of projects, only indicated differences in the degree of complexity to be managed. What appears to have been crucial in leading to turbulence was the institutional environment in which those changes occurred. As one of the Neddy staff directly concerned with the Large Sites Working Party remarked: "We took soundings among various interests and I think it was here we realized that large sites were a meeting point of many industries, something new in the environment."

The fact that large sites reflected the growing interdependence of several ostensibly different industries had two important implications. The first was organizational heterogeneity, and the second was the lack of institutional machinery at the industry level to focus the common concerns of the various networks of organizations.

First, increasing organizational heterogeneity is considered. The number and variety of client organizations has already been alluded to in describing the increasing technical diversity of the plants themselves. In addition, there were important cultural differences that cut across industry boundaries. Some of the clients, like the Central Electricity Generating Board, were British public sector organizations. Others — for example, Imperial Chemical Industries — were British based, private sector businesses, while still others, like Esso and Shell, were multi-nationals. These organizations brought with them different practices and expectations about the responsibilities of clients and contractors, divergent approaches to site management, and different views about how to handle labor relations.

The contractors in turn varied not only in their technical competence, but also in their approach to site activities. Some were manufacturers, contracting on a supply and erect basis, while others specialized in construction work without having a manufacturing base. In handling labor relations the contractors divided, partly as a matter of policy and partly depending on the attitudes of their clients, between those favoring a national agreement and those favoring site agreements. Institutionally, the former were mostly members of the Engineering Employers Federation and involved in manufacturing as well as construction. The latter were mainly oil and chemical plant contractors without manufacturing interests, who formed the Oil and Chemical Plant Constructors Association. Engineering Employers Federation members favored a low base rate plus incentive bonus schemes, while the others tended to favor measured day work. The Electrical Contractors Association, the Heating and Ventilating Contractors Association, and the Thermal Insulation Contractors Association also had members involved in large sites work. All of the contractors and subcontractor groups were engaged in activities beyond the boundaries of the large sites system, in other sectors of British industry or on an international basis.

On the union side, site labor was distributed among several unions, of which three were especially significant: the Constructional Engineering Union, the Boilermakers, Shipwrights, Blacksmiths and Structural Workers Amalgamated Society, and the Electrical, Electronic, Telecommunications and Plumbing Trade Union. With the exception of the Constructional Engineering Union, most of whose members were involved in large industrial construction, large sites membership only accounted for a minority of the total membership of the unions involved. In addition, there were major differences between the political postures of the unions involved; the Constructional Engineering Union had a General Secretary who was a member of the Communist Party, while the Electrical, Electronic, Telecommunications and Plumbing Trade Union had rules preventing Communists from holding office.

The second implication of the growing interdependence of several otherwise distinct industries was the lack of institutional machinery to focus the problems of the large industrial construction system as a whole. For most of the organizations involved, industrial construction was perceived as a necessary but troublesome peripheral activity, interfering with the effective performance of functions that were of more central concern. Before the Neddy Working Party was set up, there was little recognition of the extent of organizational interdependence. A government committee was set up to inquire into the problems, but it was concerned only with delays in commissioning power stations.

The emergence of turbulence

In a system growing in scale, complexity and heterogeneity, institutional weaknesses reinforced and amplified interorganizational conflicts, with consequent poor performance — escalating costs, long delays in completion and a strike record comparable to the worst in British industry. There was nowhere that clients, contractors and unions could meet and resolve their differences before a new series of problems sparked off more interorganizational conflicts. Because of the enormous national and commercial importance of prompt completion, client organizations became increasingly vulnerable to pressure. They were willing to buy their way out of disputes with their contractors or those between contractors and their labor forces. To cope with periodic surges in demand associated with fluctuations in the general level of economic activity, contractors relied on paying high rates to attract workers from each other as well as from other industries. Since site work is by its nature transient, and sites were sometimes remote, green field operations, this policy had organizational consequences beyond its intended economic effect. It encouraged an instrumental orientation to work [11] (but see also [6]), detaching site workers from a stable web of group affiliations and reducing their commitment to particular jobs and employers. By generating inconsistencies and contradictions on top of officially negotiated differentials, it created opportunities for *ad hoc* bargaining among work groups on the same site employed by different contractors, as well as bargaining based on unregulated comparisons among sites.

Under the stress of a disintegrating situation, contractors defined their obligations narrowly and rejected demands to take on wider responsibilities for cooperating in dealing with problems general to all contractors on a particular site. The feedback effect of these actions destroyed the basis for interorganizational coordination on sites, broke down the boundaries between operations on different sites, and progressively undermined the stability of the whole system. Policy differences among clients, contractors and unions hardened into ideologies and stereotypes, further obstructing the process of conflict resolution. The turbulence in the system was so severe that at one point the Central Electricity Generating Board was forced to discontinue work on one power station for a time. Other client companies with more flexibility could withdraw from the British scene and build plants elsewhere. It was against this background of conflict, disorder and poor performance that the Neddy Working Party was set up.

Large Sites Working Party recommendations

It is helpful to preface the analysis of the Working Party's contribution to managing turbulence by summarizing its terms of reference and recommendations. The terms of reference of the Working Party, which first met in July 1968, were:

To enquire into the problems of organization of large industrial construction sites with particular attention to labour relations, to investigate their causes and their effects on the cost of commissioning and operating plants, and to make recommendations [17].

The Working Party made recommendations under five main headings: (1) Management by Client and Contractor. This covered topics such as the forms of contracts clients might employ and the design of relationships among contractors, the assignment of responsibility for plant research and design, provision of site services and overall project management. (2) Training. This included craft training and management training directly related to large sites work. (3) Programming. The report discussed the utility of various management techniques for the control of individual projects. (4) Industrial Relations problems gave rise to a very extensive set of recommendations, ranging from the details of incentive schemes to the institutional requirements for administering a national agreement on pay and conditions across the whole of the Large Sites system. (5) Finally, the Working Party made recommendations for setting up institutions and implementing its findings.

Planning as an integrative bargaining process

The central problem of macro organizational management is creating a framework of institutions capable of coping with potentially destructive interorganizational conflict. The effectiveness of a macro management process depends on the existence at the system level of a network of representative organizations capable of reflecting and responding to the demands of their constituents and mobilizing their support for a coordinated attack on common problems. The measure of their effectiveness is their ability to carry their members with them in integrative, cooperative bargaining processes as well as distributive, competitive bargaining [26].

The need for macro intervention to promote integrative bargaining arises because turbulence creates managerial dilemmas analogous to those confronting the participants in prisoners' dilemma games. While problems appear to present individual organizations within win/lose choices, the interaction of low trust and competitive strategies actually has the effect of reducing the payoffs to all participants. Moreover, none of them gains by unilaterally trusting the others. Integrative bargaining addressed to the problem of increasing the outputs of the system as a whole requires a degree of mutual trust among leaders and collective commitment to cooperative strategies that is hard to establish in industrial and other situations where success is culturally defined in competitive terms.

The heart of the contribution the Large Sites Working Party made to managing turbulence was promoting an understanding of the need to redesign the inter-industry rules of the game and facilitate the development of integrative bargaining around issues affecting the long-term viability of the whole system. The unifying theme of its work was the search for an industry identity.

It is helpful to discuss the Working Party's activities and their general implications for the role of network organizations like the National Economic Development Office as a three-phased sequence: the referral process, the problem-solving process and the implementation process.

The referral process: gaining access to problems

Macro organizational management requires professional inputs by an independent agency all the participants can trust to facilitate the process of interorganizational learning. Even if such agencies exist, whether they gain access to problems depends on the structure of the referral process linking them to social systems where their skills can be applied [10]. Economic Development Committees, made up of individuals from management, trade unions and government, create a referral process for industrial problems requiring concerted action.

The referral of Large Sites problems to Neddy was complicated because they overlapped the interests of several Committees. They were first discussed in the Electrical Engineering Committee as labor problems contributing to delays in bringing new generating plants into commission. Subsequently, related problems were discussed in the Building, Civil Engineering and Chemical Little Neddies. None of them was prepared to accept Large Sites as their responsibility. Nevertheless, senior Neddy staff recognized that action was needed to deal with major problems cutting across the boundaries of several industries and absorbing a disproportionate amount of time and attention of a wide range of industry and government institutions. Preliminary discussions were conducted with representatives of contracting firms, employers associations, trade unions, consultants and client organizations.

The problem-solving process

The original intention of the Neddy staff involved in setting up the Large Sites Working Party was to assemble a small, specialized group of about eight people drawn from different elements in the Large Sites system. Their aim was to work quickly and produce an intellectually coherent set of recommendations in a short space of time. However, this proved impossible because of the many pressures for representation from interested parties when the formation of the Working Party was announced. The requests were acceded to, and the membership finally reached thirty-two.

Although a group of this size was not planned, and managing its work created problems for the Neddy staff, its structure and functioning are of wide potential relevance. Both the method of arriving at recommendations and the type of proposals made warrant attention. They reveal a good deal about the daunting complexity of the problems involved in managing turbulence and the time scale involved.

The Working Party as a model of the Large Sites system

A formal statement of the general relevance of the Working Party's composition and activities is contained in Conant and Ashby's [4] proposition that every good regulator of a system must be a model of that system (see also Starbuck [23, especially p. 481]). The first step towards effective regulation of a system, therefore, is to build a model of it.

In its final form, the Working Party could be regarded as a model of the Large Sites system. The enlarged membership formed an interpersonal network of relations that mapped in the structure of the interorganizational network. By creating a microcosm that modelled the large-scale political forces, it provided a mechanism for exploring the interconnections among problems and collectively thinking through ways of dealing with them. This innovation was carried farther in managing the Working Party's meetings. The Neddy staff, in conjunction with the independent chairman, sought to structure the face-to-face committee discussions by maintaining a wide range of relationships with members and relevant organizations outside the committee itself, and preparing papers based on their discussions. A member of the Neddy staff gave this description of the process:

There were the most laborious discussions with people as to the issues within the issues and also to see if there was a consensus about what was the way out, what was the appropriate remedy. The papers presented were not only an exposition of the issues, but what we thought was a feasible, practical and acceptable solution based on our discussions. We never put something to them cold, the answer had to emerge from the laborious and lengthy task of talking to people. The papers and meetings were twenty percent and the discussions eighty percent of the work. The formal meetings were the tip of the iceberg.

Several beneficial outcomes of enlarging the membership of the committee and using what was essentially a group feedback analysis technique [12] to manage its deliberations emerged from interviews conducted with members. The Working Party enabled representatives of all the groups involved to meet together and communicate with each other in a way that had never previously happened. Detailed analyses of complex problems over an extended period of time in a face-to-face situation helped to break down crude stereotypes and build interpersonal contacts. As members worked together, they gained respect for each other's competence, felt less need to challenge the legitimacy of each other's claims, and understood better the problems of other organizations in the system.

By producing working papers based on extensive prior discussion, the Neddy staff were able to present contentious issues as general problems to be solved without putting particular individuals in adversary relationships. This was an invaluable contribution because there were, for example, major sources of dissatisfaction among contractors with the way some clients failed to provide for adequate management of their sites. But, in the main, contractors dependent on a limited range of clients for future work were unwilling to expose the problems themselves for fear of the consequences.

The close contact the staff maintained with organizations outside had other important benefits, providing tests of the relevance and political feasibility of proposals emerging from the Working Party. By maintaining an understanding outside of the general directions its recommendations were taking, it stimulated the emergence of processes within and among organizations on which implementation depended. As several members observed, it was not just the final report that mattered, the integrative process among individuals and among organizations initiated in producing it was just as important. Nevertheless, the nature of the recommendations warrants attention from those concerned with developmental problems in many areas of public policy besides the economic sphere.

Designing interorganizational networks

The individuals and organizations for which the Working Party formed the only common focus brought to its deliberations very different policies, attitudes and beliefs, based on differences in culture, history and direct experience of the Large Sites system. The problem the Neddy staff faced was developing a frame of reference all the organizations would share, enabling them to recognize the areas in which coordination of their activities was needed. The problem raised strategic questions about the appropriate structure of the system itself and how to manage conflicts within it.

The different views expressed can be formulated theoretically as the question whether the Large Sites environment was disturbed reactive or turbulent. The design implications of the first view were that the system would be adequately regulated by competitive bargaining processes if there were improvements in project management at the site level. In this perspective, all problems were frictional, issue conflicts, rather than structural conflicts [18,20]. The alternative view, giving more weight to the heterogeneity and mutual dependence of the various networks of organizations involved, led to the conclusion that there were structural conflicts that had to be resolved at the system level and could not be decomposed into site-level issues.

The Working Party confronted this problem, and after extended and heated debates, the latter view prevailed. In synthesizing an overall design for the nascent Large Sites industry, the proposals it made incorporated guidelines for joint regulation of the system as a whole by bodies representative of clients, contractors and unions, as well as for site management.

From the previous discussion, it may seem obvious that the organizations involved could be divided into three organizational status sets [3]: clients, contractors, and unions, each heterogeneous but composed of recognizably similar institutions facing the same kinds of problems. In fact, it was difficult to overcome the effects of years of lack of contact and divisive conflict and persuade client organizations such as the Central Electricity Generating Board, Imperial Chemical Industries, Alcan, and Esso, of their common predicament. Much the same applied to contractors, who were bitterly divided over policies towards clients and labor relations. Unions, too, were concerned only with the separate interests of their own members. Without gradual acceptance of this broad, tripartite frame of reference, it would have been difficult to unfreeze defensive attachments to the *status quo* and initiate an interorganizational learning process.

While the terms of reference of the Working Party followed conventional wisdom in picking out labor trouble on sites as the main source of problems, investigations soon revealed that these were only part of a tightly interconnected complex of problems — a mutual causal process amplifying delays, conflicts and cost inflation. Confusion was compounded by the absence of any systematic data against which to test the validity of widely held, but superficial, interpretations of the situation. To produce a more thorough diagnosis, three subcommittees with overlapping memberships were set up, one to examine the problems of management by client and contractor, one to concern itself with industrial relations, and a third to provide the necessary statistical base.

Creating process designs

The three subcommittees did not produce a formula or blueprint setting out in precise detail the policies each organization should follow. The voluntary nature of the implementation process would have precluded this, even if the diversity of site situations and client needs had not. Instead, the recommendations may be seen as a pragmatic attempt to conceptualize the roles and model the integrative institutions required at site and industry levels to enable the system as a whole to function in a more intelligible and controllable manner. In effect, their purpose was to set the rules for subsequent negotiations, not to prejudge their outcomes.

The subcommittee on management by client and contractor produced recommendations that emphasized the importance of clients' contributions to site management in an environment in which many contractors and subcontractors had to work together, some bringing their own labor force, some hiring and firing as their needs changed. This emphasis implied major changes in the roles of several clients. For example, it was apparent that the managerial responsibilities of public sector clients went beyond meeting public accountability requirements. Indeed, it became clear that ritualistically meeting public accountability requirements by insisting on contractors' bidding competitively for fixed-price contracts was shortsighted. Any delay or dispute could trigger off a series of claims for a contract revision once work had begun.

The Working Party indicated the range of choices among contracts available to clients, and the interdependence between the form of contract selected and the assignment of roles in the functions necessary in site operations. It did not provide a specific structural prescription for site management. Instead, it provided a description of the design process clients and contractors should use to develop a specific structural prescription for a given site.

An emphasis on procedural rather than substantive recommendations also characterized the Working Party's approach to problems of interdependence among sites. The industrial relations subcommittee, in particular, was concerned with designing a framework of integrative institutions for regulating relations among clients, contractors and unions on an industry-wide basis. The process of recognizing the need for such institutions bit deeply into the personal and political beliefs of the members. It is not difficult to see why this should be so. Haphazard local bargaining had undermined national agreements which, in any case, were numerous, inconsistent, and drawn up without the special needs of the Large Sites system in mind. Discrepancies in pay and conditions of employment abounded and were a potent source of grievances. The willingness of some clients to permit or even encourage contractors to keep to deadlines by buying out trouble, together with the extent of casual employment, created the opportunities and the incentives to disregard whatever agreements might previously have been made. Changes in wage rates and other conditions on one site produced chain reactions accentuating basic and widespread conflicts, and destroyed the basis of agreements reached elsewhere.

While identifying the major areas for negotiation and indicating how site and industry levels of decision making should interact, the Working Party's main concern was setting in motion the process of giving institutional expression to the industry identity of the Large Sites system. Achieving this outcome depended on both the employers' associations and the unions unifying their policies, negotiating a comprehensive national agreement embodying scope for site agreements, and establishing general industry-wide standards, including trade union recognition, site amenities, lodging and travel allowances, and grievance procedures. It also called for closer contact among clients, building on the informal regional clients' clubs that had emerged in response to growing problems.

These proposals were hotly debated in the Working Party. It was argued that if sites were well managed there would be no need for any wider policy-making mechanisms. Market forces would adequately handle the problems of coordination and resource allocation among sites. This thesis was rejected, although it corresponded with the received wisdom of the report of the Donovan Commision on Industrial Relations [21] that plant bargaining should replace industry-wide bargaining because of the transfer of industrial power to the grass roots. Participation in the Working Party had made individuals, inside and outside, acutely aware of their rapidly growing but previously unrecognized interdependence. They saw that decentralized site negotiations were self-defeating in a situation where the problem to be solved was how to prevent collision and destructive conflicts among several increasingly interlocked networks of organizations. Effective coordination and resource allocation at the micro level depended on action at the macro level to manage the environment.

The implementation process

Implementation is frequently the Achilles' heel of efforts at planned social change. Initial enthusiasm often fails to survive the long drawn-out process of gaining acceptance for a complex program, even in favorable circumstances [19]. The Large Sites Working Party recognized that implementing their recommendations depended on the voluntary compliance of many different organizations with a history of mutual antagonism and conflict behind them.

In part, the difficulties were anticipated, and the implementation process was initiated well before the Working Party reported. Its composition and methods of working were designed to ensure that intra- and interorganizational learning processes were interwoven with the problem-solving process itself. By creating and expanding the network of communications and feedback loops linking the Working Party into the industry, the gradually emerging, shared frame of reference was disseminated.

Recognizing that this was no more than a beginning, the Working Party recommended that a Steering Committee of representatives of the various interests in the industry be established to follow up its work. It is important to note the difference in status of members of the Steering Committee compared to members of the Working Party. One of the conditions underlying the formation of the Working Party was that members were not representatives committing their organizations to its recommendations. The Steering Committee, on the other hand, was established to provide a continuing stimulus inside the industry to secure the adoption of recommendations. Broadly, it was concerned with the two interrelated implementation processes: reorientation of the policies and roles of existing organizations, and institution building — creating the interorganizational relations needed to steer the development of the industry as a whole.

Changes in policy at site level depended on clients reorienting their approaches and adopting more systematically thought-out contractual arrangements and management policies as new sites were opened up. The Central Electricity Generating Board has modified its approach to site management very significantly. On two new power station sites it has assigned overall responsibility for site management to a small number of main contractors, four in one case and five in the other. In the past, it has let contracts to as many as eighty or ninety direct contractors, ostensibly in the interests of ensuring their accountability.

At the industry level, there has also been progress. The strategy adopted by the Steering Committee was first to build up relationships within the groups of clients, contractors and unions, before moving on to the more difficult problems of setting a framework for future negotiations. A capital projects clients' group was set up as a means of assessing the future demands of clients on the Large Sites system and educating new clients in the design options and management problems confronting them. It was also concerned to ensure that the Engineering Industry Training Board provided management and craft training tailored to the needs of large industrial construction.

The Steering Committee also put considerable effort into promoting closer unity among the trade unions and employers' associations. Achieving unity was more difficult on the employers' side than on the unions' side. The unions, conscious of the advantages of improved recognition to them and greater stability of employment for their members as a result of an industry-wide agreement, formed a National Engineering Construction Committee which pursued an agreed policy.

The differences between the two main contractors' organizations, the Engineering Employers' Federation and the Oil and Chemical Plant Constructors' Association, were more marked and more difficult to deal with. Reducing the disparities between these groups has been a slow process because policy differences were marked, and the respective memberships were sensitive to the implications of changes for their relations with clients and unions as well as with each other. At the time of writing (January 1976), contractors and unions were preparing to negotiate the first national agreement on wages and conditions for large industrial construction. A National Joint Council to deal with training, status grading, recognition of shop stewards, and the establishment of grievance procedures as well as wage negotiations has not yet been established.

The time scale for implementing this program of institution building was about five years, and the whole process from the formation of the Working Party took about eight years. In 1974, an Economic Development Committee for Electrical and Mechanical Construction was established, symbolizing the formation of a new industry. It is building on the Working Party's activities by involving individuals from all sectors of the industry in identifying emerging problems and carrying out investigations such as international comparisons of productivity.

Conclusions

Guiding large-scale social systems through crises that threaten their integrity and the survival of the organizations composing them presents challenges that neither conventional market processes nor traditional instruments of public policy are adequate to meet. In turbulent conditions, past experience and immediate pressures prompt organizations to select strategies that individually appear rational, but are collectively irrational. Managing turbulence requires institutions and processes that go beyond the micro-level problem of redefining the strategies of individual organizations to the macro-level problems of redesigning the rules guiding the interaction of sets of organizations.

This article has drawn from a specific case the elements of an approach to managing turbulence. Beginning with the proposition that every good regulator of a system must be a model of that system, it was shown that the National Economic Development Office brought together individuals drawn from all sectors of the large industrial construction system to form the Large Industrial Construction Sites Working Party. As a network of interpersonal relations modelling the larger-scale network of interorganizational relations, the Working Party provided a means of simulating conflicts, diagnosing problems and testing the feasibility of proposed solutions.

In all phases of the Working Party's activities, the National Economic Development Office as a network organization, made a crucial contribution. Initially, it provided a common focus for referral of a series of apparently unrelated problems. Subsequently, it provided the context and the staff support for a systematic analysis that revealed the interrelatedness of these problems. The staff also developed a communications network providing feedback between the Working Party and relevant organizations, preparing the way for implementation.

The recommendations emerging from the integrative planning process the Working Party initiated did not take the form of a blueprint to be applied in all circumstances. Instead, they described the problems to be solved and prescribed a process for dealing with them: designing mutually consistent sets of organizational roles at site level and a pattern of interorganizational relations to monitor and guide the evolution of the system as a whole.

Producing a process design created the context for subsequent bargaining without threatening the autonomy of the participants to the bargaining process. The general importance of this approach is that it indicates a framework within which issues bearing on the performance and development of large-scale social systems can be identified and resolved. It shows how an interorganizational learning process can be created to manage turbulence in pluralistic systems.

References

[1] Berry, Dean F., Metcalfe, Les and McQuillan, Will, "Neddy: An Organizational Metamorphosis," Journal of Management Studies, Vol. 11 (February 1974), pp. 1–20.

[2] Buckley, W., Burns, T. and Meeker, L.D., "Structural Resolutions of Collective Action Problems," Behavioral Science, Vol. 19 (September 1974), pp. 277–297.

[3] Caplow, Theodore, Principles of Organization, Harcourt, Brace and World, New York, N. Y., 1964.

[4] Conant, Roger C. and Ashby, Ross W., "Every Good Regulator of a System must be a Model of that System," International Journal of Systems Science, Vol. 1, No. 2 (1970), pp. 87–97.

[5] Dahl, Robert A., "The Politics of Planning," International Social Science Journal, Vol. 11, No. 3 (1959), pp. 340–350.

[6] Daniel, W.W., "Industrial Behaviour and Orientation to Work – A Critique," Journal of Management Studies, Vol. 6 (October 1969), pp. 366–375.

[7] Dunn, Edgar S. Jr., Economic and Social Development, Hopkins Press, Baltimore, Md. and London, England, 1971.

[8] Emery, F.E. and Trist, E.L., "The Causal Texture of Organizational Environments," Human Relations, Vol. 18 (February 1965), pp. 21–32.

[9] Etzioni, Amitai, The Active Society, Free Press, New York, N.Y., 1968.

[10] Friedson, Eliot, "Client Control and Medical Practice," American Journal of Sociology, Vol. 65 (January 1960), pp. 374–382.

[11] Goldthorpe, John H., "Attitudes and Behaviour of Car Assembly Workers: A Deviant Case and a Theoretical Critique," British Journal of Sociology, Vol. 17 (September 1966), pp. 227–242.

[12] Heller, Frank A., "Group Feedback Analysis: A Method of Field Research," Psychological Bulletin, Vol. 72 (August 1969), pp. 108–117.

[13] Jantsch, Erich, Design for Evolution, George Braziller, New York, N.Y., 1975.

[14] Metcalfe, J.L., "Systems Models, Economic Models and the Causal Texture of Organizational Environments: An Approach to Macro Organization Theory," Human Relations, Vol. 27 (September 1974), pp. 639–663.

[15] Metcalfe, J.L., McQuillan W. and Hutchinson, P., "Environmental Selection and Organizational Strategies," Working paper, London Graduate School of Business Studies, London, England (April 1976).

[16] Mitroff, Ian I., "Who Looks at the Whole System?" in Decision-Making Creativity, Judgment, and Systems, Henry S. Brinkers (ed.), Ohio State University Press, Columbus, Ohio, 1972.

[17] National Economic Development Office, Large Industrial Sites: Report of the Working Party on Large Industrial Construction Sites, Her Majesty's Stationery Office, London, England, 1970.

[18] Pondy, Louis R., "Varieties of Organizational Conflict," Administrative Science Quarterly, Vol. 14 (December 1969), pp. 499–505.

[19] Pressman, J.L. and Wildavsky, A., Implementation, University of California Press, Berkeley, Ca., 1972.

[20] Rapoport, Anatole, Conflict in Man Made Environments, Penguin Books, London, England, 1974.

[21] Royal Commission on Trade Unions and Employers' Associations, 1965-68 Report, (Chairman, Rt. Hon. Lord Donovan), H.M.S.O., London, England (Cmnd. 3623), 1968.

[22] Scharpf, Fritz W., The Probability of Disagreement in Multi-Level Decisions, International Institute of Management, Berlin, Germany (paper presented at the International Institute of Management Conference on Interorganizational Decision-Making and Public Policy, 1975).

[23] Starbuck, William H., "Organizational Growth and Development," in Handbook of Organizations, James G. March (ed.), Rand McNally, Chicago, Ill., 1965.

[24] Stinchcombe, Arthur L., "Bureaucratic and Craft Administration of Production: A Comparative Study," Administrative Science Quarterly, Vol. 4 (September 1959), pp. 168–187.

[25] Stinchcombe, Arthur L., Constructing Social Theories, Harcourt, Brace and World, New York, N.Y., 1968.

[26] Walton, Richard E. and McKersie, Robert B., A Behavioral Theory of Labour Negotiations – An Analysis of a Social Interaction System, McGraw-Hill, New York, N.Y., 1965.

North-Holland/TIMS Studies in the Management Sciences 5 (1977) 25–42
© North-Holland Publishing Company

DESIGNING THE CAPITAL BUDGETING PROCESS *

E. EUGENE CARTER

University of Illinois, Chicago Circle

This paper discusses various issues involved in capital budgeting and the organization of that function within a firm. It is based in part on the findings from a laboratory experiment with individual managers and groups of managers who used an interactive capital budgeting system to help select a portfolio of projects for a firm. The selection of goals, the trade-offs between various goals, the attitudes toward risk, and the use of the interactive system are discussed. Attitudes toward various financial criteria and the departmental identification of managers as it influenced their capital budgeting project selection are reported. The implications of these investment decision-making research findings for organizational structure are stated throughout the paper. The conclusion stresses the interdependence of interactive computer/information systems, of capital budgeting theory, and of organizational design as it relates to the firm's budgeting process.

Studies of managerial decision making usually focus upon one of three approaches. Some studies examine the behavior of individual managers, both descriptively and normatively. Because managers have limited information and positive costs of search, the conclusions in these studies include the effect of bounded rationality, the replacement of general inoperable goals with specific operable ones, the use of multiple attributes as a response to an uncertain environment, a concern with firm risk, and the departmental identification of managers [1,13,16,30,32,35,49,51].

Other studies focus upon product pricing and stress that the behavior of managers reflects the particular activity and values of these corporate managers [2,3,9,14,21, 25,28,38,47,50,53]. These studies conclude that managers generally do not have profit maximization as a single goal, that management knowledge of cost and revenue functions is not an adequate basis from which to maximize profits, and that the interactions between departments required in the firm limit managers' abilities to concentrate on a single goal even if they desire it. Often, managers price goods in order to realize both a targeted return on investment and market share, or in order to prevent competition. Thus, while these rough heuristic rules may operate to maximize long-run profits, in the short run these rules often contradict achievement of short-run profits.

A third group of studies looks at the organizational relationships of members

* Received April 1975; revised January 1976, May 1976.

and suggests that short-term tenure in a given assignment and the project approval process within the organization often mean that capital budgets and prices are evaluated on the basis of seemingly noneconomic criteria [6,14,31,36,46,55,57]. Increased information from modern data processing systems, group versus individual decisions regarding risk evaluation, and the control process affect the risk evaluation forecasts and the decision process of projects. Cyert and March [15] use the concepts of quasi-resolution of conflict, uncertainty avoidance, problemistic search, and organizational adaptation as major explanatory variables for their behavioral theory of the firm. Carter [7] notes the impact on capital budgeting and strategy decisions of multiple organizational levels, bilateral bargaining between a project sponsor and a manager, the impact of technology, and ex-post uncertainty resolution by the Pollyanna-Nietzsche effect (in which either a rose-colored-glasses view of the world or a commitment to a positive thinking will-to-power mode of operation absorb uncertainty surrounding a project once it is accepted). Finally, Cohen et al. [12] see organizations such as universities as organized anarchies having problemistic reference to the given situation, unclear technologies and fluid participation.

These studies and others reveal that management pursues a variety of goals in the capital budgeting process. Some goals may be operational surrogates for long-run profit maximization. In addition, managers worry about major interdependencies among projects and about corporate risk, however defined.

Concurrent with these studies is an improved analysis of the capital budgeting problem. An improved theoretical basis for capital budgeting, the successful introduction of various analytical techniques in business, the development of management science models in the last twenty-five years and their successful implementation in some corporations, and the deepening of the analytical framework for the broader field of corporate strategy serve to highlight the need for knowledge about the values of managers and for consideration of organizational design changes implied by those values [5,11,20,22–24,26,27,39,44,45].

The organization's capital budgeting process has changed because of the advent of computer systems. Although these large systems usually are described more broadly as part of an information system, the heart of the capital budgeting models described above is a large computer system. Generally, writers surveyed by Whisler [56] agree that middle managers' roles will be circumscribed as the computer comes to usurp these managers in many tasks, and that top managers will have more time for goal setting and for systems design. Although some writers acknowledge that computers can promote decentralization by making information available to middle and lower managers, most writers predict that centralization will occur, in part because they assume centralized locations for computers, and they do not anticipate the expansion of time-sharing systems offering remote access. Whisler believes managers have four roles: computation, communication, goal setting, and pattern perception. While computers can aid in the latter two areas, they can dominate in computation and have strong influence in communication.

Simon [49] observes that computer systems make the decisions no longer exclusively human events but man-machine interactions. As he also observes, the scarcity in today's environment is not information but capacity to process information. The problem of decentralization for efficiency of communications versus centralization to minimize uneconomic externalities, a conflict noted many years ago, is central to his evaluation of computer systems as they affect managers.

All organizations possess information systems in some form and always have. Control of information can be a powerful organizational weapon [40]. However, the studies noted above do not directly discuss the impact time-shared computer systems have on managers' capital budgeting process, normatively or descriptively. The availability of structured information regarding cost and revenues, together with the increased analytical power provided by a time-shared system, can alter the capital budgeting process. Interaction between levels of managers should be increased because of the possibility of rapid re-evaluation of controversial results. Such immediate reanalysis was not possible prior to the time-shared system, rendering a controversial quantitative analysis as well as the basic technique (e.g., risk analysis simulation) irrelevant in many decisions. The study in [8, Chapter 3] linked and evaluated the concepts and conclusions affirmed in many of the above research reports with the interactive capital budgeting process now available to corporate managers. The study also includes conclusions on the implications of those concepts and the interactive capital budgeting process for organizational design.

To learn more about the decision process for project selection and the values pursued by managers in a management setting, an interactive simulation program was used with individuals and with groups of managers. They confronted a capital budgeting situation, and their judgments on the desirability of various projects were obtained by questionnaires. The remainder of this paper is concerned with their decisions and the implications of those decisions for organizational design. This exploration of the means by which managers reach decisions about a capital budgeting portfolio is structured in the form of various hypotheses based on previous financial and behavioral science research. Throughout this paper, a major premise is that the organization should be designed to produce a final assortment of approved capital budgeting projects (the portfolio) which meets top managers' standards.

A laboratory setting with managers allows a controlled environment. Common simulated events appear in a consistent order and time framework to the managers, the responses are recorded, and so forth. The artificiality of the techniques may be offset in this particular research project by the nature of the individuals involved; all were practicing managers with a minimum of eight years' experience.

The decision environment

The information about the situation was given to the managers in two separate packages. Package A consisted of brief outlines of 20 projects. For each project the expected value and standard deviation were provided on ten criteria: the net present value and the yearly mean for each of the next three years of cash flow, earnings per share, and sales. Each project's mean rate of return and profitability index (the ratio of the present value of inflows to outflows) were given; the managers also saw the expected cost and standard deviation of the projects.

The company was a diversified manufacturer of specialized machines for various industries. The managers knew the firm's previous years' cash flows, depreciation charges and capital outlays, and had full income statements and balance sheets for the preceding three years. Managers unfamiliar with simulation read a brief description of it. Chamberlain [9, Chapter 6] reviews the background factors to this experiment in detail.

Package B briefly described portfolio theory and presented the correlation coefficient matrix for all of the projects on each of the ten criteria. In conjunction with Package B, a computer program was made available which allowed managers to observe the effects of hypothetical decisions. For any portfolio, the program could compute the expected value and the standard deviation on any of the ten criteria the managers desired. Each manager was asked to state the standard or goals for selecting a portfolio and to select an initial portfolio from among the projects. Unfeasible project combinations (e.g., one of two new products might be launched, but not both) were excluded and current operations had to continue as explained in the packages and as built into the program.

In using this program, managers could use a number of filtering options. They could determine portfolio data for the group of projects. Confidence levels assuming normality were printed for various intervals if requested. A proposed portfolio could be compared with the current operation; for example, the managers could estimate the probability that earnings per share in the second year would be no less under a proposed portfolio. The consequences for the means and standard deviations of adding or deleting a project were given. Mean search routines permitted managers to seek altered values from the expected outcome of the portfolio for any criterion. When using this option, managers indicated the criterion and the number of proposals desired. The program printed the projects which would have the greatest effect in increasing or decreasing the expected value under consideration. Variance search routines returned a list of those projects in and/or out of the current portfolio which would most increase or decrease the variance in expected performance of a criterion.

Evaluation of data

The managers' responses to questionnaires after exposure to A and B packages were divided into goals, constraints, and risk considerations. Goals are identified as the major factors relating to which there was an implied or stated optimization process. There could be more than one major goal. A constraint involves a situation in which the objective is to meet a minimal level of achievement, such as a reasonable growth in sales. Beyond that level, the criterion is not of particular importance. Risk is considered important if a manager (1) specifically noted detailed standard deviation considerations in the questionnaire, (2) mentioned risk or a synonym in a response, or (3) stressed diversification, in some form, when describing the portfolio. In these experiments with a single-level decision and in the discussion that follows, note that the use of these terms is specifically restricted to these definitions even though goals or a concern with risk at one level of management are often translated into constraints for lower levels of management [50].

Professional background and project selection

Dearborn and Simon [16] and others present evidence that identification with a particular area of business specialization is a factor influencing the manner in which

Table 1
Proportions of respondents selecting each goal or project by professional background

	Finance	Marketing	Production	General management	Total
	(N = 20)	(N = 12)	(N = 22)	(N = 48)	(N = 102)
Goals					
Rate of return	0.55 *	0.25 *	0.46	0.31 *	0.38
Sales	0.20	0.17	0.23	0.21	0.21
Earnings per share	0.85	1.00	0.91	0.94	0.92
Cash flow	0.15	0.17	0.14	0.13	0.14
Other	0.10	—	0.09	0.02	0.05

Results are significantly different at the 10% (*) level. These results and those described in later tables were evaluated by a one- or two-tailed Chi-square test (as appropriate) with one degree of freedom in a 2 × 2 contingency table adjusted for continuity. For both large samples and interval groupings, this procedure is equivalent to the use of the Z (normal deviate) distribution. Both the Chi-square and the Z tests are approximations. Exact tests for samples of small size yield different results ([19], paragraph 21.02). Tables used for a small A or B sample (less than 20) or an A or B sample between 20 and 40 observations where the smallest absolute observation was less than five are from Finney et al. [18], following the procedure of Snedecor and Cochran [52].

N indicates the number of participants in each category.

people view a business problem. One might hypothesize that finance managers have a higher interest than other groups in rate of return and earnings per share. One also might hypothesize that marketing managers have a greater interest in sales than other managers because of their identification with sales as a goal, as opposed to earnings, rate of return, or cash flow.

Table 1 presents statistics relevant to these hypotheses. For all categories of managers, earnings per share (0.92) is dominant with some concern for rate of return (0.38). In terms of goals, sales and cash flow were rarely considered. Finance managers place more emphasis on rate of return, as hypothesized. This emphasis is significantly higher at the 10% level than the degree of concern by both marketing and general managers. Marketing managers place lower emphasis on rate of return compared to the other groups, but do not differ significantly from the others in their appraisal of the importance of sales as a goal.

Constraints on project selection

Nearly one-third of the managers place a constraint on cash flow in both the A and B trials. This constraint is typically expressed as part of their goal statement; e.g., maximize earnings per share subject to a minimum of X $ in second and third year cash flow or with a 90% confidence level for a positive cash flow in the third year. The rate of return constraint (more than 20% incidence in both trials) is often expressed as a return no less than the firm's cost of capital, although this requirement was typically ignored in the case of a particular project when the project was especially outstanding on some goal. The low incidence of earnings per share as a constraint coincides with the frequent selection of this factor as a goal; the typical goal is maximum earnings per share with no regard for any minimum level of earnings.

Number of goals in project selection

Given the availability of the computer and data which permit evaluation on many more criteria, one might expect that more goals will be considered. Alternatively, one might hypothesize that managers have multiple goals because of little confidence in the information available; multiple goals are a means of eliminating imprecision. By this hypothesis, a device to handle the important information results in fewer goals being mentioned, for managers now may focus on the goals of real importance. For example, see the Cyert and March [15] concept of quasi-resolution of conflict and their idea of multiple goals which are imprecisely fulfilled and traded off against each other.

The result of the test is inconclusive; there is no significant difference in the number of goals mentioned in the A (142 goals) and B (129 goals) packages, with the latter package being one in which the interactive system was available. The goal to which most managers turned initially is also the goal selected subsequently: earnings per share. This goal dominates others in frequency of selection by the managers, and the desertion of high-rate-of-return projects for other projects with high earnings impact is readily apparent from other data not presented here. These results imply that an organizational designer can ignore the introduction of an inter-active capital budgeting system as a major modifier of a manager's goals.

Rate of return as a standard

The exhibits presented to the managers were couched in terms of net present value although results also were given for the internal rate of return and the profit-ability index. The computer output and the tables accompanying the B package were stated exclusively in net present value terms. However, more than 80% of the managers refer to rate of return rather than net present value when evaluating projects. Furthermore, two projects with alternative rankings on NPV and ROR analysis have significantly greater acceptance for the high-ROR project.

If top managers agree to finance theory's acceptance of net present value as superior to rate of return, then several design implications exist: a training process and/or an interactive capital budgeting system which emphasizes NPV is required. In addition, the management group involved in the capital budgeting needs a force-ful proponent of top management's standard as a member of that group.

Goal divergence in project selection

If a manager has particular goals, one expects projects which are desirable along the dimension of those goals to be more frequently selected than other projects, and to be more frequently selected by that manager than by other managers. But there are difficulties in capital budgeting analysis because a manager may pursue a goal in a subtle manner. Responding to that goal fulfillment process, top managers may alter the information process or change the team involved in the decision process if the organization is to produce a portfolio of projects which meets the requirements of those top managers.

The pursuit of projects which meet the goal of managers selecting earnings per share is direct in the experiment reported here. A large proportion of the managers select earnings per share as a major goal; many express concern with a satisfactory rate of return. This latter group of managers then selects projects with high earnings per share in the earlier years but with rates of return which are exceptionally low. This selection is contrary to their stated goal of a satisfactory rate of return, suggesting that a pluralistic goal structure is not used: EPS is the only goal. For those managers who indicate rate of return as a major priority, there is evidence of a simplicity of decision making which top managers may alter by adjustment of the groups making the decisions or by signals within the information system. The evidence is that managers favoring rate of return tend to select a single, small, high rate of return project without realizing that such a decision precludes a more comprehensive project (including the smaller project as a component) whose return is far above the average of the other proposed projects. Such myopia occurs when managers focus upon the project rather than the portfolio, and it occurs with significant frequency in these experiments [8, Chapter 7]. Finally, those managers who select sales level as a goal pursue the goal with asymmetric decisions; they choose projects with high sales impact more frequently than other managers, but do not reject projects with no impact on sales (such as cost reduction of new plant facilities) with greater frequency. The lack of increased rejection of other projects, however, under any sort of budget constraint means that fewer projects generating sales increases can be selected.

The design implications suggest that the sales-oriented managers can be counter-acted by a careful screening by other managers of the sales-generating projects, for there seems to be no unusually high rejection of other projects by these managers. For other managers, explicit discussions of the goals and decision standards after the tentative portfolios are selected seems most plausible. These discussions would be beneficial to sales-oriented managers as well. The inconsistencies with top managers' standards can be exposed for discussion. Finally, rule-making routines for management application as well as for the information system need to be created. The stimulus for the particular rules can be from ex post analysis of the previous project selection. These rules are guidelines for future project selection ex ante.

Table 2
Explicit concern with risk

	Package A	Package B	Package B without computer usage	Package B with substantial computer usage
	(N = 68)	(N = 68)	(N = 11)	(N = 39)
Concern with risk in				
Rate of return	0.23	0.40 **	0.36	0.46
Sales	0.09	0.15	0.09 } 0.25	0.23 } 0.44
Earning per share	0.24	0.59 ***	0.36	0.67 *
Cash flow	0.13	0.26 **	0.18	0.38

Results significantly different for considerations of risk in the computer and noncomputer at the 10% level (*), 5% level (**) or 1% level (***), one-tailed test. Comparison is for Package A versus Package B and for Package B with and without significant computer usage. Sample size differs from Table 1 since only 68 managers had separate usable responses for each of the A and B packages.

N indicates the number of participants in each category.

Risk evaluation

The cross-tabulation in Table 2 attempts to confirm the hypothesis that there is a positive relationship between availability of information about risk and the concern with a portfolio risk profile. Given the capability for an evaluation of risk among projects in Package B, the number of managers who look at risk increases for all criteria. In Package A, risk of projects could be evaluated, but risk of the total portfolio of projects, the risk which should be of ultimate concern, is not possible.

Another hypothesis is that an interactive system is associated with greater risk evaluation. To review this question, the sample of responses to tbe B package was segmented into those managers who did not use the computer and those who were relatively heavy computer users, omitting eighteen moderate users. Those managers not using the computer have a 0.36 incidence of concern with risk on earnings per share, while those using the system have a 0.67 incidence of concern with this risk. Overall, there is an average incidence of the risk evaluation of 0.25 for those managers not using the system versus 0.44 for those using the computer in the B package analysis. The small number of those not using the computer makes the test for significance extremely restrictive in this case. However, there is a probable relationship at the 80% level. Previous studies [1,7,13,20,27,30] indicate that most managers have a concern about risk, and this study indicates that most managers use the opportunity to evaluate risk in portfolio. Additional discussion of financial conflicts (lease evaluations, merger accounting, etc.), risk-coping behavior, and cultural differences suggested by [17] may be found in [8, Chapters 6 and 7].

If top managers desire division managers to concern themselves with risk, then it is appropriate to structure the decision process to use such an interactive model as was available to managers in these experiments, for it is virtually impossible for a manager to look at portfolio risk without such a computerized model. Even project risk can be evaluated only incompletely without a computerized model, for manual risk analysis simulations are expensive to perform for a given set of assumptions about probabilities of growth, revenues, costs, etc. Changing sets of assumptions add to the cost of the analysis. An interactive model is more efficient than a batch model because of stored common terms which may be readily recalled for a retrial while the manager is still on-line.

Top managers may wish to decentralize decision making which focuses upon divisional risk rather than corporate-wide risk. In such cases, suppression of some projects and elimination of some interdependencies among projects is appropriate in the portfolio creation process. This is neither deceptive nor inefficient. Rather, such a policy recognizes the merits of decentralized attention to a limited number of items because of bounded rationality, while simultaneously acknowledging the importance of externalities in the global corporate decision [49]. Depending on the scope of the operation, top managers may insert various intermediary levels of appraisal in which more of the portfolio considerations, such as project covariances and interdependencies, are included for the intermediary level managers to evaluate.

Group versus individual decisions

After the trials described above, a new pool of managers repeated the entire experiment. For this test, the managers were divided into five- to eight-person groups. The purpose of this test is to compare the decisions of groups versus those of individuals, for any sharp differences need to be acknowledged in the design of the organization for capital budgeting analysis.

A similar frequency of projects selected by individual managers is generally found when the results from group selection are studied. The rank correlation coefficient for the individual and group decisions is 0.86 after package A and 0.90 after package B, indicating similar evaluations and frequency of selection by the managers.

Some studies of organizations suggest that an organization wishes to avoid conflict and operates by a quasi-resolution of conflict. If that judgment is true, then one would expect groups to have more goals as standards for projects. Such a selection is a way of avoiding conflict. When one person feels sales are important, another is concerned with rate of return, and a third favors a broadly diversified business active in many fields, the easiest compromise is to state all of these views as group goals. Hence, one hypothesizes that groups have more goals than individuals.

For the twelve groups on which paired comparisons are possible, the frequency of goal selection in A and B parallels the frequency found with individuals, as shown in Table 3. However, there are two major changes. First, the inclusion of the "other" category in goals is more frequent in the A and B trials for groups than individuals. Second, the goals per responding unit are increased for groups, averaging

Table 3
Comparison of group and individual goals

	Package A		Package B	
	Individuals	Groups	Individuals	Groups
	($N = 68$)	($N = 12$)	($N = 68$)	($N = 12$)
Goal				
Rate of return	0.63	0.58	0.49	0.50
Sales	0.31	0.42	0.25	0.42
Earnings per share	0.69	0.83	0.94	0.92
Cash flow	0.34	0.42	0.21	0.50
Other	0.12	0.75 ***	0.01	0.58 ***
Total goals	142	36	129	35
Per unit (N)	2.1	3.0 ***	1.9	2.9 ***

Results significantly different at the 1% level (***), one-tailed test.
N indicates the number of participants in each category.

three goals per group unit versus two goals for a typical individual manager.

These two changes are consistent with the hypothesis. As a means of avoiding conflict, groups apparently tend to approve as a goal many items which a group member thinks is reasonable whatever the inconsistency with the other goals espoused.

The main confirmations from the group experiments are the similarities in group and individual goal standards, considerations of risk, and general project selections. Of more interest is the greater number of criteria named as goals for the group and the preponderance of vaguely defined other goals compared to the individual managers.

Pluralistic goal structures and group decisions

The model used in the laboratory experiments meets the three criteria of Simon [49] for analysis: comprehensiveness, technical sophistication, and pluralism. The model permits consideration of a variety of goals using whatever optimization analysis the finance and management science specialists desire. Pluralism is accomplished by including both the goals of various levels of an organization and the multiple goals required by top managers. The pluralism implied by the greater goal specification of groups may be desirable for normative capital budgeting if one agrees that long-run economic performance and corporate social responsibility require a concern with sales, cash flow, and other goals. Such multiple goal evaluation represents a means of considering intertemporal portfolio evaluations: a growing sales rate compared to that of the competition may permit eventual domination of the market, leading to greater long-run profits. Satisfactory cash flows for future years may be established as a standard to permit a wider range of project selection in future years than otherwise would be possible. Some economists and managers argue that the single goal of profit is the only appropriate criterion for managers; the job of business is to economize in our society and this goal is the measure of performance. Even if managers reject this single-goal theory, the question they must answer is what multiple goals are appropriate for managers in their firm in their industry. If top managers agree that such pluralism is desirable, then their concern should be to impose appropriate goals and to establish how trade-offs are to be made among them.

Top managers' precise statement of goal trade-offs is a possibility, but the wide range of possible outcomes makes completion of a written manual exceedingly burdensome. A more realistic behavior is the issuance of general guidelines followed by specific judgments on particular portfolios after a first pass at the capital budget by lower manager levels. Assuming top managers have other priorities beyond capital budgeting, such as external societal relations and general strategy, a staff office concerned with the capital budgeting process for the whole corporation is sensible. This office can act as the liaison between top managers of the firm and the other managers involved in the capital budgeting process. Otherwise, intermediate level managers are required to confront top managers with many preliminary portfolios in order to establish the goal trade-offs desired.

There is an option of having different goal standards for different divisions or types of projects, segmented by type of product, by size of project relative to the firm or to the market, by consumer versus industrial goods, and so forth. Because of the imprecision in the cash flow data, a research and development project will be judged on several goals beyond a single rate of return criterion. On the other hand, relocation of a major warehouse facility can be evaluated on a simple rate of return basis, even though the cost of these two projects might be identical in a single year.

As an alternative to this variable specification of goal standards by top managers for group decisions, a chief executive might select an individual or a set of individuals who uniquely match the top manager's set of capital budgeting decision standards. If there is an intricate and involved set of standards employed, then those cognitively complex surrogates can make decisions on a decentralized basis. This organization process would require both a top manager who has a perfect idea of how to make the decisions and a cognitively complex individual who can reflect the manager's evaluations. In the absence of such a mirror, top managers probably must accept on faith the expectation that the complex individual will make desirable choices. In contrast, a top manager can assume that the pluralism and goal exchange rates found by a group are likely to be more apparent to the group members themselves and (ultimately) to the higher managers. Such visibility of standards suggests the group decision process as more desirable for most top managers because the standards of the cognitively complex subordinate are glimpsed with difficulty.

An interactive model and the organizational design

From these findings, consider the implications for organizational design of the use of some form of interactive computer model in the capital budgeting process. The results are consistent with a premise that executives can employ an interactive, portfolio capital budgeting model. Managers receive risk information and use it in evaluating projects. Many managers remarked that they vaguely knew that there were optimizing management science models which would provide risk output given their inputs, but they were uncomfortable with being asked to specify all this information ex ante. Thus, the interactive feature of the system may have been more beneficial than the creation of portfolio data. Group interaction also seemed to be heightened as a result of using the interactive model. To the extent that an organization's managers believe that such group interaction leads to a consensus which is valuable in successfully completing the firm's operations, they will favor the use of such an interactive model, for it helps achieve this behavior among an organization's members. Furthermore, an increased group awareness of the biases brought by some group members may reduce the impact of those biases. This outcome also is consistent with the desires of most corporate chief executives in capital budgeting decisions.

Regarding the introduction of an interactive system such as the one proposed here, how does one accomplish change? As opposed to a bureaucratic model or a participative model of change, an alternative is the task force with a planning elite and group involvement, facilitated by a manager who acts as an intermediary between the specialists and the group to be changed [29,37,56, pp. 96–97].

What is likely to be the impact of such a model and of information technology on tasks? Whisler [56] suggests changes do occur, and participants may be happy or sad with the changes. Personal interaction tends to increase in terms of total group relationships, but specific interpersonal interaction with other people often decreases. At higher levels of management, there will probably be greater interpersonal interaction both laterally and vertically.

A multi-pass budgeting process is also desirable. Typically, the budgeting process consists of a local division manager's decision followed by the submission of budgets to corporate headquarters. There also may be intermediate levels to whom budgets must be submitted and approved prior to the next higher submission. An interactive model permits cycling reappraisals depending on arguments or disagreements about data at any level. In addition, it offers top managers an opportunity to integrate the suboptimizing behavior of lower levels. Bounded rationality implies divisional decisions, but these decisions often suboptimize because of ignored externalities. The interactive approach permits managers to detect and to rectify suboptimizing behavior at later stages without centralizing the initial decision making. Such technological features of an interactive model suggest than an organizational redesign to accommodate the multi-pass budgeting is required for full benefit of the model. One budget decision cycle can be based on the projects alone. Later rounds of evaluation permit study of the portfolio effects at various levels of aggregation, revisions in data inputs created as a result of division externalitites, a common assessment for various macro variables (Gross National Product forecasts, expected borrowing rates, etc.), and new proposals stimulated as a result of the portfolio projections.

Using the interactive system at several levels to provoke interpersonal interaction, to force less-than-obvious conflicts between projects into the open for resolution, and to improve the analysis, is part of a requirement that projections be conserved at various levels. For example, the selection of some high return projects at the expense of others which are less than the selected projects but greater than the average remaining projects (as seen in the study reported above) should become apparent as a probably unwise decision from a portfolio analysis (versus the single project analysis) and from the group interactions following the various passes over forecasts. In a normal decision process, the quantitative analysis completed for a project at a lower organizational level is often discarded or condensed in sanitized form as the project progresses. The decision process is usually based on a quantitative hurdle at a lower management level; once that hurdle is passed, the higher managers focus upon various qualitative variables, thus exposing some conflicts which would otherwise be undetected.

Imbedding top managers' goals in the capital budgeting process

The top managers must specify more of the goal structure to be used at all levels. The coalitions within the groups implied from the experimental results often seem to accommodate all goals proposed by members, a reasonable outcome in the laboratory setting with no hierarchy of authority forced upon the groups. In a firm, carefully mandated goals from above, especially in the ranges of trade-offs which will be tolerated in various goal conflicts such as EPS/NPV, are needed to avoid dysfunctional pursuit of conflicting goals by various people from different backgrounds. For example, a sales-dominated group will readily sacrifice NPV achievement if high sales growth is present in a project, yet specification of the trade-off permitted would lessen this behavior. Again, pluralism in goals may be desired; if so, top managers need to be sure that the operant pluralism is what they wish to have in the firm. Additional issues which should be resolved from higher management levels include whether the cash flow concern of subunit managers as a risk proxy is desired (are other sources for coping with downturns in future cash flows considered more desirable by a chief executive?) and what form of risk confidence measure is appropriate for a subunit manager. Whether a probability of no loss above $X\%$ or a particular risk confidence interval are appropriate criteria for screening projects should be signalled to this subunit manager. Such signals can be provided without a computer model, but the use of a model and the resulting data mean that the rules have relevance; lacking the model, the relevance is minimal.

The top managers should use the continuous monitoring, control, and updating permitted by such a computerized capital budgeting system. By holding the forecasts for projects in the memory, an easy comparison of forecasts with actual performance is permitted. Furthermore, low performance on some goal by a particularly vulnerable project can quickly result in a signal from the model to indicate which other projects might be accelerated or expanded in scale of investment. The ready availability of such on-line information and the organizational response to the model with built-in error signals means that a firm's manager may respond rapidly to a decline in performance.

Managers learn, but changes in individuals in particular positions in the organization, changes in the standards of superiors, and imprecision in the standards mean that a particular manager in the midst of an organization often has difficulty realizing what norms are to be applied. An interactive computer model can provide more specific guidelines than normally would be present in the organization. This assertion does not mean that top management is necessarily wiser or less selfish than a subordinate management group. Top management is responsible, however, and a premise stated earlier is that the capital budgets should please that top management. Rather, what is implied is that such a recycling of the decision process for capital budgeting analysis within an interactive model framework permits the benefits of the decentralization/centralizational balance to be improved. Managers at a lower level are likely to feel more satisfied with an appraisal of a project if the appraisals include more characteristics of acceptable projects as part of the analysis, and such increased consideration of important variables is more feasible with an interactive model than with a division appraisal using the local standards of divisional managers. This comment rests on the assumption that a diversification of goals is required or desirable, a judgment which is consistent with most empirical research cited earlier; future cash flows adjusted for the correct level of risk in which managers have great confidence are typically unobtainable, contrary to financial theory.

This interactive model may be seen as a device to keep lower level managers in line, to delegate some authority without truly decentralizing if decentralizing is seen as further along the continuum of central authority to complete autonomy. It can be used for such a purpose. On the other hand, the author's view is that such a model can be used to increase decentralization in a firm. One reason more organizations are not decentralized is that top managers are concerned that capital budgeting decisions involving substantial externalities to particular projects will be reached without anyone explicitly considering those externalities. Because an interactive model can reassure top management that some major externalities such as total corporate risk will be revealed at later stages in the decision process, many more decisions in the typical firm can be decentralized. When these externalities are uneconomic, top managers will reverse or modify lower level managers' decisions. However, top managers' knowledge of such monitoring of externalities means that more decisions can be given to lower level managers. Thus, more decisions are decentralized in number, but a greater percentage of decisions may be reversed. In fact, some organizations would find the percentage of decisions reversed declining with the advent of such an interactive portfolio model because the model can also convey some of the explicit interdependencies among projects lower in the organization than is possible in the absence of the models. If the lower level managers are now able to act on information unavailable to them previously, they are more likely to reach decisions congruent with the top managers' values.

Conclusion

Managers use planning models of increasing sophistication, although there are arguments about the effectiveness and efficiency of such models. Some managers are moving to exceptionally complex models. For example, International Utilities has an interactive capital budgeting model involving mathematical programming which accomplishes many of the trade-offs suggested here, although within the context of a single goal [33,34]. Such models and a review of programming solutions for capital budgeting problems is found elsewhere [18,45]. The models themselves require organizational redesign to take advantage of their benefits. Yet, advocates of models usually ignore the organizational complexities induced by the introduction of the models. On the other hand, many organizational design experts are often unaware of the potentials of planning models. The organizational redesign implied by the use of these models has been studied to a limited degree, and the prescriptions of these laboratory results using an interactive computer model are offered as a contribution to further awareness of the interrelationship of organizational design, interactive computer systems, and the process of capital budgeting.

References

[1] Alderfer, Clayton T. and Bierman, Harold, Jr., "Choices with Risk: Beyond the Mean and Variance," Journal of Business, Vol. 43 (July 1970), pp. 341–353.

[2] Baldwin, William, "The Motives of Managers, Environmental Restraints, and the Theory of Managerial Enterprise," Quarterly Journal of Economics, Vol. 78 (May 1964), pp. 238–256.

[3] Baumol, William, Business Behavior, Value, and Growth, Macmillan, New York, N.Y., 1954.

[4] Berg, Norman A., "The Allocation of Strategic Funds in a Large, Diversified, Industrial Company," Graduate School of Business Administration, Harvard University, Boston, Mass. (unpublished doctoral dissertation), 1963.

[5] Bierman, Harold and Hass, Jerome E., "Capital Budgeting Under Uncertainty: A Reformulation," Journal of Finance, Vol. 27 (March 1973), pp. 119–129.

[6] Bower, Joseph L., Managing the Resource Allocation Process, Division of Research, Graduate School of Business Administration, Harvard University, Boston, Mass., 1970.

[7] Carter, E. Eugene, "The Behavioral Theory of the Firm and Top-Level Corporate Decisions," Administrative Science Quarterly, Vol. 16 (December 1971), pp. 413–428.

[8] Carter, E. Eugene, Portfolio Aspects of Corporate Capital Budgeting, D.C. Heath, Lexington, Mass., 1974.

[9] Chamberlain, Neil, The Firm: Micro-Economic Planning and Action, McGraw-Hill, New York, N.Y., 1962.

[10] Chambers, John C., Mullick, Satinder K. and Smith, Donald D., "The Use of Simulation Models at Corning Glass Works," in Corporation Simulation Models, Albert N. Schrieber (ed.), University of Washington Printing Plant, Seattle, Wash., 1970, pp. 349–367.

[11] Cohen, Kalman J. and Cyert, Richard M., "Strategy: Formulation, Implementation, and Monitoring," Journal of Business, Vol. 46 (July 1973), pp. 349–367.

[12] Cohen, Michael D., March James G. and Olsen, Johan P., "A Garbage Can Model of Organizational Choice," Administrative Science Quarterly, Vol. 17 (March 1972), pp. 1–25.

[13] Conrath, David W., "From Statistical Decision Theory to Practice: Some Problems with the Transition," Management Science, Vol. 19 (April 1973), pp. 873–883.

[14] Cyert, Richard M. and MacCrimmon, Kenneth R., "Organizations," in Handbook of Social Psychology, (2nd ed.), G. Lindzey and E. Aronson (eds.), Addison-Wesley, Reading, Mass., 1968, Vol. 1, pp. 568–611.

[15] Cyert, Richard M. and March, James G., A Behavioral Theory of the Firm, Prentice-Hall, Englewood Cliffs, N.J., 1963.

[16] Dearborn, Dewitt C. and Simon, Herbert A., "Selective Perception: A Note on the Departmental Identification of Executives," Sociometry, Vol. 21 (June 1958), pp. 140–144.

[17] England, George W. and Lee, Raymond, "Organizational Goals and Expected Behavior Among American, Japanese, and Korean Managers – A Comparative Study," Academy of Management Journal, Vol. 14 (December 1971), pp. 425–438.

[18] Finney, D.J., Latcha, R., Bennett, B.M. and Hsu, P., Tables for Testing Significance in a 2 × 2 Contingency Table, Cambridge University Press, Cambridge, England, 1963.

[19] Fisher, R.A., Statistical Methods for Research Workers, Oliver and Boyd, Edinburgh, Scotland, 1941.

[20] Fremgen, James M., "Capital Budgeting Practices: A Survey," Management Accounting, Vol. 54 (May 1973), pp. 19–25.

[21] Gale, Bradley T., "Market Share and Rate of Return," Review of Economics and Statistics, Vol. 54 (December 1972), pp. 412–423.

[22] Gershefski, George W., "Corporate Models – The State of the Art," Management Science, Vol. 16 (February 1970), pp. B303–312.

[23] Hillier, Frederick S., The Evaluation of Risky Interrelated Investments, North-Holland, Amsterdam, The Netherlands, 1969.

[24] Jean, William H., The Analytical Theory of Finance, Holt, Rinehart and Winston, New York, N.Y., 1970.

[25] Katona, George, Psychological Analysis of Economic Behavior, McGraw-Hill, New York, N.Y., 1951.

[26] Keeley, Robert and Westerfield, Randolph, "A Problem in Probability Distribution Techniques for Capital Budgeting," Journal of Finance, Vol. 27 (June 1972), pp. 703–709.

[27] Klammer, Thomas, "Empirical Evidence of the Adoption of Sophisticated Capital Budgeting Techniques," Journal of Business, Vol. 45 (July 1972), pp. 387–397.

[28] Lanzillotti, Robert F., "Pricing Objectives in Large Companies," American Economic Review, Vol. 48 (December 1958), pp. 921–940.

[29] Leavitt, Harold J., "Applied Organizational Change in Industry," in Handbook of Organizations, James G. March (ed.), Rand McNally, New York, N.Y., 1965, pp. 1140–1170.

[30] Mao, James C.T. and Helliwell, John F., "Investment Decision Under Uncertainty: Theory Practice," Journal of Finance, Vol. 23 (May 1969), pp. 323–338. (Also see "Comment" by Frank Jen, pp. 342–344.)

[31] March, James G. and Simon, Herbert A., Organizations, Wiley, New York, N.Y., 1958.

[32] Marris, Robin, "A Model of the 'Managerial' Enterprise," Quarterly Journal of Economics, Vol. 77 (May 1963), pp. 158–209.

[33] McSweeney, James J., "A Strategic Management System – An Operational Concept," International Utilities, Philadelphia, Penn. (unpublished paper), October 1972.

[34] McSweeney, James L., "Strategic Management Systems," International Utilities, Philadelphia, Penn. (unpublished paper), January 1973.

[35] Miller, George A., "The Magical Number Seven, Plus or Minus Two: Some Limits on Our Capacity for Processing Information," Psychological Review, Vol. 63 (February 1956), pp. 81–97.

[36] Mintzberg, Henry, Raisinghani, Duru and Theoret, André, "The Structure of 'Unstructured' Decision Processes," Administrative Science Quarterly, Vol. 21 (June 1976), pp. 246–275.

[37] Mumford, Enid and Sackman, Harold (eds.), Human Choice and Computers, North-Holland, Amsterdam, The Netherlands, 1975.

[38] National Industrial Conference Board, U.S. Production Abroad and the Balance of Payments, National Industrial Conference Board, New York, N.Y., 1966.

[39] Paine, Neil R., "Uncertainty and Capital Budgeting," The Accounting Review, Vol. 39 (April 1964), pp. 330–332.

[40] Pettigrew, Andrew, "Information Control as a Power Resource," Sociology, Vol. 6 (May 1972), pp. 187–204.

[41] Raiffa, Howard, Decision Analysis: Introductory Lectures on Choices Under Uncertainty, Addison-Wesley, Reading, Mass., 1968.

[42] Roenfeldt, Rodney L. and Osteryoung, Jerome S., "Analysis of Financial Leases," Financial Management, Vol. 2 (Spring 1973), pp. 74–87.

[43] Rotch, William, "Return on Investment as a Measure of Performance," Graduate School Business Administration, Harvard University, Boston, Mass. (unpublished doctoral dissertation), 1958.

[44] Salazar, Rudolpho C. and Sen, Subrata K., "A Simulation Model of Capital Budgeting Uncertainty," Management Science, Vol. 15 (December 1968), pp. B161–B179.

[45] Schrieber, Albert N., (ed.), Corporate Simulation Models, University of Washington Printing Plant, Seattle, Wash., 1970.

[46] Shaw, Marvin E. and Penrod, William T., Jr., "Does More Information Available to a Group Always Improve Performance?" Sociometry, Vol. 25 (December 1962), pp. 377–390.

[47] Shubik, Martin, "Approaches to the Study of Decision-Making Relevant to the Firm," Journal of Business, Vol. 34 (April 1961), pp. 101–118.

[48] Simon, Herbert A., "Applying Information Technology to Organizational Design," Public Administration Review, Vol. 33 (July-August 1973), pp. 268–278.

[49] Simon, Herbert A., Models of Man, Wiley, New York, N.Y., 1957.

[50] Simon, Herbert A., "On the Concept of Organizational Goal," Administrative Science Quarterly, Vol. 9 (June 1964), pp. 1–22.

[51] Slovic, Paul, "Psychological Study of Human Judgment: Implications for Investment Decision Making," Journal of Finance, Vol. 27 (September 1972), pp. 779–799.

[52] Snedecor, George W. and Cochran, William G., Statistical Methods, (6th ed.), Iowa State University Press, Ames, Iowa, 1967.

[53] Spitaller, Erich, "A Survey of Recent Quantitative Studies of Long-Term Capital Movements," International Monetary Fund Staff Papers, (March 1971), pp. 189–217.

[54] Vancil, Robert F. and Anthony, Robert N., "The Financial Community Looks at Leasing," Harvard Business Review, Vol. 37 (November-December 1959), pp. 2113–2140.

[55] Wallach, Michael A., Kogan, Nathan and Bem, Daryl J., "Group Influence on Individual Risk Taking," Journal of Abnormal and Social Psychology, Vol. 65 (1962), pp. 75–86.

[56] Whisler, Thomas L., Information Technology and Organizational Change, Wadsworth, Belmont, Ca., 1970.

[57] Woods, Donald H., "Decision Making Under Uncertainty in Hierarchical Organizations," Graduate School of Business Administration, Harvard University, Boston, Mass. (unpublished doctoral dissertation), 1965.

North-Holland/TIMS Studies in the Management Sciences 5 (1977) 43–54
© North-Holland Publishing Company

DESIGNING ORGANIZATIONAL RESPONSES
TO AN INFLATIONARY ENVIRONMENT *

RICHARD F. VANCIL and STEVEN C. WHEELWRIGHT

Harvard University

The impact of increased inflation on business is pervasive and yet highly situation specific. Through use of PRISM, a corporate simulation model designed to examine the impact of rapid inflation on a firm and to evaluate alternative managerial responses, these premises are illustrated. A conceptual framework for managerial autonomy in a decentralized organization is then presented and used as the basis for guiding the control and implementation of the diverse managerial responses identified through use of PRISM.

The impact of inflation on an organization that fails to respond appropriately is dramatic and often swift, as has long been recognized. Managers and theorists have documented numerous successes and failures and have also published many prescriptions about appropriate decisions and actions, e.g., [15,17]. However, these works have usually been too general to provide managers with specific guidelines. Furthermore, there has been a lack of prescriptive approaches that consider both policies appropriate to inflation and the managerial actions needed to implement such policies.

A useful, though artificial, conceptual dichotomy commonly applied in examining organizational responses to inflation distinguishes analysis from instrumentation. An analysis deals with a specific problem. Alternative policies and managerial actions are evaluated to select optimal ones for the organization. Analyses stimulated by inflation usually involve tighter control of working capital and slower rates of growth.

In instrumentation, the decisions made in the analysis of the problem are implemented. These decisions commonly relate to the distribution of authority. Responses to inflation, especially by large corporations, have frequently neglected the designs of instrumental activities; consequently analyses have not been implemented or have resulted in serious problems when implemented.

The prescriptions proposed here, though not dramatic, are workable. They are based on two models. The first is a computer simulation model that can be used to predict how inflation affects the performance of an organization. The second is a conceptual model of how changes in the environment change the distribution of

* Received July 1975; revised February 1976, June 1976.

authority in a hierarchical organization. This model is useful in designing instrumental activities.

Inflation and performance

As the rate of U.S. inflation has increased beyond the historical levels of two or three percent per year, most managers have realized that they should adjust their policies and actions accordingly; however, few have felt they had adequate knowledge of how inflation had changed their problems and still fewer have known how to modify their usual policies (strategies) and actions (operations) appropriately.

Because high rates of inflation are recent in the U.S., the literature has described mainly how inflation caused poor performance, except for the prescriptive recommendations of Wheelwright [15], Vancil and Kelly [14] and Winkler [17] and for the particularly relevant empirical information and prescriptive theory in the literature on multinational organizations. These organizations have experienced extreme inflation in some of their foreign subsidiaries for over a decade, and the literature presents prescriptions for compensating for currency revaluations or for inflation in measuring and reporting performance.

Since foreign exchange rates are related to inflation rates, managerial actions recommended for coping with exchange fluctuations may be relevant to those for responding to inflation, as indicated by such authors as Lietaer [6], Rutenberg [8], Shapiro [9], and Wheelwright [16], who have presented prescriptive models for the response of organizations to currency fluctuations.

There are many unsupported generalizations about the influence of inflation and about apprpriate responses to it; for example:

1. Inflation must be financed much as growth is, but without the advantages of growth.

2. Inflation causes narrowing of profit margins as the costs of an organization tend to increase faster than it can raise its prices.

3. Inflation penalizes the shareholders because the real value of dividends decreases when inflation exceeds the rate of dividend growth.

4. Inflation alters the appropriate level of working capital investments because the associated higher interest rates increase the benefits of tighter control.

5. Inflation causes a form of involuntary liquidation of capital because plant replacement costs substantially exceed funds provided through depreciation.

6. Inflation increases the effective income tax rate by including illusory inventory profits in taxable income.

To determine which of the generalizations applies to an organization and what the implications are for managerial action, it would be necessary to understand the interrelationship of the many activities of the organization and the relative influence of the many different decisions and environmental characteristics on its performance.

A general corporate model referred to as PRISM (Price Inflation Simulation Model) was developed and is sufficiently detailed in representing the characteristics and environment of the organization to permit investigation of how inflation (and higher interest rates) influence an organization's performance. The model was designed to give output results in terms of conventional (historical cost) and price-level-adjusted (constant dollar) financial statements.

PRISM is an analytical model that provides the content of prescriptions, such as, days of inventory on hand, delay times for paying suppliers, and rates of growth; therefore it can be useful in identifying appropriate organizational changes in response to inflation. PRISM appears to represent the interaction of prescriptive variables with inflation realistically (see, e.g., [14,15]).

Results of simulations using PRISM

Table 1 summarizes the initial characteristics of two organizations, a retail grocery chain and a basic steel producer, each of which has the median characteristics for its industry in 1973. These two industries differ greatly in profit margins,

Table 1
Assumptions used for simulating performance of a grocery chain and a steel producer

1973 Median Data *	Grocery chain	Steel producer
Profit after tax/net sales (%)	0.91	3.19
Gross margin (%)	20.8	28.7
Return on equity (%)	9.41	9.39
Sales per net fixed assets	17.01	3.52
Debt/equity	0.44	0.29
Pricing margin (profit before tax) (%)	2	7
Inventory accounting	First in first out	First in first out
Inventory turnover	25 days	46 days
Payment lag in accounts payable	18 days	38 days
Collection lag in accounts receivable	0 days	46 days
Operating cash	15 days	33 days
Other assumptions **		
Dividend payout (%)	50	60
Sales growth (annual, real volume, %)	1.5	3
Productivity increase (annual, %)	0.31	2.3
Pricing lag	1 month	2 quarters

* *Duns Review*, "Ratios for Retailing," September 1974. *Duns Review*, "Ratios for Manufacturing," November 1974.

** Chosen by the authors as representing typical policies and performance during a period of low inflation.

investment requirements, elements of working capital, and so on, and were chosen because of their differences. Understanding the differences among different organizations and industries is particularly critical to predicting the economic effects of inflation on a specific organization because inflation may affect different organizations, even in the same industry, in different ways, so that the appropriate policies and actions will differ.

In the example chosen, the model was first used to predict the base-line performance of each organization over the period 1974 through 1978, assuming that the managerial policies and actions remained unchanged and that only prices changed. These predictions are shown in the first row of Table 2 and indicate that continuation of policies, unchanged, leads to rapidly deteriorating performance in both organizations.

Next, changes in particular policies and actions were simulated. Table 2 shows the effects of four such changes. These changes improve performance in the two organizations, although the fourth policy does not necessarily improve performance.

Finally two composite policy changes were simulated, one including the first three, largely operational, and the other including all four. The results (Table 2) show that both organizations benefit from implementing the first three policies; but when the fourth is included, the benefits for the grocery chain are not nearly as great as those for the steel producer.

A somewhat simplistic interpretation of the results in Table 2 made by many managers and researchers is that increased financial control — that is, minimum cash and receivables, maximum payables, quick response to cost increases, prices high enough for constant margins, and greater inventory turnover — leads to improved performance in inflation. Multinational organizations that have made decisions and taken action in response to inflation have largely centralized the control of liquid assets in the treasurer's office. Although centralization facilitates making decisions on policies and actions for the particular organization, it clearly influences the distribution of responsibility throughout the organization. Because large diversified organizations have had success with decentralization, it may not be desirable for them to become strongly centralized over long periods, even in order to adapt to inflation.

To identify alternative policies and actions that would help an organization to adapt to inflation, it is instructive to classify the decisions analyzed with the PRISM model as tactical or strategic. Tactical decisions are those which are so important in their effect on the performance of the organization or a segment of it, that the decision maker responsible for the decision wishes a prior review of the action proposed by a subordinate, even though the subordinate has been delegated the authority to take the action. Day-to-day decisions affecting elements of working capital, such as accounts receivable, inventory, and accounts payable, are clearly tactical, as are cost-price adjustments (which might also be delegated to operating managers in diversified organizations). Strategic decisions are those which are so important in their effect on the performance of the organization or a segment of it, that the deci-

Table 2
PRISM results for 1974–1978

	Compound annual change in earnings per share (%)		Return on equity (%)		Debt/equity (%)		Selling price (1973=100)	
	Grocery	Steel	Grocery	Steel	Grocery	Steel	Grocery	Steel
Base case (policies as in Table 1; 10% inflation per year)	−2.5	−11.3	9.6	4.9	67	73	96.7	83.0
Management policies								
Reduction in cash and receivables (10%) and lengthening of payables (10%)	0	−8.2	10.7	5.7	42	57	96.7	83.0
Improvement in inventory turnover (10%)	−1.1	−9.8	10.3	5.3	51	66	96.7	83.0
Reaction time to higher costs cut 50%	+5.3	−0.3	12.9	8.3	50	62	97.1	84.7
No growth in real volume, but a slightly higher selling price	−1.4	−5.9	9.9	6.4	46	25	97.0	84.0
Composite management policies								
First three items	8.2	2.5	14.3	9.4	29	42	97.1	84.7
All four items	9.2	5.9	14.6	10.8	29	23	97.6	86.0

sion maker responsible for the decision wishes to have a prior discussion of the proposed action with peers and/or supervisor, even though he or she has been delegated the authority to take the action.

Decisions relating to growth and overall pricing policies would undoubtedly be considered strategic in most organizations and would reflect (1) corporate-level knowledge of investiment opportunities and resource constraints and (2) division-level knowledge of competitive conditions, market opportunities, and investment requirements. Decisions on resource allocation always involve complex trade-offs, and rapid inflation increases the complexity of these trade-offs. Consequently the authority of a division manager to promote growth may be somewhat reduced, but even without extreme inflation, division managers have only limited influence on factors promoting growth. Their influence was due chiefly to their opportunity to make and defend investment proposals; the top managers controlled the funds.

Implementing tactical decisions is important, as shown in Table 2, and will directly affect divisional responsibilities so that a conceptual model is needed for implementing tactical decisions in a decentralized organizational structure. The model of instrumental activities that follows is particularly useful for formulating instrumental activities in the response of an organization to inflation.

Authority in hierarchies

If large diversified corporations are to survive and grow they must decentralize decision making to be able to continue to adapt to changing market and technolog-ical environments (see e.g., [4,12]). The total task of the organization is thus progressively subdivided, and the heads of subdivisions have a certain amount of authority (or autonomy) to act within their assigned spheres of responsibility. How is that certain amount determined in the complex decision making of a hierarchical organization?

The pyramidal hierarchy is the basic structure of most organizations. Manager A may be several levels from the top of the organization but is still at the top of a pyramid of his own. Most large organizations are composed of dozens or hundreds of such interlocking pyramids. Such hierarchical structures permit specialization and division of labor [11] which makes efficiency possible. However, achieving the objectives of the organization must not be sacrificed to efficiency. Manager A has a broader perspective than subordinate managers at the successively lower levels B and C. Still A has a problem because he is responsible for the actions of his sub-ordinates, although forced to delegate authority for action to them because of the magnitude of his task.

A simplistic concept of delegation of authority implies that the main tasks of Manager A are selecting the managers to fill the positions at level B, assigning spheres of responsibilities to them and then holding them accountable for their performance. But A's responsibilities include a great many operating decisions, which are critical to the successful implementation of policies and actions made at higher levels.

The anomaly of most organizational structures is that many of the decisions supposed to be made by A are, in fact, within the sphere of responsibility A has delegated to B. But the old maxim, "No responsibility without authority," while useful, is an oversimplification of how managers work together [5]. The relationships of manager B with a manager one level above (A) and another one level below (C) illustrate the problem. As Mintzberg [7] has so well documented, most of the purposeful contact between B and C takes place in a decision-making context. They cannot operate independently, restricting themselves to their assigned spheres of responsibility, which exist only in the organizational chart. Their formal and informal contacts with other managers, shown by the shaded areas in Figure 1, are the very essence of decision making. Some examples follow:

1. Sometimes the decision to be made is obvious enough that the B-C discussion is described as "keeping the boss informed." But informed on the before-the-fact

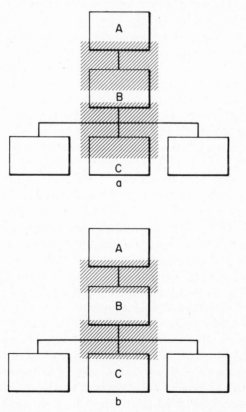

Fig. 1. Development of autonomy in decision making with time: Early (a) and mature (b) relationships of B to A and C.

basis is quite a different thing — from the point of view of both men — than C's allowing B to learn of the action later.

2. Sometimes the B-C dialogue is one of "check my logic." Manager C has identified a problem on which action is required, has isolated two, or three, or four alternative actions and analyzed them, and has decided which one should be adopted. Even though such a manager knows that the decision is within the official scope of his authority, he feels a need to discuss his analysis with someone before taking an irrevocable action. He fully expects B to concur in the recommended course of action and does not regard discussing the decision with B as a diminution of his authority.

3. Sometimes the problem, or incipient problem, is still ill defined and C's request of B is to help formulate the problem. A brief discussion at this stage may lead to a subsequent discussion a few hours or a few days later of the type just described in which C presents alternatives and solutions developed.

4. Sometimes, of course, the B-C discussion is a formal meeting, scheduled well in advance, to review recent performance and/or to discuss formal plans and budgets for the future.

If B managers are to fulfill their responsibilities, they must remain aware of the problems of their subordinates, because like most managers they are in the middle of hierarchies, being responsible to their superiors for the actions of their sub-ordinates. Consequently, B managers (that is, all but top-level and bottom-level managers) must continually respond to questions because the environment changes: (1) Are opportunities being exploited? (2) Are the activities and efforts of sub-ordinate units appropriately coordinated and balanced? (3) Are current policies and procedures still appropriate? In addition, because people change, are subordinates adequately challenged and yet adequately effective in their jobs?

These questions concern B managers because of their own professional standards of performance and because A managers are also concerned with these questions. The need for exchange of this information to arrive at consensus on decisions about policies and actions facilitates the development of decision channels. The role of such channels can best be seen by first considering the types of decisions that concern B managers. The various decision typologies proposed — non-programmed [10], strategic, operating, and administrative [1], strategic and tactical [3] — all focus on the substantive content of decisions, whereas in this study, the focus is on the decision-making process.

Strategic decisions

In Figure 1a, although B may have the authority to take action within the sphere of responsibility defined by all B managers, because of the mutual need that A and B have for a decision channel, B's decisions may be further subdivided into strategic, tactical, and positional decisions. Strategic decisions, those that B wants to discuss with A before taking action, are represented by the upper area in B's organization cell. Many factors are involved in determining the importance of a strategic decision: (1) the time required to implement it; (2) the duration of its effect; (3) its magnitude compared to that of the usual decision; (4) its reversibility; and (5) the cost of a wrong decision (its magnitude multiplied by the degree of uncertainty that the decision is incorrect).

In an early A-B relationship, both managers grope for a mutual understanding of which decisions are important enough for B to review with A. As the relationship evolves, the number of decision channels may change radically, with the amount probably decreasing with time as shown in Figure 1b. Managers B and C must also share in decision making for manager C's strategic decisions, and these constitute the tactical decisions shown in the lower section of manager B's cell (Figure 1a).

Positional decisions

Finally, the third segment of Manager B's decisions is that lying between the upper and lower sections shown in Figure 1. These positional decisions are those which (1) the decision maker has not delegated to a subordinate because the action may affect the activities of several subordinates, or for other reasons, and (2) the decision maker is willing to make a resource commitment without prior review with the superior.

These three types of decisions, collectively, are intended to encompass all of the decisions that B might take, except that some of manager C's strategic decisions will be of sufficient importance that they will also fall in B's strategic set; that is, although C may have the responsibility for analysis and recommendation, the decision will be of such importance that even B will wish to review it with manager A. Such interrelated decision making is not illustrated in Figure 1.

This three-way division of a manager's decisions is a useful way of thinking about what autonomy really means in a hierarchical organization [2]. As Figure 1a indicates, when B is new to the job, he or she is very aware that his/her positional authority is low. A may have delegated substantial responsibility to B, but both A and B will want to review many of B's proposed decisions before action is taken. Similarly, B must also develop a relationship with C, and so C's definition of strategic decisions is suddenly — and usually briefly — expanded.

The rate at which the relationship of A, B, and C evolves to that shown in Figure 1b is affected by many factors. If C has had long experience, B may be able to re-establish C's autonomy rather quickly. Similarly, B's prior experience in other positions may soon lead A to demonstrate confidence and respect for B's abilities. Some managers are more interested in the details of their subordinates' activities than other managers. The division of a manager's decision into three segments is determined not so much by a carefully worded position description as it is by the abilities, experience, and personality of the managers that he must work with in the hierarchy.

Mature autonomy relationships can be disrupted by environmental changes, such as those resulting from inflation. The tactical decisions treated in Table 2, traditionally handled as positional decisions by subordinates in mature relationships, need at least temporarily to be redefined as strategic, so that higher-level managers can assist their subordinates in adjusting their decisions to take account of inflation. This involves changing the mature relationship between A and B and that between B and C, shown in Figure 1b, to something more like the earlier relationship between those managers shown in Figure 1a.

Managers might choose to become more involved with their subordinates in areas that would include not only the management of working capital and more rapid cost-price adjustments, but also in the establishment of performance measures that reflect the new performance goals of the organization. Over time, as these performance goals become established and accepted, and as incentives are brought into line with the new goals, the relationship would return to the mature form shown in Figure 1b.

The speed with which a firm will be able to move effectively to the early relationship and then return to the more stable mature relationship will depend partly on the organization. For example, an organization that has a financial function which includes a controller in each operating division should be able to implement procedures for tightening control of working capital at the operating level more quickly than an organization that must do this by going through the usual line-management chain of command because a division controller at the site can quickly place more emphasis on control of working capital at the operating level.

Application of models

By combining the use of the simulation model (PRISM) of operating performance and a conceptual model of managerial autonomy, appropriate action for coping with inflation can be developed. Some of the results of organizations using this approach follow:

1. A large regional utility perceived that two areas of strategic action might require change — long-term capital structure and government-approved depreciation schedules. Both the need for such changes and the specific action to be taken were identified using PRISM. The decisions being strategic, action was implemented by the corporate headquarters.

2. A multinational manufacturing organization identified the need for tighter control of working capital — cash, inventories, receivables, and payables — in its foreign subsidiaries because of increased inflation. Wanting to maintain decentralization of operating decisions, top management chose to define corporate policies regarding capital, but left the implementation of tactical decisions to local management.

3. A publishing organization with ten decentralized plants in the U.S. applied PRISM to determine the influence of increased inflation under existing management plans. While the results clearly identified the importance of operating deci-

sions, top management chose to reduce its growth goals in order to maintain existing decentralization rather than to change its organizational structure.

4. The financial planning staff of a large manufacturing corporation used PRISM to estimate the hurdle rate appropriate for divisional capital investments in order to achieve the corporate goal of real return on investment. They also used PRISM to teach division managers about the influence of inflation on performance, but avoided seeking specific solutions for divisions in order to maintain the autonomy of divisions.

Summary

In identifying the kinds of organizational change a company needs in order to adapt to inflation, one can see that a large number of diverse management actions are relevant. Since most organizations find it extremely difficult to change several policies or actions at the same time, they should first identify those that are most important for their poblems and give them priority. Over time, the organization could then build upon that basic set of altered management policies and actions in order to align its management decision making more closely to the changing environment.

As illustrated in this paper, design of an organizational response to inflation can be usefully considered as consisting of two parts — one analytical and one instrumental, with the analytical part further subdivided along the dimension of tactical and strategic.

From experiences where the simulation model, PRISM, was used to identify the specific decisions about management policies and actions needed to adapt to increasing rates of inflation, it became clear that such identification was only a part of the task. Equally important was the identification of ways to implement those policies and actions while maintaining the management philosophy and the basic authority structure of the organization. In other words, the simulation model and the conceptual model complement each other in helping an organization to adapt itself to inflation.

References

[1] Ansoff, H. Igor, Corporate Strategy, McGraw-Hill, New York, N.Y., 1965.

[2] Dalton, Gene W., Barnes, Louis B. and Zaleznik, Abraham, The Distribution of Authority in Formal Organizations, Graduate School of Business Administration, Harvard University, Boston, Mass., 1968.

[3] Drucker, Peter F., The Practice of Management, Harper and Row, New York, N.Y., 1954.

[4] Lawrence, Paul R. and Lorsch, Jay W., Organization and Environment, Graduate School of Business Administration, Harvard University, Boston, Mass., 1967.

[5] Learned, Edmund P., Ulrich, David N. and Booz, Donald R., Executive Action, Graduate School of Business Administration, Harvard University, Boston, Mass., 1951.

[6] Lietaer, Bernard, Financial Management of Foreign Exchange, M.I.T. Press, Cambridge, Mass., 1971.

[7] Mintzberg, Henry, The Nature of Managerial Work, Harper and Row, New York, N.Y., 1973.

[8] Rutenberg, David P., "Maneuvering Liquid Assets in a Multi-National Company: Formulation and Deterministic Solution Procedures," Management Science, Vol. 16 (June 1970), pp. B671—B684.

[9] Shapiro, Alan, "Optimal Inventory and Credit-Granting Strategies Under Inflation and Devaluation," Journal of Financial and Quantitative Analysis, Vol. 8 (January 1973), pp. 37—46.

[10] Simon, Herbert A., The Shape of Automation, Harper and Row, New York, N.Y., 1965.

[11] Stieglitz, Harold, "On Concepts of Corporate Structure," The Conference Board Record, Vol. 11 (February 1974), pp. 7—13.

[12] Thompson, James D., Organizations in Action, McGraw-Hill, New York, N.Y., 1967.

[13] Treuherz, Role, "Forecasting Foreign Exchange Rates in Inflationary Economies," Financial Executive, Vol. 37 (February 1969), pp. 57—60.

[14] Vancil, Richard F. and Kelly, James N., "Get Ready for Price-Level-Adjusted Accounting," Harvard Business Review, Vol. 53 (March-April 1975), pp. 6—8.

[15] Wheelwright, Steven C., "Management by Model During Inflation," Business Horizons, Vol. 18 (June 1975), pp. 33—42.

[16] Wheelwright, Steven C., "Applying Decision Theory to Improve Corporate Management of Currency-Exchange Risks," California Management Review, Vol. 17 (Summer 1975), pp. 41—49.

[17] Winkler, John, Company Survival During Inflation, John Wiley, New York, N.Y., 1975.

North-Holland/TIMS Studies in the Management Sciences 5 (1977) 55—69

PROFESSIONALS IN BUREAUCRACIES: A STRUCTURAL ALTERNATIVE *

JANET SCHRIESHEIM

Kent State University

MARY ANN VON GLINOW and STEVEN KERR

The Ohio State University

Many difficulties arise from potential incompatibilities between professionals' characteristics and the bureaucratic structures and assignment of authority based on hierarchical position of most organizations. These incompatibilities may lead to dysfunctional conflict between professionals' role expectations and organizational requirements. Some organizations are attempting to deal with conflict by adopting dual hierarchies — separate hierarchies for managers and professionals — in place of single hierarchies. Existing evidence indicates, however, that dual hierarchies are generally ineffective for handling such conflict. Innovative triple hierarchies designed to better manage this conflict and facilitate the integration of professionals into organizations are discussed in this paper. These triple hierarchies combine the advantages of separating professional from managerial hierarchies with the benefits of providing a hierarchy of integrators to manage professional-managerial relations in areas where conflict is most likely to occur. Evidence supporting the conflict management potential of triple hierarchies is drawn from several sources, most notably the literature on Likert's linking pin [25,26] and Lawrence and Lorsch's integrator [24].

There is some disagreement in the literature about which characteristics serve to define a professional, but several definitional criteria are used most frequently. These are:

Expertise. Professionals possess expertise, that is, specialized training in a body of abstract knowledge (e.g., [13,23,44]).

Ethics. Professionals maintain codes of ethics requiring that they behave toward clients with neutrality and without emotional involvement or self-interest, and by applying universalistic standards (e.g., [8,13,17,45,49]).

Collegial maintenance of standards. Professionals believe that they alone have the technical competence and ethics necessary to police their specialty and to assure quality service [17,43,44].

Autonomy. To a greater degree than nonprofessionals, professionals demand self-control over both decisions and work activities [11,19,34]. Autonomy is sought concerning innovation, individual responsibility, and free communication [50],

* Received June 1975; revised February 1976, July 1976.

particularly in areas where professionals perceive that they alone have the expertise that is required.

Commitment to calling. Professionals feel a strong sense of calling to their fields, careers, and work, and believe that their professions perform valuable, even indispensable services to society (e.g., [15,23,43]).

Identification with profession and fellow professionals. Professionals feel a strong identification with their chosen professions, and use fellow professionals and professional associations as important referents (e.g., [8,34,44]). They typically maintain stronger commitments to specialized role skills and to their professional subculture than to their employing organizations (e.g., [7,16,30]).

Obviously, no one individual will possess in full measure the six characteristics identified above. Rather, these characteristics collectively describe a stereotypical ideal, and organizational employees are defined as more or less professional as they approach or depart from the ideal. Professionals may therefore be thought of as specialists who also maintain the above-mentioned values and attitudes. Whereas specialists may be willing to forego practice in their specialties to perform other organizational functions, professionals are extremely reluctant to relinquish their professional activities.

Professionals in bureaucracies

As an ideal type, the bureaucratic model consists of several dimensions, including: hierarchical authority structures; spheres of influence determined by division of labor; webs of formally established rules and regulations for the coordination of activities; appointment to administrative positions by superiors rather than election by peers; promotion according to some combination of seniority and achievement; and impersonality in relations with both clients and other organizational participants [8,12]. No organization can be expected to fit the ideal bureaucratic model in every aspect; however, almost all organizations employ the bureaucratic model to some degree as a structural strategy.

Some aspects of the bureaucratic model conflict strongly with the values and attitudes of professionals. Typically, hierarchical authority structures emphasize direction from administrative superiors, who relay orders and instructions downward to hierarchically lower members. These structures, particularly in the business organization, usually accompany a management culture stressing financial soundness, organizational loyalty, conformity with rules and procedures, and growth in production output, volume, and size. Control mechanisms and criteria for evaluation are similarly formed according to these emphases [21].

Professionals, however, have been inculcated with certain attitudes and values which are not discarded upon assuming organizational roles, but continue to influence their behavior while they enact these roles. They may therefore rely upon self-determination, collegial maintenance of standards, and interaction with fellow professionals for task performance and for coordinating their activities with those of other organizational participants. Professionals may therefore be subject to role conflict resulting from discrepant professional values and attitudes and bureaucratic organizational requirements, particularly regarding authority, evaluation and control. As a result, unless the leader is also recognized as a professional, professionals may question his or her competence to evaluate them, and have authority over them. They may reject rules and standards developed by nonprofessionals and maintain only conditional loyalty to the organization.

Scott [39, p. 266] summarizes two general reasons for conflict between professionals and bureaucratic organizations:

First, professionals participate in two systems – the profession and the organization – and their dual membership places important restrictions on the organization's attempt to deploy them in a rational manner with respect to its own goals.

Second, the profession and bureaucracy rest on fundamentally different principles of organization and these divergent principles generate conflict between professionals and their employers in certain specific areas.

Specific professional-organizational conflicts may relate to any of the six professional characteristics mentioned earlier. For example, organizations may find professionals' expertise, acquired through specialized training in a body of abstract knowledge, too abstract and overly specialized. At the same time, professionals may be impatient with an organization's relatively unscientific, seat-of-the-pants problem-solving approaches. Professional codes of ethics and client orientations may conflict sharply with an organization's overt and sometimes deceptive marketing of products and services, with a firm's claims of the right to own and keep secret new products and processes, and with an organization's disregard of ethical considerations in using research results (recall, for example, the atomic scientists' battle against the utilization of their research data to develop the hydrogen bomb). Peer control and maintenance of standards may be inconsistent with the organization's authority, evaluation and control structures [31]. Professionals' autonomy demands may clash strongly with the network of rules which binds bureaucratic organizations, and their external identification and commitment to calling may run counter to organizational demands for allegiance.

Professionals' external identification and commitment to calling may also determine their attitudes toward hierarchical advancement. If professionals remain within their technical specialties, in single hierarchies they will likely forego the increased pay, power, status symbols and other amenities associated with higher office. Furthermore, in most cases they will continually be subjected to such constraining uncertainty reduction devices as job descriptions, rules, and standard operating procedures [46]. They may also be labeled failures, since personal success is typified by the income and social prestige which so often depend upon hierarchical advancement [18]. As Victor Thompson [47, p. 508] observed, "To be socially defined as 'successful' in our culture, one must proceed up *some* hierarchy. To have public recognition and esteem, hence self-esteem, one must succeed hierarchically."

On the other hand, should professionals seek promotion to higher organizational levels, they must often perform administrative or managerial duties. Thus they must choose between remaining in their professional specialties and tolerating numerous interferences with their autonomy, or relinquishing precisely those tasks which permit them to employ their professional knowledge and skills.

Entry to higher organizational levels in single hierarchies normally depends less upon specific skills, knowledge and outstanding performance in professionally-oriented activities than upon evidence that individual and organizational goals are congruent. The critical test, as J.D. Thompson [46] notes, is whether the individual holds values and loyalties considered important by the organization. Hierarchical advancement therefore means not only that the professional will face increasing amounts of nonprofessional work, but also that organizational tests of loyalty and goal congruence will replace professional criteria.

The dual hierarchy

In an attempt to remove the sources of professional-organizational conflict described above, and to provide professionals with an alternative career path and reward opportunity, some organizations utilize a dual hierarchy structure whereby an additional set of positions is established parallel to the managerial hierarchy. These positions comprise a professional hierarchy of equivalent rank with the managerial hierarchy, but with evaluation, control, authority and advancement criteria consistent with the professional characteristics described earlier. The specific objectives of using the dual hierarchy are to (1) provide advancement opportunities for professionals unable or unwilling to ascend the managerial hierarchy; (2) permit successful professional personnel to earn compensation, recognition and prestige equivalent to that of successful managers; (3) provide professionals with opportunities for greater autonomy; and (4) create a set of positions where administrative duties do not interfere with professional contributions [18,20,-23,40].

The dual hierarchy is intended to help manage conflict between professionals and their employing organizations by facilitating pursuit of professional objectives within the organization. While many objectives of the dual hierarchy are often pursued informally by organizations which have only a single hierarchy, such informal processes cannot provide the professional with meaningful career alternatives to advancement on the managerial hierarchy.

Figure 1 illustrates the single and dual hierarchy structures. Dual hierarchies are occasionally used by research-oriented corporations, hospitals, and often by colleges and universities, where research professorships and university chairs may offer prestige and financial benefits comparable or even superior to administrative positions.

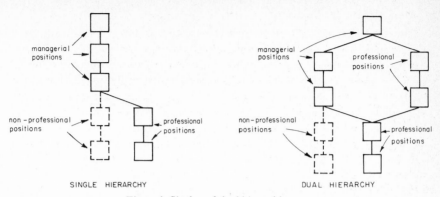

Figure 1. Single and dual hierarchies.

An example of the dual hierarchy in industrial research is provided by Hallenberg [18]. The dual hierarchy at Westinghouse Research Laboratories provides comparable salary ranges, but differing duties and appointment criteria, for positions on the two hierarchies. The management hierarchy consists of a director, department manager, section manager and supervisor. Equivalent positions on the professional hierarchy are titled director, consultant, advisory scientist (or advisory engineer) and fellow scientist (or fellow engineer).

The promotion procedure has three stages. First, the professional is nominated by a manager (for a fellow position), or a director (for an advisor or consultant position). Then the nominee's qualifications are considered by an examining board consisting of laboratory directors and the manager of administrative services, and the board makes a recommendation to the vice-president of research. Finally, the vice-president of research makes a decision based upon several criteria: mastery of scientific and technical field (usually Ph.D. or equivalent in research accomplishments); ability to plan independently and follow through on programs; professional accomplishments such as number and quality of internal and external publications, discoveries leading to company benefits, recognition by peers, strong consulting activities, invited participation in professional societies; and ability to exert influence, exercise judgment in matters affecting the laboratories, assume responsibility for special tasks and guide (though not necessarily supervise) the work of others. Evidence of competent supervision of other technical personnel is not required for promotion on the professional hierarchy, although it is a major criterion for those on the managerial hierarchy.

A review of the literature indicates that dual hierarchies have generally been unsuccessful at resolving conflicts between professionals and their employing organizations, and at providing alternative career paths and reward opportunities. The following problems are primarily responsible for this lack of success:

Lack of power

The most important reason dual hierarchies fail is that promotion on the professional hierarchy is, by definition, a movement away from power [2,6,15,28,36,37, 42]. By freeing professionals from budgeting, staffing, purchasing and other managerial activities, dual hierarchies simultaneously separate professionals from major rewards and resources which serve as sources of power within the organization. In a few cases, research grants or other nonorganizational sources of support may provide freedom for professionals, but usually the adoption of a dual hierarchy results in increased, not decreased, dependence upon nonprofessional management.

Sign of failure

Accurately or not, the professional hierarchy may be viewed by professionals as a face-saving device for persons who have failed in their managerial careers. In some instances, professional employees reported that if an individual possessed managerial talent he or she was encouraged to advance on the managerial rather than the professional hierarchy. Transfer to the professional hierarchy was therefore interpreted as a sign of the individual's inability (rather than unwillingness) to fulfill a managerial role. Shepard [42] suggests that since managerial talent is considered in our society to be highly desirable, an organizational employee who is unable to fulfill a managerial role is considered a failure. In fact, some organizations actually have used the professional hierarchy as a place to transfer incompetent managers so as to remove them from power without forcing them from the organization altogether [9,35–37,41,42]. On the other hand, in some organizations (in particular those where professionals perform primary functions, such as in hospitals and universities) powerful norms may develop which cause movement to the managerial hierarchy to be interpreted as a sign of failure.

Lack of equity with managerial hierarchy

Another difficulty is that organizations may fail to provide equal benefits for parallel positions on the two hierarchies [4,15,29,35,36,38]. This may result from inadequate attention to equalization on the part of the organization, differences in market value of the skills of professionals and managers, or other constraints beyond the organization's control (e.g., required adherence to a prespecified personnel grading system in public agencies).

Inadequate number of professional hierarchy positions

In some organizations the number of positions on the professional hierarchy was found to be so few that its incentive value was small [42]. This may result from lower prestige and income ceilings for those on the professional hierarchy was compared to the managerial hierarchy [35], or from a scarcity of positions in the middle levels of the professional hierarchy. Whyte [48, p. 600] points out that this may be caused by organizations promoting only those professionals who have made spectacular contributions:

When a man holding a supervisory position is promoted, transferred, retired, fired, or buried, this creates a vacancy, and the logic of the chart demands that a blank box be filled in with a new name as soon as can be arranged. If no fully qualified candidate for the position is available, the position must be filled, so management assumes that the new man will grow into his new responsibility. The scientific side provides no such ready-made boxes. Scientists claim that their superiors do not advance them on the scientific ladder, while expecting them to grow into the larger responsibilities. They rather demand that the scientists prove outstanding capacity before they are recognized.

Inequitable evaluative criteria

In some organizations studied, evaluations concerning professional ladder appointments and advancements were made solely by nonprofessionals. Under such circumstances choices may be made without respect to professional criteria, and the legitimacy of such choices therefore may be questioned by professionals:

First, professionals may deny that their hierarchical superiors have the skills to determine whether performance standards are being met. From the professional's viewpoint, only fellow professionals know enough about their work to evaluate it competently. Second, professionals may deny that their superior's performance standards are even relevant [12, p. 385].

It is clear that most of the reasons why dual hierarchies fail reflect implementation difficulties rather than problems inherent in the structure. As noted earlier, however, the single most important reason for failure is that the professional hierarchy separates professionals from key sources of organizational power, increasing professionals' dependence upon nonprofessional management. This is not an operational problem, but is rather a fundamental paradox of the dual hierarchy concepts.

A few successful implementations of dual hierarchies have been reported [8,18, 21], but all of these reports are based on anecdotes and managerial opinions; none is based upon rigorous research. Overall, the literature suggests strongly that the dual hierarchy has not been effective. The remainder of this paper will therefore discuss an alternative to the single and dual hierarchies which has not been explicitly considered in the literature, but which is consistent with existing theory and research. This alternative is designed to be congruent with professionals' characteristics, while simultaneously providing them with power and organizational resources adequate to maintain professional standards and values.

Triple hierarchies

An innovative structure designed to manage professional-organizational conflicts more successfully than single or dual hierarchies is the triple hierarchy. The triple hierarchy structure (shown in Figure 2) provides three different advancement opportunities. The managerial hierarchy is available to those who desire advance-

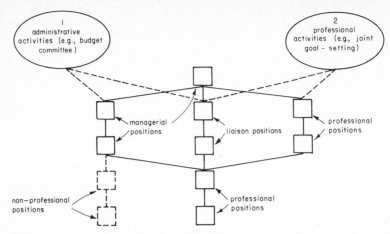

Figure 2. Triple hierarchy.

ment to managerial positions. For those professionals wishing only professional duties, the professional hierarchy remains a viable option. The third, liaison hierarchy is occupied by professionals in key administrative areas who have regular professional duties, but who also have hierarchical authority over professional hierarchy occupants in areas where professional values and organizational requirements are most likely to diverge. Note that in these areas individuals on the managerial hierarchy have no authority. Where serious divergence does not exist, liaisons — as occupants of this third hierarchy will be called — have no hierarchical authority, and in these areas occupants of the professional hierarchy continue to be dependent for resources and services upon the managerial hierarchy. Positions on all three hierarchies must be carefully established so as to permit equivalence with regard to salary, office appointments, etc.

Specific areas of authority to be assigned to liaisons must vary according to organizational circumstances; however, in most cases, duties would be assigned in the manner similar to that suggested by Table 1.

No implication is intended that the impact of managerial hierarchy activities upon professionals' working environments will be trivial. As under single or dual hierarchy structures, how well nonprofessional individuals and resources are managed will strongly affect the degree to which professional objectives are met. The important point is that authority will be assigned based upon the likelihood that divergent values will increase conflict between professionals and managers, and impair efficiency and morale. At least in theory, nonprofessionals can perform activities assigned to the managerial hierarchy in Table 1, and these activities are unlikely to result in professional-managerial conflict. Of course, other kinds of conflict, such as those concerning equitable resource allocations among work units, will be as likely to occur under the proposed structure as under any other.

Table 1
Illustrative areas of authority

Managerial hierarchy	Liaison hierarchy
Purchasing of general clerical supplies and equipment.	Purchasing of specialized technical supplies and equipment.
Selection and training of office and low-level administrative personnel.	Selection and training of professional and technical personnel.
Supervision of nonprofessional managerial and office personnel.	Supervision and coordination of professional activities.
Responsibility for evaluation of office and low-level administrative personnel.	Responsibility for conducting or coordinating professional employee performance appraisals.
Distribution of resources required by nonprofessional employees.	Distribution of resources required by professional employees.
Budgeting for nonprofessional activities.	Budgeting for professional activities.

Liaisons as described would be in a position to represent the interests of both managerial and professional subgroups within the organization. They would be involved in important organizational processes such as controlling and planning, and would therefore acquire an understanding of the limitations on resources and other constraints which act upon professional employees. Liaisons would thus be better equipped than their managerial hierarchy counterparts to mold professional expectations based upon these limitations. They would also be in a good position to establish and maintain professional controls through participative and collegial methods of desicion making, goal setting, and evaluation.

In addition to acting upon professional expectations so as to increase conformity to administrative constraints, liaisons would also ensure that professional requirements were brought to the forefront in organizational policy, goal setting, and resource allocation matters; in this role they would serve as legitimate representatives of the professional group. The organization could therefore depend on the liaisons to see that organizational objectives are not ignored by a professional group grown independent, while the professional could depend upon them to minimize organizational interference with primarily professional activities.

With respect to the problems with the dual hierarchy discussed earlier, the triple hierarchy addresses two of these in particular. They are:

Lack of power. The most important reason why dual hierarchies fail, and the reason which was said to constitute an inherent deficiency of the dual hierarchy concept, is that professionals on the professional hierarchy are separated from power, and must depend on nonprofessionals for resources and services. The triple hierarchy, on the other hand, limits managerial hierarchy authority to acquiring and administering nonprofessional resources and services. In other areas professional hierarchy occupants depend upon liaisons. These liaisons are clearly different from those on the professional hierarchy, as evidenced by their willingness to occupy liaison positions. Nonetheless, liaisons are far more likely than managers to share professional values and to comprehend professional expectations and requirements.

Poor and inequitable evaluative criteria. The major difficulties in this area were earlier said to be (1) denial by professionals that those who evaluated them had the skills to do so, and (2) disagreement between professionals and their evaluators concerning which performance standards are relevant. The triple hierarchy is more likely than the dual hierarchy to solve this problem, since evaluations and recommendations for promotion of professionals are made by liaisons, not by managers.

The other problems with the dual hierarchy — lack of equity between the hierarchies, inadequate numbers of professional positions, and perceptions of movement onto the professional hierarchy as evidence of failure — all have the potential to occur under the triple hierarchy as well. However, while the triple hierarchy would not automatically resolve these potential difficulties, neither would it automatically bring them about. Careful attention to these factors during the construction of the triple hierarchy would probably prevent the first two, and proper use of the professional hierarchy by the organization should, over time, minimize the third.

Liaisons as linking pins

Although the liaison position as described in this paper does not formally exist, and has not therefore been explicitly considered in the literature on organizational design, some insights may nevertheless be drawn from related theory and research. Inasmuch as liaisons serve important mediating functions, it is fruitful to compare them to Likert's [25,26] linking pins. Linking pins are individuals who have memberships in several groups, so that each group overlaps with other groups in the organization. Although Likert has been concerned primarily with vertical linkage, that is, with building bridges between different hierarchical levels, he also believed that lateral linkages between hierarchically equal groups were important.

It is basic to both Likert's linking pin structure and to our proposed triple hierarchy structure that, for an organization to function properly, neither professional nor managerial requirements can be ignored. The overlapping-group form of organization, when accompanied by a high level of group interactive skills, presents a structural mechanism to aid integration by increasing communication and information exchange, and by providing new channels through which influence may be exerted. Linking pins obtain influence, as would liaisons, because the members of each group accept and trust the linking persons more than a nonmember. In general, influence derives from being able to speak the language of both groups and from sharing to some extent the norms, values, needs, knowledge, vocabulary and objectives of each group to be linked. Likert also noted that where the divergences between groups in these areas are great, the task of a single linking pin becomes extremely difficult. Use of several positions, as in a liaison hierarchy, should alleviate this problem.

If a further analogy may be drawn between Likert's overlapping group model and the triple hierarchy it might be expected that, like the linking pin individual, liaisons will function variously as superiors, colleagues, and subordinates. Therefore, they need skill in both leadership and membership role behaviors.

Liaisons in practice: The integrator role

Some evidence pertinent to the triple hierarchy structure stems from the work of Lawrence and Lorsch [24], whose research highlighted the importance of the role of integrators in facilitating cooperation among different components of organizations in dynamic and diverse environments. One conclusion from their research which is particularly relevant is the following:

> If the integrators had developed goal, time, and interpersonal orientations equidistant among those of the managers in the various departments they were linking . . . they would be more effective in resolving conflicting viewpoints than if they tended clearly toward one orientation . . .. In essence, if the integrators thought and behaved in ways that were not too dissimilar to those of each of the departments with which they had to work, they would be better able to communicate with all these departments and thus to help solve interdepartmental disagreements [24, pp. 58–59].

It is likely that liaisons would adopt the intermediate orientations described by Lawrence and Lorsch. Their formal training and early professionally-related organizational experience should serve to develop and maintain professional values, while continual interaction with managerial hierarchy incumbents should acquaint them with the resource, functional and interpersonal constraints operating on the organization. The tendency to adopt an intermediate orientation would be strengthened by the formal reinforcement of such an orientation by the organization.

Another variable which affected performance in Lawrence and Lorsch's research concerned the basis of the integrator's influence. In the more effective plastics firms studied, integrators were seen as highly competent, and possessed influence primarily because managers valued their knowledge and expertise. In the relatively ineffective organizations integrators were not seen as particularly expert or knowledgeable.

While the triple hierarchy structure offers no guarantee that managers would view liaisons as highly competent, such perceptions are clearly more likely than under single hierarchy systems. Furthermore, liaisons would be less dependent than are most staff personnel upon informal influence in their interactions with managers, since they would have formal authority in areas where professional expertise is required.

Further support for the rationale underlying the triple hierarchy comes from Baumgartel's [5] and Pelz's [33] findings that when research director or research administration positions were held by individuals with professional or scientific backgrounds, researchers felt more protected and work units had higher productivity and morale. They found that the ideal situation occurred when the research directors had both technical/professional backgrounds and a thorough knowledge and understanding of their roles as administrators. Such individuals would most likely have joint loyalties to both their professions and their employing organizations.

Another description of a single position similar in some respects to a liaison is offered by Marcson [29]. While conducting research in a large electronics firm, he discovered an executive-level job for which the selection criterion was expertness — in science, not in management. Thus, indirectly, authority in this case derived from scientific expertise as well as from occupancy of the position.

Some important liaison functions are also performed by the expert manager described by Mintzberg [32]. As heads of staff groups these individuals appear to act both as managers and as experts, in that they must manage their organizational units while simultaneously serving in an advisory staff capacity. As specialized centers of information they advise other managers and are consulted regularly on specialized problems. Mintzberg pointed out that since much of the expert manager's work is tied in with his specialty function, typically managerial work aspects are less pronounced; however, they are present to some degree.

While theory and research related to the triple hierarchy suggest that important benefits might accrue from using the proposed structure, the research literature contains evidence of dysfunctions which would also be likely to result. Foremost among these is the probability of role conflict. For example, Kornhauser [23] has shown that the research director and research supervisor typically occupy "man in the middle" roles, with loose linkages between researchers and higher management. One result is that they are constantly exposed to conflicting demands, and are likely to experience considerable strain because of the cross-pressures. Other studies [1,22] have also found that integrators are apt to experience higher levels of conflict and tension because of the variety of roles they are required to assume in carrying out their integration responsibilities. It is probable that incumbents of the liaison hierarchy would be subject to similar conflict and tension.

Formalizing the professional-liaison role

Although the liaison hierarchy proposed in this paper has neither been recognized in the literature nor formally adopted in practice, some of its functions are often carried out through a variety of mechanisms. Committees, task forces and related structures may perform integrating and linking pin activities but, as noted earlier, cannot provide professionals meaningful career alternatives. Informal individual and group actions also result in integration; however, Galbraith notes that:

> These processes do not always arise spontaneously from the task requirements, especially in highly differentiated organizations. When the relevant participants have different and sometimes antagonistic attitudes ... the effective use of joint decision making requires formally designed processes [14, p. 47].

Based on a review of Lorsch [27], Lawrence and Lorsch [24], Burns and Stalker

[10], and Woodward [51], Lynton [28] concluded that under conditions of high differentiation and subsystem autonomy effective linkage mechanisms are usually organized formally and on a permanent basis. In his own work as well, temporary ad hoc linkage mechanisms often resulted in failure. These data suggest that problems of integration and professional accommodation are more appropriately addressed through permanent formal means such as the proposed triple hierarchy than through informal or temporary structural mechanisms.

In addition to formalizing the structure, specification of the areas of formal authority assigned to liaisons provides them with legitimate power within the organization, preventing them from having to rely solely on informal influence processes for performance of their integration functions. While influence may be obtained to some extent without formal authority, legitimation of activities by the provision of formal authority enhances this influence, and also reduces stress accompanying role conflict.

Conclusion

This paper recommends the creation of triple hierarchies to facilitate the integration of professional employees into bureaucratic organizations. These structures would help professionals by (1) providing advancement opportunities for individuals who wish to move from their professional specialties into administrative positions; (2) establishing promotion channels for professionals who lack the skill or ambition for managerial responsibilities; (3) granting liaison personnel adequate authority to assure that professional values and standards will not be compromised, nor organizational objectives ignored; and (4) creating mechanisms to reduce conflict between professionals and their employing bureaucracies. Thus, the triple hierarchy is designed to meet the aforementioned objectives underlying adoption of the dual hierarchy, while avoiding that structure's most important pitfalls.

The triple hierarchy would also be beneficial to managers. Activities most likely to generate conflict with their professional constituencies would be removed from their areas of authority, and they would benefit from frequent communications with liaisons who are at least somewhat sympathetic to their problems, and who are knowledgeable about practical realities and organizational constraints.

Clearly, the triple hierarchy could not fully replace other mechanisms used to resolve problems of conflict and integration. Its proper use would be in combination with other organizational methods (such as committees, task forces and other integrators) for effective integration of goals and activities within the organization.

It is obvious that a great deal of trial and experience would be necessary before the structure proposed in this paper could be considered a viable mechanism to meet the problems of conflict and integration of objectives described in this paper. We do know, however, that neither single nor dual hierarchies have been particularly successful in this regard. Although tentative, the structure proposed here seems a promising alternative.

References

[1] Adams, J. Stacy, "The Structure and Dynamics of Behavior in Organizational Boundary Roles," in Handbook of Industrial and Organizational Psychology, Marvin D. Dunnette (ed.), Rand McNally, Chicago, Ill., 1976, pp. 1175–1199.

[2] Argyris, Chris, "Interpersonal Competence, Organizational Milieu, and Innovation," Research Management, Vol. 9 (March 1966), pp. 71–88.

[3] Argyris, Chris, "On the Effectiveness of Research and Development Organizations," American Scientist, Vol. 56 (Winter 1968), pp. 344–355.

[4] Barber, Bernard, "Some Problems in the Sociology of the Professions," Daedalus, Vol. 92 (Fall 1963), pp. 669–688.

[5] Baumgartel, Howard, "Leadership Style as a Variable in Research Administration," Administrative Science Quarterly, Vol. 2 (December 1957), pp. 344–360.

[6] Beer, John J. and Lewis, W. David, "Aspects of the Professionalization of Science," Daedalus, Vol. 93 (Fall 1963), pp. 764–784.

[7] Berger, Philip K. and Grimes, Andrew J., "Cosmopolitan-Local: A Factor Analysis," Administrative Science Quarterly, Vol. 18 (June 1973), pp. 223–235.

[8] Blau, Peter M. and Scott, W. Richard, Formal Organizations, Chandler, San Francisco, Cal., 1962.

[9] Bralley, James A., "Proceedings of Industrial Research Institute Study Group Meetings: Job Status as an Award for Scientific and Administrative Accomplishment," Research Management, Vol. 3 (Winter 1960), pp. 227–238.

[10] Burns, Tom and Stalker, G.M., The Management of Innovation, Tavistock, London, England, 1961.

[11] Engel, Gloria V., "The Effect of Bureaucracy on the Professional Autonomy of the Physician," Journal of Health and Social Behavior, Vol. 10 (March 1969), pp. 30–41.

[12] Filley, Alan C., House, Robert J. and Kerr, Steven, Managerial Process and Organizational Behavior, Scott, Foresman, Glenview, Ill., 1976.

[13] Freidson, Eliot and Rhea, Buford, "Knowledge and Judgment in Professional Evaluations," Administrative Science Quarterly, Vol. 10 (June 1965), pp. 107–124.

[14] Galbraith, Jay R., Designing Complex Organizations, Addison-Wesley, Reading, Mass., 1973.

[15] Goldner, Fred H. and Ritti, R. Richard, "Professionalism as Career Immobility," American Journal of Sociology, Vol. 72 (March 1967), pp. 489–502.

[16] Gouldner, Alvin W., "Cosmopolitans and Locals – Toward an Analysis of Latent Social Roles I," Administrative Science Quarterly, Vol. 2 (December 1957), pp. 281–306.

[17] Hall, Richard H., "Professionalization and Bureaucratization," American Sociological Review, Vol. 33 (Feburary 1968), pp. 92–104.

[18] Hallenberg, Edward X., "Dual Advancement Ladder Provides Unique Recognition for the Scientist," Research Management, Vol. 13 (May 1970), pp. 221–227.

[19] Haug, Marie and Sussman, Marvin B., "Professionalization and Unionism," American Behavioral Scientist, Vol. 14 (September 1971), pp. 525–540.

[20] Healey, Frank, "Job Status for the Research Scientist," Research Management, Vol. 3 (Winter 1960), pp. 239–244.

[21] Hower, Ralph and Orth, Charles D., Managers and Scientists, Division of Research, Harvard Graduate School of Business Administration, Boston, Mass., 1963.

[22] Kahn, Robert L., Wolfe, Donald M., Quinn, Robert P., Snoek, J. Diedrick and Rosenthal, Robert A., Organizational Stress: Studies in Role Conflict and Ambiguity, Wiley, New York, N.Y., 1964.

[23] Kornhauser, William, Scientists in Industry: Conflict and Accommodation, University of California Press, Berkeley, Cal., 1962.

[24] Lawrence, Paul B. and Lorsch, Jay W., Organization and Environment, Harvard University Press, Boston, Mass., 1967.

[25] Likert, Rensis, New Patterns of Management, McGraw-Hill, New York, N.Y., 1961.

[26] Likert, Rensis, The Human Organization, McGraw-Hill, New York, N.Y., 1967.

[27] Lorsch, Jay W., Product Innovation and Organization, MacMillan, New York, N.Y., 1965.

[28] Lynton, Rolf P., "Linking an Innovative Subsystem into the System," Administrative Science Quarterly, Vol. 14 (September 1969), pp. 398–417.

[29] Marcson, Simon, The Scientist in American Industry, Princeton University Press, Princeton, N.J., 1960.

[30] Merton, Robert K., Social Theory and Social Structure, Free Press, Glencoe, Ill., 1957.

[31] Miller, George A., "Professionals in Bureaucracy: Alienation Among Industrial Scientists and Engineers," American Sociological Review, Vol. 32 (October 1967), pp. 755–767.

[32] Mintzberg, Henry, The Nature of Managerial Work, Harper and Row, New York, N.Y., 1973.

[33] Pelz, Donald C., "Some Social Factors Related to Performance in a Research Organization," Administrative Science Quarterly, Vol. 1 (December 1956), pp. 310–325.

[34] Perrucci, Robert and Gerstl, Joel E., Profession Without Community: Engineers in American Society, Random House, New York, N.Y., 1969.

[35] Raudsepp, Eugene, Managing Creative Scientists and Engineers, MacMillan, New York, N.Y., 1963.

[36] Ritti, R. Richard, "Dual Management – Does it Work?" Research Management, Vol. 14 (January 1971), pp. 19–26.

[37] Ritti, R. Richard, The Engineer in the Industrial Corporation, Colombia University, New York, N.Y., 1971.

[38] Schoner, Bertram and Harrell, Thomas W., "The Questionable Dual Ladder," Personnel, Vol. 42 (February 1965), pp. 53–57.

[39] Scott, W. Richard, "Professionals in Bureaucracies – Areas of Conflict," in Professionalization, Howard Vollmer and Donald Mills (eds.), Prentice-Hall, Englewood Cliffs, N.J., 1966, pp. 265–275.

[40] Secrist, Horace, "Motivating the Industrial Research Scientist," Research Management, Vol. 3 (Spring 1960), pp. 57–64.

[41] Shepard, Herbert A., "Nine Dilemmas in Industrial Research," Administrative Science Quarterly, Vol. 1 (December 1956), pp. 295–309.

[42] Shepard, Herbert A., "The Dual Hierarchy in Research," Research Management, Vol. 1 (Autumn 1958), pp. 177–187.

[43] Snizek, William, "Hall's Professionalism Scale: An Empirical Reassessment," American Sociological Review, Vol. 37 (Feburary 1972), pp. 109–114.

[44] Strauss, Anselm L. and Rainwater, Lee, The Professional Scientist, Aldine, Chicago, Ill., 1962.

[45] Strauss, George, "Professionalism and Occupational Associations," Industrial Relations, Vol. 2 (October 1963), 7–31.

[46] Thompson, James D., Organizations in Action, McGraw-Hill, New York, N.Y., 1967.

[47] Thompson, Victor A., "Hierarchy, Specialization, and Organizational Conflict," Administrative Science Quarterly, Vol. 5 (March 1961), pp. 485–521.

[48] Whyte, William Foote, Organizational Behavior: Theory and Application, Irwin-Dorsey, Homewood, Ill., 1969.

[49] Wilensky, Harold L., "The Professionalization of Everyone?" American Journal of Sociology, Vol. 70 (September 1964), pp. 137–158.

[50] Wilson, Robert N., "Patient-Practitioner Relationships," in Handbook of Medical Sociology, Howard E. Freeman, Sol Levine and L. Reeder (eds.), Prentice-Hall, Englewood Cliffs, N.J., 1963.

[51] Woodward, Joan, Industrial Organization: Theory and Practice, Oxford University Press, London, England, 1965.

North-Holland/TIMS Studies in the Management Sciences 5 (1977) 71–88
© North-Holland Publishing Company

ORGANIZING MULTIPLE-FUNCTION PROFESSIONALS IN ACADEMIC MEDICAL CENTERS *

MARTIN P. CHARNS

Carnegie-Mellon University

PAUL R. LAWRENCE

Harvard University

and

MARVIN R. WEISBORD

Organization Research and Development

Contingency theory was used to analyze the organization of nine academic medical centers. Substantial differences existed among important characteristics of five functions – undergraduate medical education, graduate degree education, housestaff education, research, and patient care – and among the specialty departments of the centers. Individuals performing combinations of functions reported blurred perceptions of functions' characteristics. Traditional departmental structures did not facilitate an individual's shift in orientations from one function to another, nor was the academic department structure most appropriate for all functions. A matrix organization design was suggested as an alternative organizational form for medical centers and possibly for other complex professional organizations where individuals perform multiple diverse functions. In a matrix design individuals are responsible both to a department chairman and to different directors for each function they perform.

Environmental changes have created new stresses and opportunities for American medical schools and teaching hospitals. Meeting these stresses and seizing these opportunities will require reorganization. However, no empirically validated theory has been available for evaluating alternative arrangements. This paper shows how a theory developed in studies of industrial firms can be applied to academic medical centers and begins validating the theory with data drawn from nine medical centers. In addition, the paper presents a new approach to the difficult problem of relating complex professional roles to task requirements.

The conventional structure of medical centers reflects prescriptions of classical organization theory [5,15,16] in organizing work by specialities, such as biochemistry, internal medicine, psychiatry, and surgery. Increasing in importance are interdepartmental programs in education, research and health care delivery which

* Received May 1975; revised February 1976, April 1976.

cut across the traditional organizational boundaries — specialty departments in the medical school and specialty services in the hospital. For example, in education alone, experimental curricula are organized around organ systems or focal problems rather than traditional disciplines, and ask students to meet behavioral criteria in addition to demonstrating substantive knowledge. Research in cancer, and delivery of preventive, comprehensive, and family- and community-oriented medicine are other examples of programs requiring interdisciplinary collaboration.

Because these programs cut across organizational boundaries, they place increased demands and strains on the existing organization and management. The greatly increased turnover among American medical school deans is a symptom of this management problem. The mean tenure in office has declined from 12.4 years for those deans appointed before 1960 to 4.7 years for those appointed since [17].

To cope with these pressures, some academic medical center leaders have been improvising on classical designs by adding other organizational arrangements on a trial-and-error basis. However, they seem to lack an alternative organization theory that would help them respond to these pressures in a more basic way. Organizing and managing programs in each of the areas of education, research, or health care delivery presents a substantial complexity in its own right. Organizing for all simultaneously is a process far more complex than can be handled by traditional organization theory.

Preceding a description of the direct application of contingency theory [2,12,18] to medical schools and teaching hospitals, these organizations are compared to industrial firms. Contingency theory and its extension to academic medical centers then are presented, followed by the results and implications of empirical work in nine centers.

Organizational structure of the academic medical center

The reader may be accustomed to viewing the academic physician's job as a blend of roles, often combining in the same event education, research, and patient care functions. For example, medical student teaching often is combined with the delivery of patient care in a clinic or ward. This study tests the alternative hypothesis that an academic physician's job consists of several functions having important differences in their performance requirements. Whether they can be handled as a single professional role is problematic and depends to a considerable extent on organizational arrangements.

To examine the organizational implications of differences among functions, first consider the usual structure of an academic medical center. It is composed of a medical school and its affiliated teaching hospitals. These major organizational units are further partitioned by scientific disciplines and medical specialties, represented by departments in the medical school. Clinical departments are paralleled in the hospital affiliates by clinical services representing specialties or finer partitions representing subspecialties. Although this is the apparent structure of a medical center organization, it is overly simplistic. Focusing on the key members of the organization — the medical school's faculty and hospital's attending physicians — provides greater insight into the organization.

Most key professional members perform not one but a combination of education, research, and patient care functions. Each function has its own identifiable sub-environment and constituency, presenting different organizational opportunities and pressures. The organization is built upon the combined work of these multiple-function professionals (MFP), most of whom perform three or more substantially different functions. The authors consider this arrangement to contrast sharply with industrial firms, where most members perform a single function in one unit most of the time. For example, an industrial employee does primarily research or production or sales work. Even managers focus primarily upon the work of their functional units [12]. Only top management and a few individuals in coordinating positions continually bridge several diverse functions and associated sub-environments. This contrast between the MFP in academic medicine and the single-function person in a typical industrial firm is shown in Figure 1.

Use of multiple-function professionals can be attributed largely to the Flexner Report [7], which in 1910 encouraged the upgrading of medical education by merging of education, research, and patient care activities into the same organization. In performing multiple functions it was asserted the MFP potentially could integrate advancements in one area directly into the other areas. This close association among functions undoubtedly has contributed greatly to American medicine's substantial achievements in providing a scientific foundation for medical practice. However, since World War II advances in medicine itself, as well as societal changes, have greatly increased the complexity of academic medical center functions. Observers of American medicine, commenting on the dissatisfaction with the performance of academic medical centers, have called attention to the MFP. For example, one eminent observer of American medicine said:

... The individual faculty member is the key member of two large complex enterprises and carries three different major assignments, which are important elements in each of the two enterprises. He is both a faculty member and a member of the hospital staff, and he is engaged in [the functions of] teaching, research, and patient care. Called upon to wear so many hats [each corresponding to a different function], he finds it simpler most of the time to wear his own ... [1, p. 133].

A member of the faculty in one of the medical schools participating in this study commented:

... There's a lot of talk today that medical schools are failing to address the great issues of society. As a member of the system, I feel frustrated .... Faculty members have three basic areas — service [patient care], teaching, and research .... They should be mutually reinforcing, but for the most part they're not .... Faculty members' time is divided between these three competing realities. There are all kinds of big gaping cracks for things to fall into. When you put all of us together, the whole is more inadequate than the sum of its parts.

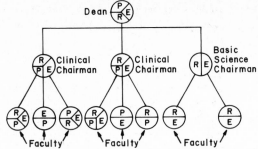

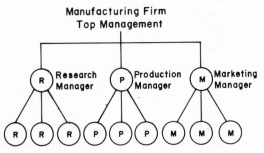

Figure 1. Distribution of functions of MFP's in academic medical centers contrasted with typical manufacturing firm.

One medical school dean said of his faculty's MFP's, "What we have here are a bunch of switch-hitters, who are batting about 0.150 from either side of the plate . . .." Contingency theory provides a framework for examining in more depth each of the functions of the academic medical center, the MFP's tendency to "wear his own hat," or blur the particular requirements of each function, and the possible consequences for center performance.

Contingency theory

The basic premise of contingency theory is that there is no one best way to structure and manage all organizations. Rather, organizational arrangements — such as structure, reward systems, information systems, management styles, contractual arrangements, budgeting, and other procedures — that are congruent with a particular task's requirements and its associated environment contribute most to organizational performance. By measuring task and environmental characteristics in terms of uncertainty, Lawrence and Lorsch [12] empirically validated this concept of differentiation in ten organizations in three diverse industries. Additional research also has supported these findings [10,13].

The concept of organizational differentiation is loosely analogous to specialization of function in biological systems. Given the different functions and requirements of the lungs and the liver, for example, it is appropriate that they have different structures and operating characteristics.

Similarly, different task characteristics in an organization require different structural arrangements and different cognitive and emotional orientations by organization members. When a member's cognitive map of the significant variables and causal relations for a particular task matches the reality for that task, it is more likely that high performance will be attained. It is not surprising that different orientations are required for research and production functions in industrial firms. This paper investigates the differences in orientations required for most effective performance of the MFP's different functions in the medical center.

Research design

A central purpose of this research was the extension of contingency theory and its application to analysis of medical center organization. Both interviews and questionnaires were used for data collection, and a pilot study was performed before continuing the major data collection effort.

Pilot study

The pilot study refined data collection procedures and instruments specifically for academic medicine, while building upon earlier research in other settings. The detail of this study is reported elsewhere [3]. It should be noted here that data from four diverse sites were collected through extensive interviews with all members of the dean's office, all chairmen of departments and key faculty committees, officers of the faculty senate or governance organization, university officials, and administrators of all affiliated teaching hospitals. The researchers also observed activities in both hospitals and medical schools, and attended a diverse array of meetings in each school.

Utilizing knowledge gained through interviews and observations, a comprehensive questionnaire was developed. Several items asked for respondents' perceptions of the task uncertainty of the various functions. Several other items asked for organizational arrangements, such as need for formal rules, required by each function. The pilot study led to item revisions to improve their clarity for medical respondents.

Second phase of the study

Five additional sites were chosen, attempting to maximize diversity among their organizations and environments. Two of the medical schools were public and three private. One was very new and the others well established. Three were in or near large urban areas, and two in smaller cities. Two had major affiliations with hospitals with substantial primary and secondary patient care responsibilities – such as community hospitals – and three were affiliated with tertiary, highly specialized referral hospitals. Sites included one of the outstanding medical research centers in the world and a school noted for its innovative curriculum.

Interviews were held with faculty and administrators and focused upon specific issues facing each particular center, similarities and differences among the center's research, education, and health care delivery functions, and local organization and management practices.

The questionnaire

Only questionnaires returned by faculty members were analyzed, and administrators' responses were excluded from analysis. Questionnaire items, sampling and distribution procedures are described in the Appendix. For each function, a set of items asked for perceptions of required organizational arrangements and of task and environmental uncertainty. The seven items, shown in the Appendix, were asked in reference to each of the following five functions:
    (1) undergraduate medical education, leading to an M.D. degree;
    (2) graduate degree education, leading to an M.S. or Ph.D.;
    (3) housestaff education, post-M.D. training of interns and residents;
    (4) research, and
    (5) patient care.
Individuals answered the set of items for a particular function only if they considered it to be a significant part of their work. Although estimates could have been collected of the percentage of time allocated to each function, interviewees indicated that such questions would not provide reliable data and would antagonize respondents.

Hypotheses

Since the sites had been chosen to maximize diversity, it was expected that significant differences would be found in reports of task characteristics among sites. Each school especially approached undergraduate medical education and health care delivery with different philosophies and organizational arrangements. Therefore, it was hypothesized:

H1. *Significant differences in reported task and environmental characteristics exist among the five sites.*

Interviewees described substantial differences among different specialty departments. Each department was an organizational unit in the center, and sometimes had its own building. Each had an identifiable knowledge base and a different specialty training program and professional organization. Frequently, faculty referred to differences in training, orientations, and ways of getting things done among different departments. Therefore, it was expected that the substantial differences among specialties would be reflected in the questionnaire data on task characteristics. It was hypothesized:

H2. *Medical center departments are significantly different from each other.*

Based upon observations and interviews with both faculty and administrators, the authors believed substantial differences also existed among the five functions. It was hypothesized the questionnaire data would show:

H3. *Medical center functions are significantly different from each other.*

The authors were aware of no organization theory which would predict *a priori* whether greater differences existed among functions or among departments. Many interviewees asserted that greater differences existed among the specialty departments. Some key administrators, however, questioned this prevailing view. Based upon their comments, the authors hypothesized that questionnaire responses from faculty members would show:

H4. *Greater differences exist among the departments than among the functions.*

Results

A 60% final response rate was obtained. Each of the 740 respondents might perform more than one function; thus 2386 sets of task characteristics for the five functions were available for analysis.

To determine whether the data reflected the two constructs — task uncertainty and required organizational arrangements — that the instrument was designed to measure, the items were correlated and three orthogonal components, accounting for 60% of the variance in the correlation matrix, were extracted through principal components analysis and varimax rotation. Rotated component loadings are shown in the Appendix. The first two components, uncertainty and formality of structure, corresponded to the dimensions expected in the questionnaire design. The third component consisted of the single item, repetitivity. Since empirically it was not highly correlated with uncertainty, as was expected, repetitivity was treated

Table 1

Mean values of task uncertainty reported by faculty members in five academic medical centers

Functions Departments	Undergraduate medical education	Graduate degree education	Housestaff education	Research	Patient care
Medicine	1.11 * 134 **	0.74 66	0.83 128	−1.07 97	−1.02 132
Pathology	0.73 42	0.69 24	0.81 38	−0.40 36	−0.92 29
Pediatrics	1.04 54	0.20 24	0.78 51	−0.79 34	−1.49 56
Psychiatry	0.71 62	0.33 40	0.75 54	−0.11 34	−0.10 54
Surgery	1.16 58	1.60 25	0.48 65	−0.39 39	−1.80 76
ALL	0.86 590	0.51 337	0.61 498	−0.86 460	−1.18 501

* Mean − Higher number indicates greater uncertainty.
** Number of respondents.

separately in subsequent analyses. Scales were constructed as an unweighted linear combination of items, standardized across the 2386 responses. For example, means for the uncertainty scale for the five functions in five departments are shown in Table 1.

The data were investigated further through analysis of variance. For each of the 2386 observations, the three scales were used as the dependent variables in separate analyses. Independent variables were (1) respondent's department coded as nine zero/one variables, (2) respondent's site coded as five zero/one variables, and (3) a set of five variables coded zero/one indicating the five functions. Variance explained and F-statistics for incremental contribution by each of the independent variables are shown in Table 2.

Results of the analysis were similar for all three dimensions. First, the site independent variable explained the smallest amount of variance. The incremental contribution of site to variance explained was statistically significant ($p < 0.01$) for two of the three dimensions, but it was also extremely small. Second, on all dimensions, function and department both explained statistically significant ($p < 0.001$) and substantial amounts of variance. Most striking is the finding that function far dominated both site and department in variance explained.

That there are greater differences among the functions than among the departments is contrary to hypothesis *H*4. However, it coincides with the perceptions of some administrators and with the fact that the different functions have identifiable

Table 2
Variance (R^2) in reports of task characteristics explained by function, depeartment, and site and F-statistics for incremental contribution of each

Variance (R^2) explained:

Independent variables	Dependent variables		
	Uncertainty	Needed structure	Repetitivity
Function	0.189	0.064	0.120
Department	0.022	0.050	0.069
Site	0.005	0.005	0.007
Function and department	0.215	0.105	0.167
Function and site	0.194	0.066	0.125
Department and site	0.027	0.056	0.078
Function, department and site	0.220	0.108	0.173

F-Statistics for incremental contribution to R^2:

Independent variables	Degrees of freedom	Dependent variables		
		Uncertainty	Needed structure	Repetitivity
Function	4,2368	146.5 **	34.5 **	68.0 **
Department	9,2368	8.8 **	12.4 **	15.3 **
Site	4,2368	3.8 *	2.0	4.3 *

$$F_k = \frac{(R_{ijk}^2 - R_{ij}^2)/(df_k)}{(1 - R_{ijk}^2)/(n - df_i - df_j - df_k - 1)}, \quad \text{for incremental contribution of } k.$$

n = Number of responses.
** $p < 0.001$.
* $p < 0.01$.

subenvironments, each with its own constituents wanting particular outcomes. By considering as a baseline the large differences among specialties, it is fair to conclude that the differences among functions are not trivial, but substantial. Contrary to fairly widespread assumptions in the field, the MFP does perform a set of very different activities that do not blend easily into a single homogeneous role.

Blurring perceptions of characteristics of multiple functions

Given the substantial differences among the several functions in the medical center, the application of the contingency theory concept of differentiation leads one to ask whether the MFP's perceive these differences accurately. From earlier research [12] one would expect higher organizational performance when individuals' perceptions of task characteristics are appropriate to the actual task. It is important to examine MFP's perceptions of each of their functions, since each has different characteristics. If the MFP's perceptions of any one function were affected by the other functions the MFP also performed, then one would expect that the MFP's orientations would be less than fully appropriate for the task requirements and, consequently, that organizational performance would suffer.

From the interview data it appeared that MFP's tended to blur together perceptions of their several functions. They described differences between any two of their functions as less than differences apparent to the authors from their observations and their interviews with administrators. The questionnaire data provided a means of testing the occurrence of such blurring in a more systematic way.

Reported function characteristics from people performing each combination of functions were compared to corresponding reports from MFP's performing the particular combination plus one other function. Adding the additional function to the original combination could show reports of each of the original functions moving either toward or away from the additional function. Movement away from the additional function would indicate MFP's performing several functions tend to contrast them and focus on differences among them. On the other hand, movement toward the additional function would indicate that MFP's blur the differences.

For example, consider reported uncertainty in pediatrics for M.D. education and for the additional function patient care. The mean uncertainty of M.D. education reported by pediatricians performing only M.D. education (M_m) is 0.77, the mean uncertainty of patient care reported by pediatricians performing only patient care (P_p) is -3.00, and the mean uncertainty of M.D. education reported by pediatricians performing both functions (M_{mp}) is 0.06. Note that M_{mp} is less than M_m, and P_p also is less than M_m. This situation is one of blurring uncertainty of M.D. education towards uncertainty of patient care. Similarly, for the group of people performing any combination of one to four functions, the mean of each task characteristic of each function reported by all people performing the given combination of functions can be compared to the mean reports of all people performing the given combination of functions plus one additional function. When the mean from the second group moves away from the mean of the first group toward the mean reports of people performing only the additional function, then blurring is indicated.

Since earlier analysis showed that specialty departments were significantly different, it is inappropriate to examine blurring by using respondents from several departments simultaneously. Thus, separate analyses were performed for each of the five specialties having the largest number of respondents for all of the functions. These departments were internal medicine, pathology, pediatrics, psychiatry, and surgery. Within each department, 480 comparisons over the three dimensions of the five functions were conducted.

If blurring did not occur systematically, then for a characteristic of any given

Table 3
Occurrences of blurring of function characteristics when an additional function is added to combination of functions performed

Function	Department					Sum over five depts.
	Internal medicine	Pathology	Pediatrics	Psychiatry	Surgery	
Undergraduate medical education	55 *	71	68	49	43	286
	57% **	74%	71%	51%	45%	60%
Graduate degree education	58	55	67	56	66	302
	60%	57%	70%	58%	69%	63%
Housestaff education	36	59	57	50	75	277
	38%	61%	59%	52%	78%	58%
Research	52	53	46	62	44	257
	54%	55%	48%	65%	46%	54%
Patient care	43	57	59	62	60	281
	45%	59%	61%	65%	62%	59%
Sum over five focal functions	244	295	297	279	288	1403
	51%	61%	62%	58%	60%	58%

* Number of cases showing blurring out of 96 possible comparisons for each function in each department
** Percent of cases showing blurring.

function it is equally likely that people performing N functions report the characteristic numerically greater than or less than reported by people performing the N functions plus an additional function. Thus, due solely to chance one would expect half of the comparisons to yield results similar to blurring and half to indicate contrasting. For each of the five departments, the number of comparisons and the percent of all comparisons showing blurring are presented in Table 3.

A systematic pattern can be seen in Table 3; blurring occurs substantially more often than the 240 cases expected solely by chance for each function and for each department. The incidents of blurring range from 244 cases in internal medicine to 297 cases in pediatrics, and from 257 cases for research to 302 cases for graduate degree education.

Performance issues

Previous organizational research found that the highest performing organizations were those that adopted different organizational arrangements and structures for tasks with different degrees of uncertainty [2,12,18]. Within each department of most academic medical centers, however, approximately the same organizational arrangements are used for all functions. The MFP usually is responsible to a department chairman and subject to the same organizational rules for all functions, and is evaluated and promoted mainly for outstanding academic performance — most often demonstrated by research publication. Given the differences in functions, it is questionable whether the same organizational arrangements are appropriate for all functions. The academic department and norms of academic medicine seem to be most appropriate for research and for graduate education. However, when the organizational structure, rules, reward system, and norms of the academic department are applied simultaneously to other functions such as patient care, one would reason that they are inappropriate, since these functions present very different organizational requirements.

In addition to the direct relationship between organizational arrangements and performance, one also should consider the relationship between individuals' cognitive and emotional orientations and performance. When the orientations are appropriate for a particular task, then high performance is expected to result. However, if individuals tend to blur the distinctions among their several functions, then their orientations are somewhat inappropriate for some functions. Dissonance research [6] suggests how blurring is often functional for individuals, allowing them to maintain psychological well-being by not having to respond to the demands and differences from diverse functions. Psychologically, it is much simpler for individuals to treat multiple functions as if they were more similar than they actually are. However, blurring is dysfunctional for organizational performance. Minimizing differences among functions implies that subtleties go unrecognized, opportunities go unnoticed, and pressures and conflicts are denied.

Two examples of behavior associated with blurring are the teacher who uses a disproportionate amount of class time to discuss rare diseases and interesting research cases at the expense of basic medical topics, and the bedside clinician-teacher who discusses a case with medical students without awareness of heightening a patient's anxiety.

Based on these lines of analysis it is hypothesized that the customary organizational arrangements of academic medical centers are substantially handicapping their performance. Testing this hypothesis must await further research that solves the very difficult problem of measuring task performance in health settings. Even without the benefit of widely accepted performance measures, however, it seems reasonable to pursue the logic of these findings and to discuss their implications for organizational design of academic medical centers.

Organizational design questions

The central organizational design question raised by these research findings is: Can an academic medical center be organized in ways that better fit its several diverse program requirements and offset the probable dysfunctions of MFP blurring of education, patient care, and research?

The most direct implication of these findings is that different organizational elements should be employed to supervise the different functions. MFP's should be responsible to different individuals, be subject to different reward and evaluation systems, have different potential career ladders, and operate under different kinds of organizational controls and rules for each assigned function. The degree of formal organization and specificity of rules should range from least for research to most for patient care.

As an extreme structural solution one might consider disbanding the academic departments and grouping faculty around the different functions. Such an alternative could be expected to have major dysfunctional effects, for it would hinder coordination across functions and also make it more difficult for the organization to respond to differences among specialties. The long-term consequence of organizing solely by function would be the downgrading of specialty competence.

The complexity of academic medical centers is not readily handled by traditional organizational models, with their focus on hierarchical structure. The simultaneous requirements of responding to both technical specialties and function differences strongly suggests the use of a matrix organization design [4,8,11].

In a matrix organization, most individuals are responsible to two or more people for different areas of activity. The application of a matrix organization to an academic medical center is shown schematically in Figure 2. The MFP is responsible to a department chairman for general professional development. For each function performed, the MFP is responsible to a different program director. Thus, the chief of the hospital specialty service would be a different individual from the person responsible for an educational program in which the MFP taught. Moreover, the MFP's department chairman would be still a third person. Each program director would be expected to communicate regularly with the MFP about program requirements and would judge the MFP's work in terms of program performance criteria.

One could argue that the matrix form of organization heightens conflict and is unworkable in practice. For several years, the matrix organization has been used in aerospace and other high technology industries performing complex programs in diverse environments, and evidence of its effectiveness has been shown [9,14]. Separating responsibility for different functions does increase the level of manifest conflict in the organization. However, this conflict is latent already; the functions themselves are inherently conflicting in terms of both time and other resource demands and the behavior required of the MFP. By bringing the conflict to a manifest level, where it can be dealt with openly and rationally, better decisions can be reached [12]. Implementing a matrix organization and managing the inherent conflict places major strains on the organization and on the individual. Successful implementation of the matrix requires not only changes in organizational structure, but also development of management and process skills to a degree not found presently in most academic medical centers.

Even if this matrix structure carries advantages at the organizational level, does it have merit at the level of the individual MFP? The matrix form should contribute

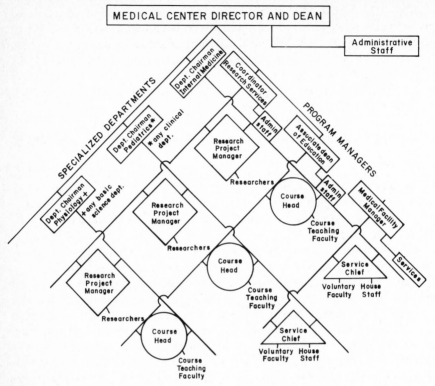

Notes:

[1] Position on diagram does not indicate organizational status. A faculty member may appear in several places on the diagram.

[2] Dean and hospital director ("medical facility manager") may be responsible to the same person, such as a vice president for health sciences. Sometimes, however, they are responsible to different individuals and even different organizations.

Fig. 2. Schematic display of one possible matrix organization for an academic medical center.

to MFP's differentiating among their several functions. Having different individuals serving as advocates for each function should facilitate the MFP's cognitive shift among functions. This shift can be facilitated further by separating the location of function performance in time and place. However, highlighting differences among functions might increase individual stress. Some people probably would not be able to work under such arrangements. Others may be able to work effectively on two functions for any one period of time, but not on four or five functions.

Effectively utilizing skills of these MFP's requires clearly specifying expectations in advance and then assessing performance for each function. From year to year, such contracts could be altered to fit the needs of both the individual and the organization. All individuals need not perform the same proportion of each function, and the organization should be flexible enough to utilize the best talents of each individual. In addition, such clearer contracts should reduce role ambiguity, and by bringing expectations and aspirations into the open improved manpower planning could be attained. Individuals may be able to work on combinations of activities they see as more desirable for their personal skills, values, and orientations. However, effective implementation of such organizational changes probably would require considerable alteration in the reward system. Academic promotion and other rewards would have to be provided for excellence in education and patient care in addition to research.

Implications for future research

Thus far, task perceptions were modeled as dependent upon those functions an individual performs, and a pattern of blurring of function characteristics was observed. It remains to refine these models to assess the degree of blurring and the direct relationship between perceptions of function characteristics and performance. Further analysis also is required to include in the models the effect of organizational arrangements on task perceptions. One must question why the site accounted for so little of the explained variance in reports of task dimensions. Is the culture of academic medicine so similar across the five sites in this study, or will more detailed specification of organizational arrangements in the different sites lead to more robust models?

At present this research cannot answer these questions, but the findings at one of the sites are suggestive. At this site, a number of small-scale organizational experiments were underway and beginning to move this medical school toward a matrix structure. For example, program directors had been appointed for three education programs and for two distinct patient care programs. Most of these program directors were very influential people. Further, the school was beginning to use program budgeting as well as departmental budgeting. They were beginning to collect systematic data on teaching as well as research performance and feeding these data into the evaluation process. Whether these changes in structure and process have effects upon MFP's perceptions of their multiple functions or upon organizational performance awaits further research.

Conclusion

Through an extension of the differentiation concept, task characteristics and the organizational arrangement of the multiple-function professional have been examined. Additional research is needed to refine the model and relate task perceptions to organizational performance, but already, serious questions need to be raised about the present organizational design and management of academic medical centers. If one accepts the premise that lack of sufficient differentiation is dysfunctional for organizational performance – as was found in industrial settings, where performance could be measured more easily than in medicine – one must conclude that the present organizational structure and procedures, which reduce required differentiation, do not contribute to performance.

The multiple-function professional is found not only in academic medical centers, but also in universities, consulting firms, and other professional organizations. It is an arrangement that raises new organizational design issues. Consideration of differentiation – in addition to the traditional emphasis on coordination – is an important design issue in academic medicine and in other complex organizations dominated by professionals.

Appendix

The questionnaire was sent to a sample of 50% of the medical school faculty, stratified by department then selected randomly, plus all of the school and hospital administration – all members of dean's office, department chairmen, and hospital administrators. A cover letter from the researchers described the study, assured confidentiality of responses, and asked for individuals' perceptions to be reported candidly. A cover letter from the school's dean indicated his belief that the research was important and asked for participation and cooperation. All questionnaires were distributed through the center's internal mail system. Completed questionnaires were returned by respondents directly in a postage-paid return envelope addressed to the researcher. Respondents were identified by an identification control number known only by the research team, and nonrespondents were sent a follow-up letter and additional copy of the questionnaire.

Items in the questionnaire were intended to tap respondents' perceptions of characteristics of their functions and organizational arrangements required for each function. These items, shown below, were asked in reference to each of the respondent's five possible functions. As shown, the items were worded for the PATIENT CARE function. Items for the other functions appeared in similar format with the name of the function replacing "PATIENT CARE" in each item.

References

[1] Brown, Ray E., "Dollars and Sense in Medical School-Teaching Hospital Relationships," Journal of Medical Education, Vol. 40 (November 1965), Part 2, pp. 126–136.

[2] Burns, Thomas and Stalker, G.S., The Management of Innovation, Tavistock Publications, London, England, 1961.

[3] Charns, Martin P., "The Organization of Multiple Task Professionals: A Study of Four Academic Medical Centers," Harvard University Graduate School of Business Administration, Boston, Mass. (doctoral dissertation), 1972.

We are interested in your perceptions of your PATIENT CARE activities. In answering the following questions reflect upon the few most important PATIENT CARE activities you perform.

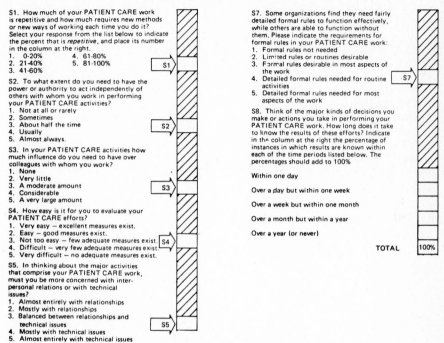

S1. How much of your PATIENT CARE work is repetitive and how much requires new methods or new ways of working each time you do it? Select your response from the list below to indicate the percent that is *repetitive*, and place its number in the column at the right.
1. 0-20%   4. 61-80%
2. 21-40%   5. 81-100%
3. 41-60%

S2. To what extent do you need to have the power or authority to act independently of others with whom you work in performing your PATIENT CARE activities?
1. Not at all or rarely
2. Sometimes
3. About half the time
4. Usually
5. Almost always.

S3. In your PATIENT CARE activities how much influence do you need to have over colleagues with whom you work?
1. None
2. Very little
3. A moderate amount
4. Considerable
5. A very large amount

S4. How easy is it for you to evaluate your PATIENT CARE efforts?
1. Very easy — excellent measures exist.
2. Easy — good measures exist.
3. Not too easy — few adequate measures exist.
4. Difficult — very few adequate measures exist.
5. Very difficult — no adequate measures exist.

S5. In thinking about the major activities that comprise your PATIENT CARE work, must you be more concerned with inter-personal relations or with technical issues?
1. Almost entirely with relationships
2. Mostly with relationships
3. Balanced between relationships and technical issues
4. Mostly with technical issues
5. Almost entirely with technical issues

S7. Some organizations find they need fairly detailed formal rules to function effectively, while others are able to function without them. Please indicate the requirements for formal rules in your PATIENT CARE work:
1. Formal rules not needed
2. Limited rules or routines desirable
3. Formal rules desirable in most aspects of the work
4. Detailed formal rules needed for routine activities
5. Detailed formal rules needed for most aspects of the work

S8. Think of the major kinds of decisions you make or actions you take in performing your PATIENT CARE work. How long does it take to know the results of these efforts? Indicate in the column at the right the percentage of instances in which results are known within each of the time periods listed below. The percentages should add to 100%

Within one day

Over a day but within one week

Over a week but within one month

Over a month but within a year

Over a year (or never)

TOTAL   100%

Varimax Rotation of Two Principal Components
Based Upon Seven Task Characteristics
in Five Academic Medical Centers

Item	Communality	Factor 1	Factor 2
Repetitivity	.122	.142	.319
Need Power to Act Independently	.236	.481	-.068
Need Influence Over Peers	.444	.019	.666
Difficulty in Evaluating Results of Efforts	.584	-.761	-.077
Orientation Toward Relationships or Technical Issues	.513	.459	-.549
Need Formal Rules	.438	.021	.661
Timespan of Feedback	.509	-.647	-.301

[4] Evans, John R., "Organizational Patterns for New Responsibilities," Journal of Medical Education, Vol. 45 (December 1970), pp. 988–999.

[5] Fayol, Henri, Industrial and General Administration, Dunod, Paris, France, 1925.

[6] Festinger, Leon, A Theory of Cognitive Dissonance, Row, Peterson, Evanston, Ill., 1957.

[7] Flexner, Abraham, "Medical Education in the United States and Canada, A Report to the Carnegie Foundation for the Advancement of Teaching," The Management Press, Boston, Mass. (Bulletin No. 4), 1910.

[8] Galbraith, Jay, Designing Complex Organizations, Addison Wesley, Rading, Mass., 1973.

[9] Goggin, William C., "How the Multidimensional Structure Works at Dow Corning," Harvard Business Review, Vol. 52 (January-February 1974), pp. 54–65.

[10] Khandwalla, Pradip N., "Mass Output Orientation of Operations Technology and Organizational Structure," Administratibe Science Quarterly, Vol. 19 (March 1974), pp. 74–97.

[11] Kingdon, Donald Ralph, Matrix Organization, Tavistock, London, England, 1973.

[12] Lawrence, Paul R. and Lorsch, Jay W., Organization and Environment, Division of Research, Harvard Business School, Boston, Mass., 1967.

[13] Lorsch, Jay W. and Morse, John, Organizations and Their Members: A Contingency Approach, Harper and Row, New York, N.Y., 1974.

[14] Marquis, Donald G., "A Project Team + Pert = Success. Or Does It?," Innovation, No. 5 (1969), pp. 26–33.

[15] Urwick, Lyndall F., "Organization as a Technical Problem," in Papers on the Science of Administration, L. Urwick and L. Gulick (eds.), Institute of Public Administration, Cornell University, New York, N.Y., 1937.

[16] Weber, Max, The Theory of Social and Economic Organization, (translated by A.M. Henderson and Talcott Parsons), Free Press, New York, N.Y., 1947.

[17] Wilson, Marjorie P., "Academic Administration: Opportunity or Futile Career Development," Clinical Research, Vol. 24 (January 1976), pp. 2–4.

[18] Woodward, Joan, Industrial Organization: Theory and Practice, Oxford University Press, London, England, 1965.

North-Holland/TIMS Studies in the Management Sciences 5 (1977) 89–97
© North-Holland Publishing Company

DIAGNOSING LATENT RELATIONSHIPS FOR COORDINATION *

VAL SYLBEY [†]

Florida International University

In this study lexical analysis was applied to documented functional statements in an organization manual to identify latent relationships for coordination. For the study of a large government department, 171 functional statements of eighteen organizational units, in five agencies were analyzed and clustered on the basis of similar functional statements. The analysis identified seventy relationships within agencies as candidates for coordination in addition to 184 already documented, and 559 interagency relationships in addition to the sixty-one documented. It was concluded that lexical analysis can therefore be used as a diagnostic tool to check the consistency of organizational documentation.

Every organization has the problem of coordinating activities to achieve its objectives, but the larger an organization, the more difficult it becomes to determine where coordination is needed. The traditional bureaucratic approach in designing organizations is to show structure by organization charts and to describe the activities assigned to the various units in the organization manual [10,13,16–18]. The actual activities of an organization may, however, differ from the activities planned in the manual [9,12].

Organization analysis is an attempt to understand the general interrelationships among organizational units. Lexical analysis, a "technique for making inferences by objectively and systematically identifying specified characteristics of messages" [11, p. 14], is a method for identifying these relationships by a context analysis of the organization manual. The relationships sought are latent since in the independent definition of functions by different people in different places and at different times organizational consistency is not required. Moreover there is no assurance that relationships are in fact active.

Context of problem

No one individual in a large organization can know about all the activities being performed. To coordinate the various activities requires a means for identifying

* Received April 1975; revised January 1976, May 1976.
[†] The author thanks the referees, the editors, Antoinette Wilkinson, Steve Altman, Robert House and Karl Magnusen for their comments.

candidate relationships for coordination and the possible content of the coordination. The chief problem is the assignment of the same function to more than one organizational unit, resulting in overlap or conflict.

Functional statements as data

Conceptually, a functional statement is a linguistic mapping of one facet of organizational behavior. A functional statement describes both activity and product, but also includes elements that define goals, constraints, inputs, outputs and so on. For example, the functional statement, "Prepares, submits and justifies budget estimates for approved development programs in accordance with appropriate budget directives," represents the general content of the assigned function, budgeting, and two constraints — one on the product and the other on the activity. Details of the performance of the function are not identified, so that additional search of documents is required to uncover the approved development programs and the appropriate budget directives.

The next step might be to identify the same function in other organizational units, but this may be difficult because of stylistic and syntactic variations in functional statements. To extract only the activity-product component of a functional statement, it must be classified. Any natural language provides much flexibility in the choice of words to express an idea and in the variety of structures for combining these words. Standardizing both content (words) and structure reduces the ambiguity of the actual descriptions. For example, lexical analysis identified the following two functional statements as being similar: (1) "Formulates technical and operational requirements for needed developments in the engineering sciences," and (2) "Provides technical guidance to the engineering activities of the aeronautical center engaged in the fabrication and manufacture of equipment and components for air navigation, air traffic control, and communication facilities." Classifying the elements of these different functional statements into categories and comparing the categories highlighted the procedural similarities and therefore the need to coordinate the two functions to prevent conflicting or inconsistent guidance and requirements.

Lexical analysis

Lexical analysis was applied to 171 functional statements in an organizational manual [6] that represented the planned rather than the actual operation of a large governmental organization. The method consists of three steps: classifying functional statements, calculating similarities, and clustering [22].

Step 1. Classifying

Classifying functional statements separates the various elements contained in a functional statement into distinct categories. In addition to the semantic classification of words, typically used in content analysis [11,23], two additional types of categories are needed: theme categories and term categories. A theme reflects the general content of a syntactic phrase and serves as a unit of expression [2,21]. When thematic categories are included as an element of analysis, the analysis is not restricted by the fact that the same idea can be expressed in different syntactic structures in a natural language [5,7]. Term categories identify the use of a word within a theme. Therefore the categorization scheme covers not only the content of words, but also their use in the different phrases of the functional statements.

The first example is a basic task description: "Maintains large-scale computer equipment configuration including software and peripheral equipment." The only theme in this functional statement is the task (task is the name of a theme category). The basic terms define an activity — "maintains" — and the object — "configuration." "Software" and "peripheral equipment" are subsidiary products (a term category), of the main product, configuration. "Large-scale computer equipment" defines the meaning of configuration. This sequence of words is composed of two nouns — "computer" and "equipment" — and a qualifier "large-scale," which is not measurable. Excluded from the classification are the words "including" and "and." Although they convey meaning to the analyst when coding, the formal structure of the functional statement does not provide for their inclusion, so they are ignored.

In summary, this example of classification contains one theme — a task, and the following words and their term categories:

Word	Term Category
Maintains	Activity
Configuration	Product
Software	Subsidiary product
Peripheral equipment	Subsidiary product
Large-scale	Qualifier
Computer	Product modifier
Equipment	Product modifier

The next functional statement analyzed is: "Prepares, submits, and justifies budget estimates for approved development programs in accordance with appropriate budget directives." This functional statement contains three themes: the task itself — "prepares, submits and justifies budget estimates," and two constraints on the task. The product, "budget estimates," is limited by the product constraint "approved development programs;" and the activity "prepares, submits, and justifies" is limited by an activity constraint "appropriate budget directives." The word "for" and the phrase "in accordance with" are ignored in the coding since the

relationship they represent was included in the classification of the themes. The classification of this functional statement can be summarized as follows:

Word	Theme Category	Term Category
Prepares	Task	Activity
Submits	Task	Activity
Justifies	Task	Activity
Estimates	Task	Product
Budget	Task	Product modifier
Approved	Product constraint	Activity modifier
Development	Product constraint	Activity modifier
Programs	Product constraint	Product
Appropriate	Activity constraint	Qualifier
Budget	Activity constraint	Product modifier
Directives	Activity constraint	Product

It is necessary to keep the various themes and their respective use of words separate in order to make valid comparisons. This classification provides inputs for calculating similarities between functional statements.

Step 2. Calculating similarities

The input data for similarity calculations are a list of objects and a list of properties for each object [14,20]. Similarity coefficients define quantitatively the relationship between two sets of objects. In this study, the objects are functional statements, and the words serve as properties of the functional statements. According to the previously described classification, each word in its category is considered a dimension in n-dimensional space [3]. Within this n-dimensional space, similarity coefficients define a distance that can be used to compare the difference between any two pairs of functional statements [8,15].

A functional statement is envisioned as a subset in this n-dimensional word space. The absence of a word from a functional statement would be reflected by a zero value on that dimension, and common absences when comparing any two functional statements would not affect the result. Multiple occurrences of a word increase the value of a functional statement on a dimension. The similarity coefficient, d^2, between any two functional statements, say A and B, is defined by the following formula:

$$d^2_{AB} = \sum_{X=1}^{m} (X_A - X_B)^2 ,$$

where X is the value of a functional statement on a dimension and m is the number of dimensions for A and B.

For example, the following matrix shows the assignment of five different words (numbered 1 through 5) for five functional statements (labelled A through E):

Functional statements	words				
	1	2	3	4	5
A	1	2	1	0	0
B	1	0	1	1	0
C	0	1	0	0	1
D	2	0	1	2	0
E	0	0	1	0	1

In this matrix, the word numbered 2 occurs twice in functional statement A, once in functional statement C and does not occur in functional statements B, D and E. From the distance equation, the similarity-coefficient matrix for the functional statement is:

	A	B	C	D	E
A	0	5	4	9	6
B	5	0	5	2	3
C	4	5	0	11	2
D	9	2	11	0	9
E	6	3	2	9	0

In this matrix, the d^2 distance between a functional statement and itself is zero. The distance between functional statements D and B is 2, but the distance between D and C is 11. This means that with respect to D the functional statement describing B is closer than that describing C. The matrix of similarity-coefficients serves as input to the clustering program.

Step 3. Clustering

Clustering of functional statements is performed in a three-program sequence. The first program reads the functional statements, selects the categorized words and performs the similarity calculations described above. The second program performs the clustering according to the Bierstone algorithm [1,9]. This algorithm determines whether the d^2 value for a functional statement indicates a high similarity to any other functional statement and assigns similar functional statements to a common cluster. The functional statements in one cluster are, therefore, more closely related to each other than to functional statements in other clusters. However, a functional statement may be assigned to more than one cluster if the content is similar along different dimensions to two or more clusters. After the clusters have been generated at one level of similarity, the process is repeated for a lower level of similarity, that is, for a larger d^2 value. In the third program, the clusters are printed with appropriate descriptions.

Results and discussion

From a methodological viewpoint, lexical analysis is a more rigorous and consistent means of revealing the content of organizational structure than impressionistic reading [4] of organization manuals. Also, compared to interviewing and observation of organizational activities, analysts using lexical analysis are unobtrusive [24].

Although actual activities change over time, the lag involved in updating the organization manual precludes continuous documentation of those changes. While this may be considered a drawback of lexical analysis, the stability of the data does have the advantage of capturing organization structure at a given time, and so permits the replication of an analysis by other researchers.

A substantive perspective is gained by examining the clusters generated from functional statements. In the organization manual, 171 functional statements were selected for analysis from eighteen organizational units, within five different agencies. Each agency developed its functional statements independently, but some awareness of organizational interdependencies existed. Functional statements in the organization manual documented the need for coordination both within and between agencies. The documentation of the coordination needed is summarized at the agency level in Table 1.

The table shows that most of the coordination needed was internal to a given agency — over half of the documented relationships (184 out of 334) in contrast to 89 external and 61 interagency relationships. Furthermore, the lack of symmetry in Table 1 indicates that the need for coordination recognized by one organiza-

Table 1
Documentation of coordination needed

Agency documenting	Agency referenced					External organizations
Coordination needed	V	W	X	Y	Z	
V	60	12	12	12	12	43
W	2	41	–	–	1	24
X	–	–	16	–	–	3
Y	2	1	1	13	1	2
Z	4	1	54	–	–	17

Table 2
Clustered relationships with $d^2 \leqq 2$

Agency	Agency				
	V	W	X	Y	Z
V	24	16	1	18	9
W	16	17	1	13	7
X	1	1	–	1	–
Y	18	13	1	1	5
Z	9	7	–	5	2

tional unit does not require recognition of the need by the reciprocal organizational unit, internal or external.

Lexical analysis bypasses this problem. Interagency similarities are treated in the same way as intra-agency similarities. The clustering, by definition, recognizes a reciprocal relationship between any two units of analysis. This symmetry is shown in Table 2, which summarizes at an agency level the relationships between the functional statements with a d^2 value less than or equal to two.

Table 2 shows the relationships latent in the 171 functional statements, with pairs of functional statements containing no more than two dissimilar words. In Table 2, more than half of the identified relationships are between agencies (71) in contrast to forty-four relationships internal to an agency. Furthermore, the symmetry of the table about the main diagonal indicates the reciprocal nature of these relationships. A comparison between documented and computer-generated relationships is summarized as follows:

		Computer-generated		
Relationship	Documented	$d^2 \leqq 1$	$d^2 \leqq 2$	$d^2 \leqq 3$
Intra-agency	184	8	44	254
Interagency	61	19	71	559
External	89	–	–	–

In this summary, the computer-generated relationships are grouped by the maximum difference (d^2 value) of the clustering. External relationships were not identified by the analysis, because the organization manual contained no functional statements of external organizations.

Results indicate that coordination documented in functional statements is primarily· internal and that computer-generated relationships are predominantly between agencies. Because the relationships defined by the clustering algorithm are based on objectively calculated similarities, one might expect that they provide a more thorough explanation of the relationships in the organization. It appears that human limitations prevent the identification of organization-wide relationships.

Summary and conclusion

In large organizations many complex relationships are not readily apparent to designers of organizations. Lexical analysis is an attempt to identify organizational relationships hidden in the organization manual. When comparing the clusters generated by this analysis from the organization manual, lexical analysis uncovered more interagency relationships than were perceived by the designers of the organization. Furthermore, detailed identification of specific relationships and the possible content of the coordination were specified. This analysis can only serve as a diagnostic tool: actual coordination requires a manager aware of these relationships and willing to effect the coordination where necessary. However, designers can use this tool to check the internal consistency of their designs: to assure that coordination documentation in the organization manual is reciprocal and that all coordination requirements are considered in the design.

References

[1] Auguston, J. Gary and Minker, Jack, "An Analysis of Some Graph Theoretical Clustering Techniques," Journal of the Association of Computing Machinery, Vol. 17 (October 1970), pp. 571–588.

[2] Baxendale, P.B., "Machine-Made Index for Technical Literature – an Experiment," IBM Journal of Research and Development, Vol. 2 (October 1958), pp. 354–361.

[3] Bonner, R.E., "On Some Clustering Techniques," IBM Journal of Research and Development, Vol. 8 (January 1964), pp. 22–32.

[4] Carney, Thomas F., Content Analysis: A Technique for Systematic Inference from Communication, University of Manitoba Press, Winnipeg, Canada, 1972.

[5] Chomsky, Noam, Aspects of the Theory of Syntax, The MIT Press, Cambridge, Mass., 1965.

[6] Department of Transportation, Organization Manual, Department of Transportation, Washington, D.C., March 1968, with changes up to March 1969.

[7] Goldman, Neil M., "Sentence Paraphrasing from a Conceptual Base," Communications of ACM, Vol. 18 (February 1975), pp. 96–106.

[8] Green, Paul E. and Carmone, Frank J., Multidimensional Scaling and Related Techniques in Marketing Analysis, Allyn and Bacon, Boston, Mass., 1970.

[9] Gulick, Luther H., "Notes on the Theory of Organization," in Papers on the Science of Organizations, Luther H. Gulick and Lyndall F. Urwick (eds.), Institute of Public Administration, Columbia University, New York, N.Y., 1937, pp. 2–46.

[10] Heberling, R.H., Organization Research and Job Analysis as an Aid to Setting and Installing Standards for Budgeting, American Management Association, New York, N.Y. (General Management Series No. 80), 1929.

[11] Holsti, Ole R., Content Analysis for the Social Sciences and Humanities, Addison-Wesley, Reading, Mass., 1969.

[12] Katz, Daniel and Kahn, Robert L., The Social Psychology of Organization, Wiley, New York, N.Y., 1966.

[13] Koontz, Harold and O'Donnel, Cyril, Principles of Management, (3rd ed.), McGraw-Hill, New York, N.Y., 1965.

[14] Kroeber, Alfred L. and Chretien, C.D., "Quantitative Classification of Indo-European Languages," Language, Vol. 13 (April-June 1937), pp. 83–103.

[15] Majone, Giandomenico and Sanday, Peggy R., "On the Numerical Classification of Nominal Data," in Explorations in Mathematical Anthropology, Paul Kay (ed.), The MIT Press, Cambridge, Mass., 1971, pp. 226–241.

[16] Maple, Eugene B., Administration Planning – A Method of Management, American Management Association, New York, N.Y. (General Management Series No. 156), 1946.

[17] March, James G. and Simon, Herbert A., Organizations, Wiley, New York, N.Y., 1958.

[18] Marsland, H.A., Alling, N.D. and Baechtold, E.L., Charts and Manuals in Organization Work, American Management Association, New York, N.Y. (Annual Convention Series No. 50), 1926.

[19] Mulligan, Gordon D. and Corneil, D.G., "Corrections to Bierstone's Algorithm for Generating Cliques," Journal of the Association for Computing Machinery, Vol. 19 (April 1972), pp. 244–247.

[20] Needham, R.M., "Computer Methods for Classification and Grouping," in The Use of Computers in Anthropology, Dell H. Hymes (ed.), Mouton, The Hague, The Netherlands, 1965.

[21] Sedelow, Sally Y. and Sedelow, Walter A., "Categories and Procedures for Content Analysis in the Humanities," in The Analysis of Communication Content, George Gerbner, Ole R. Holsti, Klaus Krippendorff, William J. Paisley and Philip J. Stone (eds.), Wiley, New York, N.Y., 1969.

[22] Silbey, Val, Lexical Task Similarities and Clustering for the Coordination of Organizational Activities, University of Pennsylvania, Philadelphia, Pa. (unpublished Ph.D. dissertation), 1974.

[23] Stone, Philip J., Dunphy, Dexter C., Smith, Marshall S. and Ogilvie, Daniel M., The General Inquirer: A Computer Approach to Content Analysis, The MIT Press, Cambridge, Mass., 1966.

[24] Webb, Eugene J., Campbell, Donald T., Schwartz, Richard D. and Sechrest, Lee, Unobtrusive Measures: Nonreactive Research in the Social Sciences, Rand McNally, Chicago, Ill., 1966.

North-Holland/TIMS Studies in the Management Sciences 5 (1977) 99–110
© North-Holland Publishing Company

A GOAL APPROACH TO ORGANIZATIONAL DESIGN *

PATRICK E. CONNOR and STEFAN D. BLOOMFIELD

Oregon State University

An initial task in organizational design or redesign is identifying the organization's goals. Complex organizations, however, characteristically pursue numerous goals, of which many must be inferred from broad and often politically oriented statements issued at many managerial levels. To introduce structure to the goal identification process, an appropriate goal typology can be developed, inducing a ranking among the individual goals. Specifying structural properties that will facilitate accomplishing the ranked goals provides the basis for a new organizational design. A case study is presented illustrating the application of these procedures in a public agency.

Using organizational goals as a starting point in an organizational design study is suggested by the concept of organizational rationality. The predominant view in the literature on organizations – from the classicists [9,21], to the open-systems advocates [11,19], to the empiricists [1,10,17] – has been that "the organization is conceived as an 'intrument' – that is, as a rationally conceived means to the realization of . . . goals" [4, p. 404]. Indeed, the essential purpose of formal organizations is "the pursuit of relatively specific objectives on a more or less continuous basis" [18, p. 488]. Thus, as Gross [6, p. 277] observed, "The central concept in the study of organizations is that of the organizational goal . . . . It is the presence of a goal and a consequent organization of effort so as to maximize the probability of attaining the goal which characterizes modern organizations."

This viewpoint establishes a rationale for organizational structure: "The specific goals pursued will determine in important respects the characteristics of the structure" [18, p. 290]. That is, within the framework of rationality, organizational structures are the tools for effectively pursuing organizational goals [4]. The resurgence of contingency theories of organization reflects this idea; organizations are designed, continually redesigned, and managed to best accomplish their purposes under prevailing conditions. Borrowing from engineering terminology, goals are the specifications to which organizations are designed.

When goals serve as the basis for organizational design, the set of goal specifications must be comprehensive, yet analytically and operationally tractable. Unfortunately, the process of specifying goals is usually arduous and frustrating. Organizations have multiple goals [10,16], of which many are difficult to define and

* Received March 1975; revised January 1976, April 1976.

often seemingly contradictory[22]. Although goals such as production quotas, profit levels, and product parameters are relatively easily stated, goals relating to quality of service, internal morale, external image, and organizational flexibility are usually difficult to specify quantitatively. The familiar dependence on proxy variables in such cases may yield precise results only at the expense of significant distortion in later evaluation and analysis [3].

As a consequence, an attempt to elicit a comprehensive list of organizational goals usually produces a lengthy and awkward compilation of statements — some relating directly to specific structural properties, and others phrased in lofty generalities with heavy political overtones. Procedures must then be developed to reduce such sets of goal statements to a form more amenable to analysis. In particular, the goals must be arrayed in a way that facilitates assigning priorities among goals, and allows for their operational restatement.

Structuring organizational goals

The need suitably to structure sets of organizational goal statements is addressed by a developing body of evidence which finds that there exists only a limited number of distinct goal types [10]. Perrow [16], for example, observed that organizations are subject to many influences, and as a result pursue five major goal categories. While differing in some respects from Perrow's formulation, the findings of Edward Gross [6–8] support the categorization of organizational goals into five goal types. The work of Bertram Gross [5] on organizational effectiveness led him to identify seven different goal types for organizations.

These typological approaches to defining organizational goals share two important properties. First, each recognizes that organizations are characterized by a variety of goals; as on-going social systems, organizations maintain activities and resources directed to many purposes. But, significantly, these purposes can be conceptually grouped into a small number of well-defined categories. Second, output goals constitute only one goal type in each of the formulations, although these goals are usually distinguished by their importance to organizational survival and prosperity. In comparison, other types may be most properly viewed as support goals [6,8].

A typological approach to organizational goals provides a helpful mechanism for dealing with "complex sets of . . . attributes by identifying a more parsimonious set of constructs" [13]. Of course, organizations vary in the relative emphases given to different categories of organizational goals, particularly the support goals. Identifying the set of relative emphases, the organization's goal mix, establishes a ranking of individual goals corresponding to the ranking of their goal category. For goals that suggest specific structural properties [12,14,18], this ranking may be extended to the subsequent selection of design characteristics, providing a mechanism for resolving conflicts among such characteristics. Finally, the structure imposed on the goal identification process through use of a typology serves an auditing function by pointing out duplication within the list of goal statements, and by revealing areas in which important organizational goals may have been inadvertently omitted.

Specifying organizational correlates

A goal approach to organizational design requires specifying structural properties which will facilitate the accomplishment of these goals. That such a specification is possible follows from Etzioni's [3] concept of a real goal (or what Perrow [16] terms an operative goal): one that is actively being pursued by a substantial part of the organization. This pursuit is reflected in members' activities and resource utilization patterns. Directing resources toward goal accomplishment, however, requires a variety of organizational design characteristics — control mechanisms, departments, communication links, and so on. These characteristics comprise what may be termed the goals' organizational correlates. Conflicts between different organizational correlates may be resolved by reference to the priorities previously assigned to the goals themselves through use of the typology.

The specific methods used to categorize goals, assign priority rankings, identify organizational correlates, and specify a final organizational design probably will vary considerably among different types of organizations and between differently constituted organizational study teams. The following case study illustrates these methods.

An application

A unit of a large federal agency used a goal approach for their organizational redesign. The agency maintains its principal offices in Washington, D.C., with subordinate units at regional, local, and field office levels. A formal line and staff structure exists at the Washington offices, creating a clearly defined hierarchy for both staff specialists and line officers. Staff positions correspond to the agency's traditional missions, called functions. Staff personnel ostensibly act as technical specialists in their respective functional areas, reporting to and advising line officers. The line officers are delegated the sole authority to issue directions and orders within their specified areas of responsibility.

Two principal factors prompted the agency's decision to explore possible organizational redesign. The first was the gradual expansion of the agency's roster of functional specialists, paralleling the emergence of specialized technical disciplines within universities. The attempt to incorporate these disciplines into the prevailing organizational structure revealed basic incompatibilities between the traditional functional areas and the new technical specialties. These difficulties were compounded by the need to accommodate new interdisciplinary, and consequently interfunctional, specialties. Agency management believed that the resulting structural arrangements blurred the established functional roles, promoting interfunctional rivalry and reducing organizational effectiveness.

The second factor was a growing tendency for functional staff personnel to bypas designated line authority and to issue orders directly. This was most noticeable in the functional areas central to the agency's primary missions. The tendency of staff personnel to oversee directly operations within the central areas was extremely frustrating to the line officials whose managerial prerogatives were being usurped, especially since these line officers – in contrast to many other federal agencies – were career officials rather than political appointees.

These developments led agency management to believe that the formal organizational structure was no longer adequate to administer effectively the agency's missions. Therefore, selected regional and local offices were directed to develop new structures more appropriate to their individual needs. One such unit was a local office, of about 550 employees, that had played a flagship role in several aspects of the agency's missions.

Rather than unilaterally developing and imposing a new organizational design, local management appointed a study team of employees to propose a new organizational structure. The team was composed of six employees representing several different hierarchical levels and functional areas. These members were selected on the basis of their observed interest and commitment to the organization, without regard to their overall knowledge of the organization or their previous managerial experience. The resulting lack of managerial expertise within the team, coupled with a restrictive time constraint, precluded the use of many sophisticated procedures otherwise appropriate in such a redesign study. The authors participated in the study as technical resource personnel, charged with providing occasional guidance to the study process and monitoring its validity. In order that the final recommendations be credible as an in-house product, the authors were cautioned that all value judgments, decision criteria, and ultimate design specifications should be those of the study team members solely.

To augment its limited knowledge of the local office's missions, the design team initially compiled a comprehensive list of goal statements for the organization. This list was generated by soliciting inputs from employees at all levels of the local office, as well as obtaining official guidelines issued from the Washington and regional offices. This produced a set of forty-six goal statements, ranging from quite specific to extremely general. Several goals related directly to structural properties of the organization, and others had no apparent organizational correlates. The length and extreme diversity of this set of goal statements suggested the need for a goal typology to facilitate the analysis.

The goal typology

Selection of an appropriate goal typology was governed by three criteria: the typology must be scientifically supported, directly applicable to the organization, and meaningful to the design team. The authors suggested the classification scheme developed by Edward Gross [6–8] categorizing organizational goals into five principal classes as follows:

1. Output Goals. Those goals that are reflected in products or services intended to affect society.

2. Support Goals. *a.* Adaptation Goals – Those goals reflecting the need for the organization to cope effectively with its environment; these concern the need to attract clients and staff, to finance the enterprise, to secure needed resources, and so on.

b. Management Goals – Those goals reflecting the need to administer the organization, to handle conflict, and to establish priorities for attending to output goals.

c. Motivation Goals – Those goals directed toward developing a high level of satisfaction on the part of staff and clients.

d. Positional Goals – Those goals aimed toward maintaining the organization's position and image in comparison to other organizations in the same industry, and in the face of attempts or trends to change its position.

The authors considered the validity of this typology to compare most favorably with those of Perrow [16], Bertram Gross [5], and others [2,15,20]. Edward Gross's categorization appeared to be the result of more systematic examination than the others, having been derived as part of an extensive empirical research program [7,8].

The design team agreed that Gross's typology was pertinent and would be useful. Team members endorsed the notion that output goals form a superordinate class of their own – the raison d'etre of the organization. Other goals, by contrast, were seen as ends intended to better facilitate achievement of the output goals. The support-goal subcategories, moreover, seemed well-suited to the organization. Being employees of an agency subject to extensive and often sensitive dealings with the public, team members readily acknowledged the existence and importance of adaptation goals. Although lacking formal managerial training, team members appreciated the need for well-coordinated organizational maintenance activities, and thus endorsed the necessity of management goals. Finally, as representatives of different constituencies within the organization, team members expressed strong concern that the organization maintain as favorable a working climate as possible, and strive to retain the unique character distinguishing it from its sister agencies. This concern led the team to support identification of motivational and positional goals.

Establishing the goal mix

Realizing that the original list of goal statements might yield conflicting prescriptions for organizational structure, the study team thought it prudent to identify the agency's goal mix early in the redesign process. The team recognized, moreover, that assigning priorities to the categories of the goal typology would serve not only to establish corresponding rankings for individual goals, but also would encourage team members to adopt a total-organization viewpoint emphasizing large-scale, overall goals.

The process used to assign goals to the five categories of the typology was tedious but straightforward. Each goal was thoroughly discussed and assigned — by consensus — to one or more categories. Many goals addressed several classes of organizational goals. For example, the goal statement, "Decision making . . . must de-emphasize intuitive reliance in favor of the increased capability and options offered by sophisticated analytical and computer systems," clearly pertained to the class of management goals, but was also thought to reflect adaptation and positional goals; it was therefore assigned to all three categories.

The subsequent process of assigning priorities to the typology was conditioned strongly by the context of the redesign study. Although many mechanisms exist for formally gathering and incorporating wide-scale organizational input into such a

Table 1
Goal typology adopted by the organization

Priority	Goal type	Organizational description
1	Output	The organization exists for the purpose of producing output. Normally output is tangible, although some may be intangible and feature lack of organizational activity such as pleasant experiences on the part of the public served.
2	Adaptability/ Flexibility	This class of goals deals with the ability of the organization to respond to external stimuli whether they come from out-of-agency or from other and/or higher units in-agency. Examples: severe budget cut, increase in delegation to units, changing program needs, public concerns, emergencies.
3	Motivation	Synonym is morale. This class of goals involves maintenance and improvement of those forces which cause employees to want to perform tasks for the organization. A normal organization cannot function in the absence of employee motivation.
4	Positional	This class of goals speaks to the character of the organization as the public, customers, politicians, employees, and prospective employees see it. This is the general tenor of the organization; the impressions it gives to those that come into contact with it. This is what makes one organizational unit appear somewhat different from another. These goals are closely allied to motivational goals.
5	Management	Organizations have goals as to how they wish to administer organization resources in terms of such organizational properties as structure, communication processes, lines of authority, decision-making processes, and control processes.

ranking task, the study team rejected such efforts as impractical within their time constraints. Instead, since the team was formed to represent several employee constituencies, team members decided to rely on their own perceptions of the agency's role, as reinforced or modified by the now-categorized goals. The goal typology, therefore, was extensively discussed within the group until a consensus was achieved for the assignment of priorities. Table 1 presents the goal typology as rewritten by the study team, and as ranked to display the agency's goal mix.

Developing organizational correlates

Developing structural properties corresponding to the set of goal statements was also a relatively straightforward, albeit judgmental, process. The design team examined each goal statement to identify one or more organizational correlates. For example, one goal statement was: "Increase public confidence in the organization's competence and credibility in long-range planning, especially by providing that decision making be open and visible to the public." The design team decided that pursuit of this goal would be facilitated by creating "a formal long-range planning unit whose charge includes acquiring input from the public." This organizational correlate was then designed into the emerging structure.

Through these activities, decision-making units were formed, linking pins were established, formal communication paths were identified, and job descriptions were modified. In short, a variety of organizational correlates were specified by the team and were then assigned priorities corresponding to those of the goal statements from which they derived.

It should be noted that the process of developing organizational correlates was actually less tidy than is suggested here. Each goal statement was exhaustively discussed and analyzed to isolate any content relevant to structural properties of the organization. Some goal statements had no implications for structure – for example, "Utilize available local unit personnel skills and training to meet program requirements." It was also discovered that many of the organizational correlates were implied by more than one goal statement; in such cases, the correlate was assigned a priority equal to that of the highest ranked statement. In all, the forty-six goal statements produced twenty-six distinct organizational correlates. Finally, many goal statements concerned factors not necessarily appearing on an organizational chart, but rather relating to tasks for managers or their departments. These tasks were described in a narrative forming an integral part of the redesign proposal.

Table 2 presents an illustrative sample of some goals and their organizational correlates.

Developing the organizational design

The final task facing the study team was to develop a new organizational design incorporating the organizational correlates. First, each team member independently

Table 2
Selected goal statements and their corresponding organizational correlates

Goal statement	Goal type	Organizational correlate
1. (a) Provide for an organization which can adjust to the imposition of additional work loads, changes in direction, and the addition of new skills.	Adaptation	Provide as few distinct organizational units as possible consistent with smooth organizational functioning (Priority 2).
(b) Develop an organization which can respond to nonrecurring goals by adjusting current goals and subunit resource allocations as imposed goals are received.		
(c) Provide an organization having flexibility in program execution to respond quickly to emergency situations.		
2. Decision making ... must deemphasize intuitive reliance in favor of the increased capability and options offered by sophisticated analytical and computer systems.	Adaptation Positional Management	Provide a unit charged with computer and systems development, capable of analytical work to furnish technical assistance to all levels of the organization (Priority 2).
3. Increase public confidence in the organization's competence and credibility in long-range planning, especially by providing that decision making be open and visible to the public.	Positional Management	Identify a formal long-range planning unit whose charge includes acquiring input from the public (Priority 4).
4. Provide for the minimum number of necessary reviews and review levels consistent with the costs, the risks of unsatisfactory performance, and the evaluation skills available.	Motivation Positional Management	Maintain absence of identifiable "review" units in the local office (Priority 3).
5. Provide for program execution based upon short-range planning and programming.	Management	Provide short organizational links between short-range planning and the program execution level (Priority 5).
6. A more precise control device needs to replace present accountability procedures as a means to effect accountability among agency subunits.	Management	Maintain in the local office an identifiable group with capability to audit or inspect against goals and standards (Priority 5).

developed a broadbrush design comprised solely of organizational elements implied by the correlates. This demonstrated the degree to which the correlates were perceived to specify an organizational structure. With these initial designs displayed before them, the team members developed their final recommendations after extensively discussing the strengths and weaknesses of their individual designs.

Specification of the final design was considerably simplified by the substantial overlap among the broadbrush designs, due in large measure to the high priority assigned to minimizing distinct organizational subunits. The extensive consolidation of tasks and functions implied by this organizational correlate was a clear distinguishing feature of each individual's design. Thus, the final design task was reduced primarily to rearranging five or six major organizational subunits to facilitate the communication needs addressed by other correlates. That being accomplished, equitable distribution of resources and power among the primary line officers was the criterion for final design selection.

The final design differed substantially from the existing organizational structure, shown in Figure 1. The existing structure had emphasized differentiation by function — that is, mission — with staff specialists ostensibly serving in an advisory capacity to line officials. As may be inferred from the organizational chart, this distinction between line and staff was often unclear, particularly to the line officials at the field office level. The new design, Figure 2, produced an organizational structure relatively free of functional emphasis. Instead, the design emphasized fundamental organizational processes, such as long-range planning and resource planning, through integration of the functional areas into these major processes.

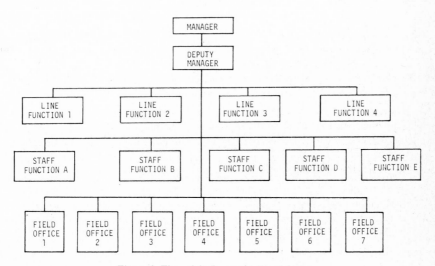

Figure 1. The original organizational design.

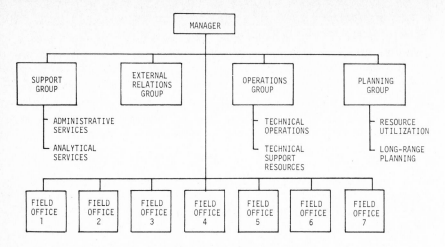

Figure 2. The new organizational design.

Outcomes of the redesign

To integrate functional tasks into the organizational process units — support, operations, planning — the staff specialists' role was redefined explicitly as support to the decision makers. To emphasize this distinction, staff members were no longer invited to formal discussions among line officers except when specifically needed, and then were dismissed after their contribution had been made. The results of this change were threefold: line officers, especially at field office levels, became considerably more confident of their role as decision makers; staff officers went through a period of disorientation and anxiety with regard to their reduced role in the decision-making process; and lines of decision responsibility and accountability were significantly clarified, to the relief of top management and their line officers.

Because local unit management could not be persuaded to conduct a formal evaluation, no systematic assessment of the new design's effectiveness can be presented. However, a series of interviews with top and middle managers revealed general agreement on two significant outcomes of the redesign. First, local-unit flexibility was improved. The new design allowed, even encouraged, an increased level of collaborative activity when unexpected events required a rapid organizational response. Officers directing the major organizational-process units report that they were able to quickly shift their personnel and resources to meet changing functional demands. Although increased flexibility within these large units was achieved at the expense of more formal communication needs between units, the trade-off was perceived to be greatly to the organization's advantage.

Second, the new design appeared after two years of operation to have been wholly accepted by the organizational membership. Local-unit management reported little tendency by organizational members to revert to previous modes of operation. The discomfort and disorientation initially experienced by many staff personnel appreciably eased, aided by the traditionally high personnel transfer rates within the agency and by personal counseling services made available during the reorganization. On balance, management concurred that the new design enabled a more effective pursuit of organizational goals.

References

[1] Blau, Peter M. and Schoenherr, Richard A., The Structure of Organizations, Basic Books, New York, N.Y., 1971.

[2] Etzioni, Amitai, A Comparative Analysis of Complex Organizations, Free Press, New York, N.Y., 1961.

[3] Etzioni, Amitai, "Two Approaches to Organizational Analysis: A Critique and a Suggestion," Administrative Science Quarterly, Vol. 5 (September 1960), pp. 257–278.

[4] Gouldner, Alvin W., "Organizational Analysis," in Sociology Today, Robert K. Merton, Leonard Broom, and Leonard S. Cottrell, Jr. (eds.), Harper and Row, New York, N.Y., 1959.

[5] Gross, Bertram, "What Are Your Organization's Objectives? A General-Systems Approach to Planning," Human Relations, Vol. 18 (August 1965), pp. 195–216.

[6] Gross, Edward, "The Definition of Organizational Goals," British Journal of Sociology, Vol. 20 (September 1969), pp. 277–294.

[7] Gross, Edward, "Universities as Organizations: A Research Approach," American Sociological Review, Vol. 33 (August 1968), pp. 518–544.

[8] Gross, Edward and Grambsch, Paul V., Changes in University Organization, 1964–1971, McGraw-Hill, New York, N.Y., 1974.

[9] Gulick, L. and Urwick, L. (eds.), Papers on the Science of Administration, Institute of Public Administration, New York, N.Y., 1937.

[10] Hall, Richard H., Organizations: Structure and Process, Prentice-Hall, Englewood Cliffs, N.J., 1972.

[11] Katz, Daniel and Kahn, Robert L., The Social Psychology of Organizations, Wiley, New York, N.Y., 1966.

[12] Lawrence, Paul R. and Lorsch, Jay W., Organization and Environment, Irwin, Homewood, Ill., 1969.

[13] McKelvey, Bill, "Guidelines for the Empirical Classification of Organizations," Administrative Science Quarterly, Vol. 20 (December 1975), pp. 509–525.

[14] McKelvey, Bill and Kilmann, Ralph H., "Organization Design: A Participative Multivariate Approach," Administrative Science Quarterly, Vol. 20 (March 1975), pp. 24–36.

[15] Parsons, Talcott, Structure and Process in Modern Society, Free Press, New York, N.Y., 1960.

[16] Perrow, Charles, Organizational Analysis: A Sociological Analysis, Wadsworth, Belmont, Cal., 1970.

[17] Pugh, D.S., Hickson, D.J. and Hinings, C.R., "An Empirical Taxonomy of Structures of Work Organizations," Administrative Science Quarterly, Vol. 14 (March 1969), pp. 115–126.

[18] Scott, W. Richard, "Theory of Organizations," in Handbook of Modern Sociology, Robert E.L. Faris (ed.), Rand McNally, Chicago, Ill., 1964.

[19] Thompson, James D., Organizations in Action, McGraw-Hill, New York, N.Y., 1967.

[20] Thompson, James D., and McEwen, William J., "Organizational Goals and Environment: Goal Setting as an Interaction Process," American Sociological Review, Vol. 23 (February 1958), pp. 23–31.
[21] Weber, Max, From Max Weber: Essays in Sociology, H.H. Gerth and C. Wright Mills (eds.), Oxford University Press, London, England, 1958.
[22] Wildavsky, Aaron, "The Self-Evaluating Organization," Public Administration Review, Vol. 32 (September-October 1972), pp. 509–520.

North-Holland/TIMS Studies in the Management Sciences 5 (1977) 111–123
© North-Holland Publishing Company

MAKING SENSE WITH NONSENSE: HELPING FRAMES OF REFERENCE CLASH *

MORGAN W. McCALL, Jr. †

Center for Creative Leadership

Detecting incongruities can be a critical component of organizational adaptation. Interactions between events and frames of reference create at least four types of incongruities. Awareness of these various types of incongruities could help designers develop organizational mechanisms that create new events and help decision makers change frames of reference.

Organizations' environments are largely invented by organizations themselves. Organizations select their environments from ranges of alternatives, then they subjectively perceive the environments they inhabit. The processes of both selection and perception are unreflective, disorderly, incremental, and strongly influenced by social norms and customs. [26, p. 1069]

Of course people are the media through which organizations do the selecting and perceiving. If interpreting environmental events depends on selective perception, two main elements must be considered. The first is an objective reality consisting of numerous events: an array of situations, behaviors, objects, and data. The second is the way people interpret events in terms of their frames of reference.

Events in environments probably occur in logical sequences, but some events may not be perceived, and independent sequences may be perceived in mixtures. Hence, events may not be perceived in logical sequences, and the causal connections among them may be missed or misinterpreted. People, however, seek to understand, predict, and control events by placing them in reasonably consistent frames of reference. Thus, people make sense of events — even misperceived ones — on the basis of a priori theories and beliefs [26].

The application of frames of reference to events highlights the importance of incongruities — deviant events that will or will not make sense depending on the frames of reference applied. An organization's ability to adapt to its environment — or conversely, to shape its environment — depends on the ability of its members to

* Received October 1975; revised December 1975, May 1976, July 1976.

† A version of this paper entitled "A Systematic Look At Nonsense: The Congruous Side of Incongruity" was presented at the University of Illinois and TIMS College on Organization workshop, "Radical Approaches to Organizational Design," October 13–15, 1975. The author gratefully acknowledges assistance from Elizabeth Conklyn, Betty Everhart, Keith Murnighan, Katie Schneider, John Senger, Paul Nystrom, and especially William Starbuck.

detect and interpret changes in events. When things went wrong in Vietnam, reports were falsified to fit the existing frames of reference. As a result, it was years before the implications of events were finally acted upon. Similar failures to apply new frames of reference to events resulted in a fiasco at the Bay of Pigs.

Preserving frames of reference inclines perceivers to discount many events as random deviations. Identifying nonrandomness among deviations is important both from an evolutionary point of view and from the perspective of managers trying to respond to events. Only if deviations are detected can their significance be assessed. To the degree that people preserve frames of reference by discounting significant deviations, the chances are reduced that people, and through them organizations, will adapt.

The implications of failing to discern nonrandomness among deviations can be explored by (1) examining types of incongruities, and (2) considering ways organizations can be designed to perceive incongruites.

Sense, nonsense, and clashing frames

Subjective interpretations determine whether events will be seen as sensible or nonsensical. What happens when events do not fit the usual frames of reference applied to them?

There are at least four types of incongruities resulting from interactions between events and frames: intertemporal incongruities, congruous incongruities, falsely false incongruities, and artificial sense. [1] Intertemporal and congruous incongruities generally involve detected deviations. That is, perceivers are likely to notice incongruous events but then either ignore them or redefine them in ways that fit existing frames of reference. Intertemporal and congruous incongruities are important primarily for the ways people deal with the incongruities they notice.

Falsely false incongruities and artificial sense, on the other hand, usually involve incongruities that are missed altogether. Realization that an incongruity has occurred may come long after the events, and then only if subsequent events provide new information about previous events. Falsely false incongruities and artificial sense are important primarily because incongruities go unnoticed.

Intertemporal incongruities

Intertemporal incongruities occur when people apply their usual frames of reference to events and find things that do not fit. If managers expect monthly output to vary no more than ten percent, a twenty percent deviation would be an intertemporal incongruity. A typical action strategy based on identifying such incon-

---

[1] The first three types of incongruities have been described by R.V. Jones [10] as the key ingredients of practical jokes.

gruities is management by exception. This and similar strategies assume that deviations in events can be identified and that statistical parameters will reveal the significance of deviations. Deviations that satisfy predetermined parameters are treated as if they were nondeviant.

The importance of not ignoring intertemporal incongruities has been demonstrated by numerous major breakthroughs. Watson's discovery of the double helix [29], Woodward and Bernstein's unraveling of Watergate [33], and Roethlisberger and Dickson's findings on the effects of social factors in the work place [22] all represent instances in which incongruities that did not fit the existing frames of reference instigated revolutions.

Both scientists and managers often ignore or discount intertemporal incongruities because they are seeking lawful, orderly, predictable relationships within current frames of reference. Copernicus's and Galileo's ideas about the earth's motion were treated as nonsense by their contemporaries [15]. Darwinists violently attacked Kammerer's contradictory research on evolution [14].

Statistical procedures institutionalize particular frames of reference. Although statistics often identify intertemporal incongruities, they also help both scientists and nonscientists discount such deviations. Events which do not fit theoretical frames of reference are frequently classified as random errors. Attention typically focuses on the amount of variance explained by a theory, even when the variance attributed to random errors is as large or larger.

As Hewitt and Stokes [9] observed in their work on disclaimers, people routinely protect their definitions of events from contradictory evidence. Speer [25] pointed out that when they wiped out traditional bureaucratic procedures, Allied bombings actually helped make German production more efficient. Allied commanders noticed that the bombings were not as effective as they should have been, but the positive effects of wiping out factories reduced the impact of the important incongruity.

What determines when intertemporal incongruities will be acted upon or ignored? Under what circumstances will people interpret deviations to fit current frames of reference or recognize them as validating different, perhaps contradictory, frames?

Managers sometimes blame failures to recognize exceptions on insufficient information. Ackoff [1] has argued that the reverse is true: managers receive too much information and have problems because they can neither digest nor integrate all of it. Managerial work is characterized by fragmentation, variety, and brevity [18]. Insufficient time probably reduces the number of different frames of reference available for problem solving. If so, two factors would induce managers to miss intertemporal incongruities: not perceiving all the data, and not perceiving data in appropriate frames of reference.

In addition, powerful forces, such as cognitive dissonance, disclaiming, rationalizing, and selective perception, mitigate against viewing events in appropriate frames of reference.

Congruous incongruities

When Saturn's pernicious moon was discovered spinning the wrong way (according to nebular theory), the following ditty was written by a dismayed astronomer:

Phoebe, Phoebe whirling high
 in our neatly plotted sky
Phoebe, listen to my lay
 Won't you swirl the other way?

A recognized intertemproal incongruity, Phoebe could not be explained with traditional theories. For years Phoebe was treated as an event which could be explained with existing theory. In fact it was a congruous incongruity: an event that made no sense in any existing frame of reference but made perfect sense when viewed with a totally different frame.

Congruous incongruities lurk in situations such as this author's desk, the first day of a semester, broken plays in football, and last-minute vacation packing because they do not fit rational frames of reference of their own. These events can produce new ways of thinking when someone makes sense of them. Success in failure may lead to adaptation, as when the broken football play is added to the playbook. More often, congruous incongruities are discounted with sighs of relief or chuckles.

Tuchman's [28] study of how newspapers routinize the unexpected and Hewitt and Hall's [8] description of quasi-theories, which are post hoc rationalizations for policies, demonstrate that people try to impose order on chaos. A consequence is that congruous incongruities are rarely recognized. That is, people miss adaptive responses to congruous incongruities by perceiving events within comfortable, traditional frames of reference. They dislike pieces which do not fit. Thus a broken play is unlikely to enter the playbook because it was a fluke within the frame of reference of traditional football strategy. From a skeptical coach's point of view, the broken play is a dismissible intertemporal incongruity. From a different point of view, the fact that the play worked makes it a congruous incongruity, an event with adaptive implications.

Most people can identify a few situations that they do not expect to make much sense. One businessman was overheard saying that he has given up trying to predict what the Environmental Protection Agency would do next — "They never make any sense." For him, encounters with the EPA represented unpredictable events with no comprehensible patterns, so he was not sensitive to possible congruous incongruities.

Managers often view organizational conflicts as, at best, necessary evils, and, at worst, detrimental sources of stress that disrupt an organization's orderliness. Managers are inclined to treat conflicts as intertemporal incongruities to be discounted if possible or stopped if necessary. A different frame of reference might disclose sensible patterns with adaptive implications in the midst of disorders.

Falsely false incongruities

A scientist expecting a practical joke on April 1 was told that his laboratory had exploded. He amiably dismissed the report, only to find that his lab had in fact been destroyed. The unfortunate man's plight exemplifies a third type of incongruity. When people expect false incongruities and experience real incongruities, they may discount their experiences as being falsely incongruous.

Researchers typically expect at least one freak subject in an experiment; some businessmen expect Ralph Nader to raise a ruckus over almost nothing; some management negotiators expect unions to make nonsensical demands during negotiations. In each case, false incongruities are expected, and frames of reference are applied in advance to discount the possibility of uniquely new meanings. For this reason, falsely false incongruities are more insidious than intertemporal or congruous incongruities: at least when incongruous events are not expected, there is some chance they will be noticed.

Falsely false incongruities echo the boy-who-cried-wolf fable, and they can have similar outcomes. Like the townspeople who lost their sheep, people who do not recognize falsely false incongruities can suffer unfortunate consequences.

The false alarm problem faced by many fire departments provides an example. Firemen may arrive at a real fire and suspect that it is another false alarm. If many false alarms are turned in at this box and no one is waiting by the box when the firemen arrive, the truck may drive off.

Artificial sense

Frames of reference frequently are shaped by historical precedents or accumulations of experience. Much of the sense-making machinery is based on past events, but changing environments slowly outstrip the traditional frames of reference applied to them. The presence of obsolete frames of reference suggests a fourth type of incongruity called artificial sense. Intertemporal, congruous, and falsely false incongruities all involve the application of frames of reference that are inappropriate to specific events. These frames are accurate for explaining some events, but are inadequate for explaining others. Obsolete frames that no longer explain the events they were intended to explain create artificial sense for decision makers.

Artificial sense is particularly insidious because decision makers are still missing or responding to intertemporal, congruous, and falsely false incongruities. Since the frames of reference applied are obsolete, the meaning given to events and to the incongruities detected in them are mythical.

Organizational myths (which often turn into traditions) accumulate over time: "That's the way we do it around here." "It's your job to carry out orders." "That's what success in the oil business depends on." Frames of reference, locked in procedure manuals and organizational folklore, are the ones first applied to current events. To the extent that these frames of reference represent artificial sense, organizational survival is a matter more of luck than of decision-making skill.

Congruity and incongruity intertwined

Although it is abstractly possible to differentiate among the four types of incongruities, reality is not so readily categorized. Congruity and incongruity, and failure to recognize either, may occur for the same events. For example, a riot, earthquake, or other catastrophe elicits multiple frames of reference from the same person.

An earthquake may be an unexpected event intruding in an otherwise stable sequence of events. From that perspective, it is an intertemporal incongruity. On the other hand, the earthquake itself generates chaos, and any sensible patterns emerging in that chaos (e.g., [5]) represent congruous incongruities. Finally, the tremors may not result from an earthquake at all. Perhaps a nuclear explosion caused the tremors, and those interpreting the event as an earthquake are victims of artificial sense.

The congruous and incongruous sides of organizational environments

The influences of environmental characteristics on organizational structures have been a popular topic in the organizational literature. There is general agreement that environments affect organizations and that different environments should and do dictate different organizational structures.

Some models of organization-environment interdependence [16,21,27] classify environments according to relative certainty. An organization's environment may be described as stable or unstable, predictable or unpredictable, certain or uncertain. Structural prescriptions, such as mechanistic versus organic [2], follow from the classification assigned to the environment.

Different environments also generate different kinds of incongruities for organizational decision makers. Highly stable environments, for example, may cause decision makers to use frames of reference that are sensitive to deviations from normally recurring events and so to look for intertemporal incongruities. Whether those environments are objectively stable or not, they appear stable because other incongruities — congruous incongruities, falsely false incongruities, and artificial sense — are overlooked or misinterpreted.

Unstable environments, on the other hand, may foster sensitivity to congruous incongruities, for decision makers are striving to discern predictable patterns within normally incongruous events. Searching for patterns causes intertemporal incongruities to be misinterpreted (after all, incongruous events are the order of the day), while the patterns perceived (the congruities) slowly develop into artificial sense.

The point, of course, is that events have little objective meaning. The frames of reference applied to them define the events and determine the likelihood of recognizing incongruities. The broad-gauged approaches to organizations which treat environment and organization as separate, and which describe organizational structures in terms of environmental events, are missing the important processes by which events are interpreted and their significance appraised.

Understanding the event/frame of reference interface

Researchers and practitioners can adopt several strategies dor understanding the interfaces between events and frames of reference. They are: (1) study exceptions, (2) examine chaos, and (3) know the normal.

Exceptions are relatively easy to find, though many are dismissed or misinterpreted. The challenge lies in distinguishing incongruities which deserve attention from those which do not. Both managers and researchers tend to focus on quantifiable information. Balance sheets and statistical significance appear cold and hard, but the events they summarize are complex. Many important events cannot be quantitatively represented and never appear in the numbers.

Management information systems (MIS's) are formal mechanisms for identifying intertemporal incongruities, and they illustrate how deviations from the normal deceive. A typical information system is based on variables and relationships that existed at a certain point in time; by the time the system becomes operational, the environment has already changed. The more complex the system, the more closely it models past realities, and the harder it is to change it later on. Even though most MIS's are constantly fed new data, the postulated relationships among variables are updated infrequently. Thus managers who depend on projections and status reports generated by MIS's run the risk that the assumed relationships no longer describe reality. As reality changes, MIS's cause managers to apply inappropriate frames of reference and to operate with artificial sense. When systems designed to detect intertemporal incongruities are based on erroneous assumptions about the normal order, the chances are dramatically reduced that important exceptions will be identified.

Examining chaos (a source of congruous incongruities) is also a difficult task. Between insisting on making everything fit (e.g., systems theory) and building quasi-theories [8], people do not allow unstructured situations to persist. People also try to cram events into familiar frames of reference rather than try out totally new frames. Temporary instabilities, such as leadership succession, surprise visits from the Occupational Safety and Health Administration, and the President's tour, represent chaotic moments which carry significant messages when they are viewed as potentially congruous incongruities.

For an incongruity to affect actions, it must be noticed. But neither congruities nor incongruities are necessarily unusual — both are there all the time. A key to their recognition is knowing what frames of reference define the normal. As Koestler noted, creative discovery results from:

the displacement of attention to something not previously noted, which was irrelevant in the old and is relevant in the new context; the discovery of hidden analogies . . .; the bringing into consciousness of tacit axioms and habits of thought which were . . . taken for granted; the uncovering of what has always been there [13, p. 120].

What kinds of tools can researchers and practitioners bring to bear on incongruities? Perhaps description is a good place to start. Mintzberg [18] managed to describe the top executive's day — in spite of its chaotic array of fleeting contacts, hundreds of activities, and frequent interruptions.

Good descriptions, based on observations conducted over extended periods of time and relatively free of interpretations, would increase understanding of what is happening. By contrast, hypothesis tests and information systems assume that the important variables have already been identified, and that the relationships among them are stable. If the normal order of events were known and stable, organizations could be designed on the basis of stabilities. But the normal order is not known and is unstable, hence organizations ought to be designed around instabilities. What would organizations look like if they were designed around instabilities?

Designing incongruity detectors

At least two strategies can increase the probability that incongruities will be detected. The first is manipulating events to ensure that there will be variety in their frequency, sequence, and degree of familiarity. The second is helping people apply diverse frames of reference to the same events.

Both strategies alter event/frame of reference interactions. The first emphasizes varied events as stimuli that force shifts in frames of reference. The second attempts to change the frames of reference applied, thereby producing multiple meanings for the same events.

Before either of these strategies can be implemented, designers must engage in four basic activities:

1. Examine assumptions about the normal order of events in the environment, in the organization, and at the interface of the two. First, apply as many frames of reference as possible to the same events. Check out the assumed causal patterns and previously applied decision rules, since finding adaptive responses depends on being aware of the frames of reference used. It is particularly important to get rid of traditions and myths that no longer fit reality because, if an initial frame of reference is misleading, the organization will be trapped by artificial sense.

2. Once the normal order is analyzed, anticipate what intertemporal incongruities might occur. Intertemporal incongruities vary in content, magnitude, sequence, and frequency, and a given set may or may not endure over time. Again, be wary of assuming that the intertemporal incongruities will remain stable — do not design systems around stability when factors inevitably change in unexpected ways.

3. Identify circumstances that normally do not make sense. "This too shall pass" is a waiting strategy that can be applied to many chaotic situations, but occasionally something can be done that creates order out of chaos. Congruous incongruities represent opportunities to make adaptive responses. As is the case with normal orders and intertemporal incongruities, chaos changes over time. Are the chaotic events existing today likely to change? What form will they take in the future?

4. Identify the organization's April Fools' Days. When is the organization likely to ignore incongruities because false incongruities are expected? How does a fire

department learn to cope with numerous false alarms?

Seeing the frame-of-reference problems within organizations leads designers to think in terms of constantly changing environmental events. If events are constantly changing, then the practitioner will try to build in ways of insuring that (1) unfamiliar events constantly challenge existing frames, and that (2) recurring events get viewed with different frames of reference.

Creating unfamiliar events

One way to force frames of reference to collide is to design organizations around the dialectic. Mitroff and Betz [19], White [31], and Mason [17] have advocated the use of the dialectic, structured debate by which opposing world views are articulated.

Rotating individuals through various jobs [23] allows naïveté and inexperience to provide new perspectives. Having people reverse roles [3] is another way to change existing frames of reference.

Routine procedures use the same frames of reference repetitively. To disturb routines, organizations can use heretical activities like recess (as in elementary schools), open houses in off-limits parts of the organization, and even task-oriented applications of games and tournaments [4].

A lot of emphasis has been placed on increasing job involvement by providing feedback, autonomy, variety, and so on, but little emphasis has been placed on making work fun. However, fun can be serious — just ask a fisherman. It is hard to imagine people more motivated than those who are deeply involved with avocations like golf or model building or showing dogs.

Emporia State in Kansas provides one example of an attempt to eliminate work and to make fun [6]. To encourage spontaneity and to help people learn "to see the whole world more clearly," the Play Factory manufactures fun while avoiding rules and conventional rewards. Whether jobs take on aspects of serious or frivolous fun, unfamiliar events are an inevitable by-product.

Another strategy to create unfamiliar events is experimentation. The research that is typically sanctioned by organizations tends to be strictly problem-oriented — developing new products, projecting markets, developing communication systems. But research also can be incongruity-oriented. Designers can help organizations experiment with themselves by designing and implementing internal simulations involving different members in different roles under new sets of rules. Sometimes even the act of collecting data is an unfamiliar event that can generate new frames of reference for the participants.

Creating new frames of reference

Decision makers can break out of the ruts guiding them within narrow frames of reference. Breaking out requires decision makers to get outside of the all-consuming day-to-day processes and to look at problems in diverse and unconventional ways. What follows are three suggestions for creating new frames of reference.

1. *Be wary of theory.* Perceptions of cause-and-effect relationships are never totally accurate. Evolving theories try to account for incongruities either by redefining events or by modifying existing frames of reference. Neither strategy is particularly useful for changing frames altogether. And, theories die hard. It took centuries to dismiss the earth-centered universe.

Theories are perceivers' attempts to provide explanatory structures for their observations. As Starbuck [26] has pointed out, "To learn an environment's causal structure solely through observation of naturally occurring phenomena is virtually impossible . . . ." This means that theories are never totally correct and, while they do provide convenient ways to organize events they also trap people in limited frames of reference.

Being wary of theory (or avoiding it all together) may help problem solvers because it forces them to ask impossible questions. Whether theories are products of personal or scientific observation, they rest on assumptions about the nature of events. Avoiding theory can surface those assumptions and force the problem solver to switch frames of reference.

2. *Be playful.* Perpetual seriousness reduces the number of frames of reference available to problem solvers. If a problem is really sticky, the problem solver should find an analogy for it or make up a song, poem, or joke about it. While hardly an orthodox approach to serious problems, these playful strategies force the problem solver to look at problems differently.

A consultant to one organization knew that the employees had problems with the administration, but all his questionnaires and interviews failed to disclose the nature of them. So in a playful mode, he asked them to design Christmas cards for the President. Their playful cooperation clearly revealed the real problems.

3. *Look at systems without obvious, immediate relevance.* It may be that the way to design effective organizations is to imitate successful organizations in the same business. But this is also a good way to miss incongruities and opportunities.

Weick [30] has pointed out that looking at alternative organizations can help researchers generate better hypotheses. Designers and practitioners too might use more frames of reference and generate more possible alternatives after they look at other types of organizations.

Suppose an industrial organization has problems motivating its employees. The problem solver is likely to look at other similar industrial organizations to find out how they motivate their people. Better, or at least more unconventional, possibilities might be generated if the problem solver studies football teams, ballet dancers, forest rangers, sports fans, or orchestras.

Although studying systems without immediate, obvious relevance is not a new idea (e.g., [11,12]), translating observations to a focal system entails difficulties that scare many problem solvers away. But even a casual look at alternative organizations can produce generalizations and analogies that may be useful back home.

Even if the usefulness is restricted to redefining the original problem, the problem solver's frame of reference will shift. What is inexplicable in one type of organization may be clear in another, for the nonsense in one organization may take sense in a different one.

A concluding note

Wisdom demands minimal rationality.
Satisfaction rests upon minimal contentment.
Improvement depends on minimal consistency.
According to Hedberg, Nystrom, and Starbuck [7], these aphorisms caricature three of the dynamic balances that are essential to a self-designing system. These authors argued that organization designs should emphasize dynamic processes and should incorporate "some inconsistencies and much heterogeneity" [20].

Designing for incongruities requires the creation or discovery of inconsistency and heterogeneity. Discovering incongruities is a continuing process that allows an organization to control its evolution to some degree. By exposing alternative cause-and-effect relationships and by applying numerous frames of reference, the organization creates more opportunities.

Winterbotham's [32] account of Ultra, the Allied intelligence operation that broke the German code during World War II, demonstrates the importance of recognizing and interpreting incongruities. Although Allied commanders often knew enemy plans even before the German field commanders, the Germans never realized their code had been broken. Convoys were sunk in the fog, overwhelming air assaults were thwarted, and U-boats were inexplicably located, but the Germans never caught on. The Germans were operating with artificial sense, the assumption that their most secret code could never be broken: those incongruities that were not missed altogether were ignored, misclassified, or discounted. By providing the enemy with decoys (such as spotter planes that stumbled onto ships or fictitious spies privy to top-level plans), the Allies helped preserve the enemy's erroneous frames of reference. As it turned out, the results were great for the Allies but disastrous for the Germans.

Through his descriptions of major crises in big corporations, Richard Austin Smith provides examples that are even closer to home [24]. As Smith points out, corporate crises are seldom abrupt; they just seem to be. A crisis "... is characteristically the result of years of procrastination, of unwillingness to face up to mistakes or write off failures ..." [24, p. 15]. In Smith's accounts of major corporations in trouble, it is clear that incongruities were missed, ignored, discounted, or misinterpreted. Over time the incongruities accumulated into major crises that took years to resolve.

Not all meaningful incongruities can be identified and appropriately responded to. Many incongruities may be better left ignored. But by knowing that incongruities take several different forms and by creating both unusual events and new frames of reference that maximize the recognition of incongruities, decision makers stand a better chance of making effective decisions.

References

[1] Ackoff, Russell L., "Management Misinformation Systems," Management Science, Vol. (December 1967), pp. B147–B156.

[2] Burns, Tom and Stalker, G.M., "Mechanistic and Organic Systems," in Organizations: Systems, Control and Adaptation (Vol. 2, 2nd ed.), Joseph A. Litterer (ed.), Wiley, New York, N.Y., 1969, pp. 345–348.

[3] Coleman, John H., Blue-Collar Journal: A College President's Sabbatical, Lippincott, Philadelphia, Pa., 1974.

[4] DeVries, David L., "Teams, Games, Tournament: A Gaming Technique That Fosters Learning," Simulation & Games, Vol. 7 (March 1976), pp. 21–33.

[5] Festinger, Leon, "The Motivating Effect of Cognitive Dissonance," in Assessment of Human Motives, G. Lindzey (ed.), Rinehart, New York, N.Y., 1958, pp. 65–86.

[6] Gilbert, Bil, "Play," Sports Illustrated, Vol. 43 (October 13, 1975), p. 84.

[7] Hedberg, Bo L.T., Nystrom, Paul C. and Starbuck, William H., "Camping on Seesaws: Prescriptions for a Self-Designing Organization," Administrative Science Quarterly, Vol. 21 (March 1976), pp. 41–65.

[8] Hewitt, John P. and Hall, Peter M., "Social Problems, Problematic Situations, and Quasi-Theories," American Sociological Review, Vol. 38 (June 1973), pp. 367–374.

[9] Hewitt, John P. and Stokes, Randall, "Disclaimers," American Sociological Review, Vol. 40 (February 1975), pp. 1–11.

[10] Jones, R.V., "The Theory of Practical Joking – Its Relevance to Physics," in A Random Walk in Science, R.L. Weber (ed.), Crane, Russak, New York, N.Y., 1973, pp. 8–14.

[11] Kaufman, Herbert, The Forest Ranger: A Study in Administrative Behavior, Johns Hopkins, Baltimore, Md., 1960.

[12] Kerr, Steven, Athletic Teams as Research Samples: Toward Field Realism with Laboratory Controls, The Ohio State University, Columbus, Ohio (working paper), 1975.

[13] Koestler, Arthur, The Act of Creation, Dell, New York, N.Y., 1964.

[14] Koestler, Arthur, The Case of the Midwife Toad, Random House, New York, N.Y., 1971.

[15] Kuhn, Thomas S., The Copernican Revolution, Vintage, New York, N.Y., 1957.

[16] Lawrence, Paul R. and Lorsch, Jay W., Organization and Environment, Harvard Business School, Boston, Mass., 1967.

[17] Mason, Richard O., "A Dialectical Approach to Strategic Planning," Management Science, Vol. 15 (April 1969), pp. B403–414.

[18] Mintzberg, Henry, The Nature of Managerial Work, Harper and Row, New York, N.Y., 1973.

[19] Mitroff, Ian I. and Betz, Frederick, "Dialectical Desicion Theory: A Meta-Theory of Decision-Making," Management Science, Vol. 19 (September 1972), pp. 11–24.

[20] Nystrom, Paul C., Hedberg, Bo L.T. and Starbuck, William H., "Interacting Processes as Organization Designs," in The Management of Organization Design: Vol. I, Ralph H. Kilmann, Louis R. Pondy and Dennis P. Slevin (eds.), Elsevier North-Holland, New York, N.Y., 1976, pp. 209–230.

[21] Perrow, Charles, Organizational Analysis, Wadsworth, Belmont, Cal., 1970.

[22] Roethlisberger, Fritz J. and Dickson, William J., Management and the Worker, Harvard University Press, Cambridge, Mass., 1939.

[23] Roos, Leslie L., Jr. and Roos, Noralon P., Managers of Modernization, Harvard University Press, Cambridge, Mass., 1971.

[24] Smith, Richard A., Corporations in Crisis, Doubleday, Garden City, N.Y., 1963.

[25] Speer, Albert, Inside the Third Reich, Avon, New York, N.Y., 1970.

[26] Starbuck, William H., "Organizations and Their Environments," in Handbook of Industrial and Organizational Psychology, Marvin D. Dunnette (ed.), Rand McNally, Chicago, Ill., 1976, pp. 1069–1123.

[27] Thompson, James D., Organizations in Action, McGraw-Hill, New York, N.Y., 1967.

[28] Tuchman, Gaye, "Making News by Doing Work: Routinizing the Unexpected," American Journal of Sociology, Vol. 79 (July 1973), pp. 110–131.

[29] Watson, James D., The Double Helix: Being a Personal Account of the Discovery of the Structure of DNA, Signet, New York, N.Y., 1969.

[30] Weick, Karl E., "Amendments to Organizational Theorizing," Academy of Management Journal, Vol. 17 (September 1974), pp. 487–502.

[31] White, Orion F., Jr., "The Dialectical Organization: An Alternative to Bureaucracy," Public Administration Review, Vol. 29 (January-February 1969), pp. 32–42.

[32] Winterbotham, F.W., The Ultra Secret, Dell, New York, N.Y., 1975.

[33] Woodward, Bob and Bernstein, Carl, All the President's Men, Simon and Schuster, New York, N.Y., 1974.

North-Holland/TIMS Studies in the Management Sciences 5 (1977) 125–142
© North-Holland Publishing Company

DESIGNING INFORMATION SYSTEMS IN AN ORGANIZATIONAL PERSPECTIVE *

NIELS BJØRN-ANDERSEN

Copenhagen School of Economics and Business Administration.

and

BO L.T. HEDBERG †

University of Gothenburg.

Studies conducted in two banks reveal that technological considerations determined the objectives, constraints, and alternatives for information-systems designs. The design teams limited their responsibilities to technology, and they neither predicted nor allowed for the human consequences of technology. As a result, the information systems failed to exploit opportunities for improvement. Because information systems influence all aspects of organizations, it is realistic for design teams' responsibilities to encompass human considerations as well as technological ones. To handle human considerations adequately, design teams need expertise beyond the ranges of technological specialists. The scopes of design processes can be widened, and users can meaningfully participate in designing, but this requires changes both in organizations and in their environments. Participative designing can lead to better information systems when organizations' members share major objectives. When this is not the case, designing must be dealt with as a political process.

Writers on design of information systems increasingly emphasize that changes in information technology should be planned in their organizational contexts, and that the whole spectrum of organizational needs should govern designing, but understanding still diverges far from practice in this area [3,20,28,31].

There are many reports on information systems' dysfunctions [1,12,15,32,39], but observers rarely link these dysfunctions to design practices. Few researchers

* Received June 1975; revised February 1976, June 1976.

† The reported studies are part of the joint research project "Computer Systems and Work Design," an optional study associated with the international research project on "Automation and the Industrial Worker," administered by the Vienna Centre for Coordination of Social Science Research. Although these two studies were conducted by the authors, the research instruments were developed by a team with participants from Austria, Britain, Denmark, France, Germany, and Sweden. The financial support of the International Institute of Management, Berlin, of the Danish Social Science Research Council and of the Danish Philips foundation in 1958 is gratefully acknowledged. The authors are indebted to William H. Starbuck and Finn Borum for very constructive criticism.

have studied information systems design and little knowledge exists about how design teams perceive their tasks and roles [24,36,38]. Such knowledge would provide a basis for improving design methods and for determining the scopes of design processes.

It is reported below how two large banks designed their information systems. There are two foci of attention. One focus is on the goals, constraints, and alternatives of the design processes, and on how design teams perceived their responsibilities. The other focus is on the design teams themselves: Who participated, and who influenced the design solutions? The findings, together with other empirical studies, form a background for discussing ways of improving design methods and of removing barriers which separate theory from practice.

Two case studies

The studied banks are two of the largest ones in Scandinavia. *ALPHA* is a commercial bank with around 400 branch offices and 7,000 employees; *BETA* is a savings bank with around 200 branches and 2,000 employees. Feasibility studies and early construction work started in the late sixties in both banks, and the resulting information systems came into operation gradually between 1972 and 1975.

Both banks set out to design on-line, real-time systems for handling customer accounts, but the design team at *BETA* fell short of this goal and settled for an on-line, data-entry system as a first step towards a full-fledged real-time system. *ALPHA* had its own computer department, while *BETA* relied on a computer service bureau, shared and owned by all the savings banks in the country.

Data about the design processes and about the consequences of the new information systems were collected in 90 interviews with managers, clerks and members of the design teams. In addition, 48 members of the design teams filled in questionnaires. Top managers and the head of computer operations assured access to the banks and to the computer service bureau. No constraints were imposed on the researchers or on the selection of interviewees. The studies were paid for by independent research funds, and the respondents were assured of confidentiality.

There was general agreement that the new information systems improved on the ones they replaced in both banks. They were technologically well designed, and they performed in technologically satisfactory ways.

Respondents expressed conflicting opinions about the human consequences of the new technologies. Both design teams attempted to tailor new information technology to the existing organization and to make as few changes in work roles as possible. However, several unintended changes in work roles resulted at both *ALPHA* and *BETA*. The most pronounced changes occurred at *ALPHA,* where the most advanced computer system operated.

Other reports describe the impacts the new technologies had on work roles and users' job satisfaction [6,23]. In summary, the users' relative satisfaction with the new information systems appeared to reflect primarily that work roles changed only modestly. Because the users had feared dire consequences, and because the users sought little improvement, the new information systems rated favorably more as a result of what they did not do than as a result of what they accomplished.

Two general observations from the bank studies deserve emphasis: Firstly, the new technologies caused unintended changes in work roles and in organizational structures inside branch offices and between the latter and the central offices. Secondly, the new information systems only very marginally exploited the opportunities for redesigning these work roles and organizational structures in directions which were more conducive to human satisfactions and capabilities. The design teams gave little consideration to how the information systems could contribute to overall improvements in the organizations. Observations of the design processes reveal some reasons for this myopic orientation.

Design processes at *ALPHA* and *BETA*

Managers, design teams, and users described how the design processes started and proceeded. The descriptions centered around three questions:

(1) What were the major reasons for introducing the new information systems?
(2) How did the design teams perceive the scope of their tasks?
(3) What major constraints and alternatives did the design teams encounter?

Personnel in both banks said that new information systems had been sought because of technological innovations, increasing work loads, ambitions to cut costs, and competitors' decisions. Publicity around a major competitor's decision to install an on-line information system made *ALPHA* rush to an investment decision: the pressure changed the timing, although the firm's plans had envisioned a new system. The same incident also affected *BETA's* decision to install a new information system, when news of the pioneering bank's activities spread across national borders.

Members of both design tems defined their design responsibilities as ranging from a feasibility study to the final testing and installing of the technology. Their job was to specify hardware and software requirements, to estimate investments and production costs, and to structure and program the new information systems. Both design teams believed that other groups in their organizations should be responsible for designing work roles, informing users about the new developments, preparing and running training courses, and implementing the new technology in an organizational sense. In effect, the design teams singled out the technology as their area of responsibility. They saw the design of work roles and organizational structures as being the responsibilities of other subunits in the banks. The design teams' model of the design process did not appear to recognize performance evaluation and learning as parts of the design activities. A design process began when a mission was given, and it ended when the technical solutions were operative. It was left to others to consider and assess the individual and organizational consequences.

Personnel from organization and training departments participated in installing the new information systems and running training courses. Although the design teams rated these contributions as substantial, the man-hours invested were few. The efforts going into redesigning work roles and the organizational structures added up to only small fractions of the efforts going into technology design.

Work design lagged considerably behind technology design – to the extent that work design occurred at all. For example, the selection of computer terminals preceded any work-design discussions; personnel from organization and training departments became involved only after the technological properties of the new information systems had been determined; and computer programming continued for several years, but the programming of people for new tasks – in the form of training – took place only during the last few weeks just before the technology was installed in branch offices.

Members of the design teams said that they had experienced few design constraints, particularly in the initial phases when they decided on the systems' overall structures and when they selected equipment. Although later choices were constrained by earlier decisions, insufficient core storage (*ALPHA*) and time pressure (*BETA*) were the only severe constraints. Users' attitudes and the impacts of the new technology on users' work roles were regarded as extremely weak constraints: indeed, few members of the design teams recalled ever having considered these as being constraints. Table 1 summarizes the respondents' ranking of five kinds of constraints.

Facing few constraints and working on a design task that involved many variables and many partial solutions, the design teams could, hypothetically, have considered many design alternatives. But the members of the design teams recalled few situations where they had made explicit choices between design alternatives. Those design alternatives the respondents did recall concerned technological choices. The

Table 1
Ranking of constraints on the design process.

ALPHA	BETA
(1) Technological constraints (core storage, terminals, software, etc.)	(1) Time available for design
(2) Time available for design	(2) The previous information system
(3) The previous information system	(3) Technological constraints (core storage, terminals, software, etc.)
(4) Users' attitudes	(4) Effects of the new technology on work roles
(5) Effects of the new technology on work roles	(5) Users' attitudes

Table 2
Were there design alternatives?

- "We did not perceive it as our task to provide alternatives."
- "These decisions were already taken by management."
- "There was only one solution. We were strongly influenced by management directives."
- "We were completely constrained by the selected equipment."
- "There was no choice."
- "The directives implied that the jobs should be made more interesting."
- "The directives implied that the jobs should be more routinized."

---

design team at *ALPHA* had debated whether to use typewriter terminals or visual display terminals, and whether to select a technology with full real-time capacity or to settle for on-line interaction with batch-updated files. They had also explored alternative ways of organizing the data base. The design team at *BETA* had considered developing a multi-purpose terminal and providing question answering facilities in the new computer system. Both features could have widened tellers' work roles, but costs and ambitions to simplify programming ruled out these alternatives.

Beyond these few technological alternatives, most members of the design teams saw the design process as having been deterministic, with solutions that were given or obvious, and they thought of themselves as specialists who could tailor a new technology to an existing organization. Adapting and matching, rather than changing and restructuring, characterized their tasks. "We are merely replacing the old system. We are not changing anything for the clerks," was a typical answer. The quotations in Table 2 illustrate other characteristic attitudes.

There had been times, though, when the design teams had understood that the new technology would affect both work roles and the organizational structures. "I realized that most of the users would turn into part-time key punchers," said one designer at *ALPHA*. Another said, "The tellers' role will be changed. They'll need to know more about banking, especially about the work at the savings department." But these concerns were not brought explicitly into the design processes; they remained informal insights about possible impacts on work roles, and they were never translated into design constraints or made bases for formulating alternatives that would have met human needs better.

These were, in outline, the observations with respect to the nature and content of the design processes. Who were, then, the members of the design teams, and how influential were the represented groups within each organization?

Design team participation of *ALPHA* and *BETA*

ALPHA had high ambition for involving different groups in the design process. Installing an interactive real-time system called for an elaborate project organization with 10 project groups. The project was anchored in the formal line organization,

and the project groups included managers, administrative staff, and branch personnel. The administrative director of the corporate headquarters chaired the steering
committee, which reported to a committee of vice presidents. The special implementation group, formed towards the end of the project, included the head of the
training department and a group of former branch personnel; the latter tested and
installed the system. Ten local branch managers – selected from 550 – read written
memos and reacted to given proposals.

Management at *BETA* was less concerned participation. They saw few opportunities to involve employees in design decisions, since they believed that changes
would be marginal and that impacts on the users would be negligible. Besides,
designing a standard system for all cooperating banks took place at the service
bureau, so each bank was not directly in touch with the developments. Management
at the service bureau saw few difficulties in having the users accept the systems, and
they felt that user involvement was unnecessary until the system was ready for implementation in the branches. At this late point, *BETA's* management established
a contact group to implement their information system.

The design teams reported that technological specialists and *EDP* management
were heavily involved in initiating the design projects, whereas branch management,
clerks, and union representatives had little or no involvement. Two persons – the
manager in charge of computer operations at *BETA's* service bureau and the head
of *ALPHA's* administrative deparment – appeared to have triggered the design processes.

The design teams stated that top management were relatively important participants in the design process, because top management had to make the investment
decisions. Top management at *ALPHA* received progress reports bimonthly, and
top management at *BETA* had a representative on the board of the service bureau.
But the top managers in both banks claimed that insufficient computer knowledge
prevented them from directly influencing the detailed contents of the new system.
Having approved the investment in principle they perceived few possibilities for
influencing the development or introducing ideas.

Members of *ALPHA's* design team believed that clerks and branch managers
had been involved through the 10 representative branch managers, but interviews
revealed that branch personnel's influence had been very marginal. Because the
representative branch managers did not have time to discuss proposals with their
subordinates, the clerical staff in the branches were never actually involved in the
design process. Both branch managers and clerks said furthermore, that they lacked
proper computer knowledge and had difficulties in understanding given proposals
and in articulating their alternatives. Nobody thought that the clerks and branch
managers at *BETA* had participated in the design process. Union officials had no
participation in design at either organization. Management and the design teams
said that the administrative department at *ALPHA* and the implementation group
at *BETA* had provided for users' needs in the design, but most decisions had been
made before they became involved.

Thus, the technological specialists at *ALPHA* and at *BETA* formulated as well as translated objectives; they made the real decisions about developments. However, they did not seek such influential roles. The dominance of technological concerns in the designs was the result of the technological specialists acting in vacuums, rather than the result of deliberate grabs for power. The technological specialists did not see the absence of direct influence by users as a major problem. Because many of the specialists had worked in branches, they felt they knew enough about the users' jobs and problems. They saw themselves as professionals who understood their clients' worlds and who acted as their clients would wish.

Unfortunately, this was not so. The technological specialists' perceptions of users' attitudes were more mechanistic and less limited than those expressed by the users themselves [6,23]. The projects did not take the users' interests into consideration. Most users were represented neither directly nor indirectly in the design processes, and the technological specialists had conceptions of users and users' needs that were not shared by the users themselves.

Broadening the scopes of design processes

Observations from *ALPHA* and *BETA* suggested that technology dominated the design processes from initiation all the way through implementation. The design teams limited their areas of responsibility to the task of constructing functioning computerized systems and to the time during which they selected, programmed, and installed the technology. The triggers, constraints, and alternatives of the design processes were predominantly technological. Human needs and organizational impacts received little attention and were brought into the design discussions late, if at all.

This general pattern of design behavior is supported by observations from other recent studies. Mercer and Harris [33] found strong technological biases in a study of design processes in a British bank. Mumford and Ward [38] concluded that a sample of British computer specialists had very narrow, technological role perceptions, and that they avoided assuming responsibility for the human consequences of their designs. Lucas [30] and Davis [14] concluded that designers who develop information systems often lack proper understanding of the organizations and the users they design for, and they urged that human and organizational aspects should be considered at an early state of each design process.

In order to move from observations to prescriptions, we need to consider why design teams define their tasks so narrowly and why technology received more attention than people in design processes.

One explanation is that design teams' behavior is the logical result of self-selection processes. That is, people have to be fascinated by technology in order to devote their lives to designing information systems, and if they are fascinated by technology, they are likely to see particularly the technological opportunities and constraints in the design problems which they face. Information systems have benefited from computer developments over the last decades, and it is very likely that people who wanted to work with computers have found it particularly attractive to become systems designers.

To the extent that self-selection is a cause of the overemphasis of technology in design processes, the cure should be to attract to design teams people who expect to work with both people and computers. Also, increased awareness that technology design is but a subset of information systems design – and that many of the most difficult and challenging design problems are nontechnical – should gradually affect the self-selection processes.

A second group of explanations have to do with the conditions under which design teams operate. Although the observations from *ALPHA* and *BETA* suggested that there were few explicit constraints on the design solutions, the designers still maintained that they had acted inside given directives and that they had considered very few design alternatives. Their answers implied that the design situation contained implicit constraints which limited the design teams' perceptions of problems and solutions. One group of such implicit constraints could be the beliefs or values which guide the design team's search for problems and solutions. Hedberg and Mumford [24] found that British and Swedish computer specialists expressed more humane and nonmechanistic values when they described their general concepts of man and well-functioning organizations than when they described the specific clients for whom they actually designed and the specific organizations where they worked. The computer specialists saw few opportunities to work towards their private beliefs when designing. They felt that they had few choices to make, and that they should not question the values that were embedded in their organizations and missions.

Many forces impose values on design teams. Training and education are major influence sources. Professional societies are others. There are presently few curricula or textbooks which make information systems designers as knowledgeable about humans as about computers. Even the ambitious curriculum for graduate training of information systems designers and analysts, which a committee developed a few years ago for the Association for Computing Machinery, contains only four organization courses, while the other nine courses primarily teach technology [4]. Professional journals are also dominated by technological issues. Mumford and Pettigrew [37] found, for example, that the British Computer Society's two journals *The Computer Bulletin* and *The Computer Journal* treated human and organizational computer-related problems very rarely. Only 10 articles of 114 in 36 consecutive issues of the *Bulletin* dealt with nontechnological aspects of computer systems. Three of these 10 articles concerned the issue of privacy, and the others were articles on training and implementation. *The Computer Journal* had only articles on technology in the studied issues. Another study [47] classified articles appearing in 48 periodicals for computer professionals during 1972-1975 and used the courses of the *ACM* curriculum proposal as a classification scheme. More than 100 articles were published on each of the topics: Computer Systems, File and Communication Systems, Software Design, Introduction to Computer Systems, and Operating Systems, but only 66 articles appeared on Human Behavior, and only 55 dealt with the Social Implications of Information Systems. Outside the classification scheme, there were 721 articles on specific hardware equipment, 218 on timesharing services, and 150 articles on programming. The dominance of technology topics was massive. Computer specialists' conventions probably reflect similar topic distributions, although the authors are unaware of any studies in that area.

Another group of implicit design constraints comes from the ways in which design teams' performance is measured, and from the rewards which are attached to their performance. If performance measures are crude and partial, they are likely to direct design teams' attention mainly to the variables that are reflected in the measures. If rewards encourage only certain design considerations, other design aspects are likely to be neglected.

Top management at *ALPHA* and *BETA* supplemented vaguely expressed design objectives with cost budgets and time schedules in order to control the design processes. These performance measures spelled out time and money as important design considerations, but they did not acknowledge human needs on equal terms. The design teams were not rewarded for considering human needs, and budgets and time schedules were not planned to allow capacity for work design or reorganizing. Neither did they encourage – or even enable – members of the design teams to spend time evaluating and learning from the information systems they had installed. When one system was technically completed, another design project was waiting. The design teams' emphasis on making the technology work, and their reluctance to assume responsibility for their systems' human consequences are very understandable in view of the ways in which their performance was judged and rewarded.

To the extent that values that are communicated through teaching and professional societies limit technological specialists' connotation of designing merely to the technological aspects, the long-term cure should be to provide broader eduction, so that members of design teams understand more of the context in which they work. Technological specialists' increased awareness of the human side of information systems should then gradually change the contents of professional journals and of meetings and conventions, and these changes in the professional subculture would encourage design teams further to widen the scopes of their design processes. In the short run, at least, it should be a more effective strategy to recruit people with various educational levels and from different professional subcultures to design teams [39]. This may also be a good long-term strategy. Considering the rapid growth of knowledge both about men and technologies, it may well be impossible to provide all necessary design knowledge in one broad curriculum. There may be markets for specialists in technology, as well as in work design and organization design, in tomorrow's teams.

Organizations should, furthermore, measure design teams' performance so that human, technological, and financial objectives receive attention [35], and they should reward designers' attempts to consider the interplay between people and technology. Traditional performance measures are insufficient in this respect, as, for example, Daellenbach [11] has concluded based on studies of how management science projects are evaluated. Efforts of accountants during the last decade to develop human resources accounting and social auditing may indicate a possible route to improved measures of design performance. Although such attempts still are crude and incomplete, they could result in necessary complements to financial and technological performance measures.

But, even design teams that seek to take human needs into account and that understand the whole context in which they design may have cognitive difficulties in perceiving innovative alternatives and in deviating from professionally accepted standard solutions which overemphasize technology. Dialectic decision techniques could help such design teams in inventing design alternatives and making their underlying values and assumptions explicit [34]. Kilmann [27] has formalized notions from dialectic decision making into the *MAPS* method — Multivariate Analysis, Participation and Structure — which provides design teams a way to invent at least one counterproposal to each given design proposal and which helps design teams discover and express their different values and perceptions.

Taking cognizance of the complexity of design tasks and the illusion of finding optimal solutions, design teams should, in principle, treat each new design as an experiment and organize themselves for repeated experiments over time [43,46]. They should develop their ability to evaluate their designs so that each sequential solution could contribute to improving the next. To the extent that the logical implications of new design alternatives are difficult to work through, design teams may benefit from employing computer aids — such as simulation — to generate and to evaluate alternatives [5].

Another way to widen the scope of design processes is to widen the participation in design teams inside organizations so that diverse interests, perceptions, and experiences can influence the design solutions. The next section discusses the prospects of users' participation in designing.

Involving users in design processes

ALPHA made serious attempts to involve managers and users in designing, while *BETA* paid little attention to the issue of participation. The result was, however, about the same. The technological specialists designed the systems, and others participated only formally, or not at all.

One frequently heard argument for users' participation in designing is that involvement enables people to develop realistic expectations, and that it reduces resistance to change [7,10,21]. This argument has often a manipulative flavor and appears to pay more attention to users' feelings of influence than to their actual ability to influence. The effects of such insincere pretenses of democracy are questionable and may well counteract their purposes of facilitating change.

A second reason is that new systems may be constructed upon erroneous premises, and user participation in systems design could improve the knowledge upon which systems are built. Users typically know their jobs well, and they constitute the environment in which new systems are to operate [12,29,30]. Emery [19] summarized this point of view:

"The most adequate and effective designs come from those whose jobs are under review. It is only from people pooling their various and usually fragmented, but always very detailed, knowledge that a comprehensive and stable design can come."

A third reason represents democratic values. Because organizations ought to respect human dignity and basic human rights, all members should have a right to participate in decisions about changes that are likely to affect them [12,14,25].

Several authors have delineated models for involving users in designing; passive influence is the weakest form of participation. Design teams study users' wishes and and needs for change [26]. The technological specialists frame the questions, interpret the answers, and decide what actions to take. Users are merely objects with recognized needs. In essence, the advocates of passive influence are sending a very simple message to design teams. Be smarter and try to understand the organization you work with!

Another strategy is to use representatives on steering committees that anchor design teams in the line organization [2,21,25]. Committee members may represent important user groups, and the chairman may be a senior line manager [7,8,9]. But many cooperation problems may arise between the steering committee and the design team. Although a committee of branch managers followed the design process at *ALPHA,* neither these representatives nor their constituents felt that the arrangement allowed them to influence the design. Representatives in these arrangements may become captive participants who formally share responsibilities for decisions which they cannot actually influence.

Potential users can also be recruited for positions in the design teams [2,7,39]. Both *ALPHA* and *BETA* did this. Clerks played important roles during the installation of the systems. These recruits knew their jobs well, but they knew little about computers, so they went through intensive computer training. A result was that they gradually turned into technological specialists and were absorbed by this new profession. None returned to their earlier jobs, although most of them had intended to do so.

Extensive experimenting in Norwegian firms to employ sociotechnical techniques in designing production systems [16,18] led to elaborate organizational structures with high worker involvement. Based on these experiences, Nordby [40] recommended a project organization with three different task groups. One group – consisting of technological specialists and those users who will be directly affected by the new system – would do the technological design guided by defined objectives. The second group – consisting of users who will be less directly affected by the new system – would set systems objectives, be in charge of organizational development activities and prepare adequate information, training and instructions. The third group – representing everyone else who has a legitimate interest in the system – would meet occasionally and act as a sounding board for basic design ideas.

However, participation will not bring design changes unless users' attitudes change. Just as technological specialists have to realize that their profession extends beyond computer technology, so must computer laymen understand that they should play important roles in design processes. Laymen can and should participate in merging technological and human objectives and in disclosing implicit assumptions and values. When organizations start using technological specialists, not to design but to teach managers and workers how to design, then the ultimate in participative designing is reached; the technological specialists shift from being designers towards being facilitators and catalysts of change processes [22,43].

Elden [17] reported such an attempt in a bank where the clerks were given the opportunity to redesign their work roles and to formulate requests on the information systems, while techological specialists and researchers acted as informants when the clerks needed assistance.

When broader scopes and more participation do not suffice

The first prescriptive theme of this article asserted that the scope of design processes should widen so as to encompass not only technological and economic, but also human, aspects of information systems. Six means to that end were discussed.

1. Broader training would enable members of design teams to appreciate also the human aspects of their design problems.

2. Diversity of backgrounds in design teams would lead to more balanced attention to problems and solutions.

3. Professional societies' values and norms should be scrutinized and changed, if needed, so as to encourage design teams to design for people and with people.

4. Dialectic problem solving techniques could help design teams to perceive innovative design alternatives and to become aware of their underlying value assumptions.

5. Performance measures should reflect the fulfillment of technological, economic, and human design objectives.

6. Rewards should encourage design teams to consider as many relevant aspects as possible of the systems they design.

These prescriptions share the common aim of making design teams better equipped, more conscious, and more motivated to deal with both the human and the technological aspects which their design problems offer, and less inclined to reduce uncertainty by avoiding responsibility for the human consequences of their designs.

The second prescriptive theme suggested that users should participate to a larger extent in designing information systems. One argument for user participation is the ethical one that people should have a right to influence their own work situations. Another argument is that users who participate in designing will form more realistic expectations about new systems and will become less reluctant to accept changes in their work roles. A third argument is that user participation adds knowledge to design teams and increases the likelihood that new designs can respond to a wide range of relevant work aspects.

Both these prescriptive themes assumed that lopsided designs result from design teams' lack of factual understanding of design matters. If only technological specialists knew enough, they would design better. Now, there is a hidden assumption in this; namely, that technological specialists and users have common objectives, and that there are solutions that can satisfy everyone, if only these solutions can be found. If this is not the case, then designing must also be understood and dealt with as a political process [44,45].

Behind the case studies at *ALPHA* and *BETA* were the assumptions that technological specialists, managers, and users would have at least partially conflicting objectives with respect to the new systems. There were, however, no indications that design teams had perceived or dealt with such conflicts, except marginally. But the implemented systems met the objectives of technological specialists and managers much better than they satisfied the needs of users, and power had been redistributed inside the organizations. Still, the political aspects of the design processes had not been realized.

Failure to realize the political dimension of design tasks may well explain why many ambitiously organized design teams have turned out systems which have been less than satisfactory to the users. Design teams that have acquired broad knowledge about their design objectives may well decide to use their skills manipulatively if their objectives differ from those of their clients. User participation in design teams can easily deteriorate to hostage situations, if there are conflicting objectives between the users and the technological specialists, and if the users fail to have their viewpoints accepted or understood by the technological specialists.

Users have had poor resources so far to influence design processes. They have received little education about the new technologies, so they have had difficulties in appreciating design constraints and design opportunities; they have, as a rule, had little training in solving complex problems and have been hesitant to articulate their viewpoints and alternatives even when they had some; they had little time to become involved in design problems since they have had their normal jobs to attend to; they have had low status in their oganizations, in comparison with managers and technological specialists; and they have lacked both the rewards and the sanctions by which they could have made the technological specialists pay more attention to users' interests. It is, therefore, not surprising that users' objectives have received lower priority than economic and technological objectives in design processes.

There are at least three areas where changes could improve users' influence over design processes. Access to expert knowledge is one area of great importance. The current knowledge on information technology and design alternatives is largely inaccessible to ordinary people in organizations. Technological specialists have not been able – and maybe not even interested – in explaining to laymen the relative simplicity of their trade. Textbooks and research articles have contributed to maintaining an air of magic around computers, and they have been written from a technologist's point of view. Interesting developments in this area are going on in Norway, where several trade unions have initiated and supported research aimed at developing computer knowledge and design expertise among workers and union officials [41]. A series of textbooks [42] written in ordinary language explains to workers the major features of the new information technologies, as well as key concepts of planning, administration, decision theory and work design. A formal language for design discussions helps users formulate their demands on new information systems. The unions' initiatives have resulted in considerable activities all over the country. Local unions have suggested new information systems designs to their firms' management, and more knowledgeable workers and clerks have taught their fellow employees introductory computer courses. The Norwegian developments demonstrate very strongly that users can strengthen their influence over design processes by developing their own design expertise.

Structural arrangements which strengthen users' bargaining power and grant users the right to participate in designing form another important area. Some Norwegian trade unions' agreements with employers regulating the use of new information technologies is one example. Such agreements could, for example, specify the unions' right to early information about companies' plans to design new information systems. They could provide for a data ombudsman or a data shop-steward who is paid by the company and employed by the unions to represent the workers' interests. This representative should have full access to information systems developments. Such agreements could also regulate users' right to company-financed education so that they could participate in design teams and operate new systems more confidently. The agreements could, finally, regulate the use of personnel data and grant individuals the right to know what their personal files contain. Similar developments are under way also in Sweden and Denmark where trade unions prepare to negotiate data agreements for both white-collar and blue-collar workers. On a macrolevel, data laws being introduced in several countries point at another route to strengthen humanity's influence over information technologies.

A third area, where users' abilities to influence design processes could be improved, is that of self-reliance. He who knows and understands the new technologies will be more confident in his own proposals. She who knows that she has the right to express her view, will be more likely to dare to bring up her conflicting interests. Users have to realize that they possess important experiences which should affect new designs. They know their jobs, and they know how they react to different work arrangements [14].

The users at *ALPHA* and *BETA* did not think that they could contribute much to the design discussions, so they did not demand to become involved. They lacked confidence in their own experiences and believed that their knowledge was hopelessly inferior to that of the technological specialists. In fact, both managers and members of the design teams thought more highly of the users' abilities to contribute ot the design processes than the users did themselves [6,23]. Interviews showed that many clerks had interesting ideas which could have improved the new information systems, if they had reached the design teams.

Users who acquire design expertise and self-reliance, and who have the support of legislation or agreements to participate in designing, could well develop their own design proposals and their own information systems, as the Norwegian developments have demonstrated. When users, managers and technological specialists agree on the major design objectives, they should design jointly. When they have conflicting objectives, they should clarify how their needs and objectives differ and then negotiate and bargain until they have reached workable compromises. Users need to strengthen their bargaining positions for such instances, and attempts to do so have been promising thus far [12,41,42]. Information processing capacity is a limited resource today, and information systems designs have power implications [22,44]. Increased awareness of this among managers, technological specialists and workers is likely to bring out the political aspects of information systems designing more often than presently is the case.

Conclusions

If new information systems are to contribute profoundly to organizations' needs, the scope of design processes must be broadened, users' participation must increase, and the political aspects of designing must be recognized and dealt with.

Training, diversity, and consiousness raising, together with more diverse performance measures and supportive reward systems, can enable and encourage design teams to design with both human needs and technological possibilities in mind.

Users must improve their resources to influence design processes. mere participation is not enough. Increased self-reliance, access to expertise, and legislative support, which grants users the right to share design activities, can strengthen users' influence over design processes.

Participative designing can contribute to better designs when design teams share the major objectives. When there are many conflicting interests, information systems designing should be seen also as a political process, and designs should emerge as compromises between different organizational subgroups.

References

[1] Ackoff, Russell L., "Management Misinformation Systems," Management-Science, Vol. 14 (December 1967), pp. B147-B156.

[2] Andersen, Christian, Krog-Jespersen, Fritz, and Petersen, Anders, Syskon — En bog om konstruktion af datamatiske systemer, G.E.C. Gads Forlag, Copenhagen, Denmark, 1972.

[3] Argyris, Chris, "Management Information Systems: Challenge to Rationality and Emotionality," Management Science, Vol. 17 (February 1971), pp. B275-B292.

[4] Ashenhurst, R.L., (ed.), "A Report of the *ACM* Curriculum Committee on Computer Education for Management," Communications of the ACM, Vol. 15 (May 1972), pp. 363–398.

[5] Bjørn-Andersen, Niels, Informations systemer for beslutningstagning, Nyt Nordisk Forlag, Copenhagen, Denmark, 1974.

[6] Bjørn-Andersen, Niels, "The Design and Impact of a Batch Computer System on Work Design and Job Satisfaction," in Satisfaction, Systems Design, Work Structure, and Job Niels Bjorn-Andersen, Bo Hedberg, Dorothy, Mercer, and Andres Solé, (eds.), Pergamon Press, London, England, 1977, forthcoming.

[7] Blumenthal, Sherman C., Management Information Systems: A framework for Planning and Development, Prentice-hall, Englewood Cliffs, N.J., 1969.

[8] Bryce, M., Associates Inc., Pride-Profitable Information by Design through Phased Planning and Control, New York, N.Y. (technical report), 1974.

[9] Canning, Richard G., "A Structure for *EDP*-Projects'" EDP-Analyzer, Vol. 11 (May 1973), pp. 1–13.

[10] Coch, Lester, and French, John, "Overcoming Resistance to Change," in Group Dynamics, Dorwin Cartwright and Alvin Zander (eds.), Harper, New York, N.Y., 1968.

[11] Daellenbach, Hans G., "Note on a Survey on Evaluation of Operations Research Projects," Interfaces, Vol. 6 (February 1976), pp. 50–53.

[12] Dallinger, Alfred, "Trade Unions and Computers," in Human Choice and Computers, Enid Mumford and Harold Sackman (eds.), North-Holland, Amsterdam, The Netherlands, 1975, pp. 61–72.

[13] Davis, Gordon, B., Management Information Systems: Conceptual Foundations, Structure, and Development, McGraw-Hill, New York, N.Y., 1974.

[14] Davis, Louis E. and Taylor, J.C., (eds.), The Design of Jobs, Penguin, Baltimore, Md., 1972.

[15] Dunlop, Robert A., "Some Empirical Observations on the Man-Machine Interface Question," in Mangeement Information Systems: Progress and Perspectives, Charles H. Kriebel, Richard L. Van Horn, and J. Timothy Heames, (eds.), Carnegie Press, Carnegie-Mellon University, Pittsburgh, Pa., 1971, pp. 219–252.

[16] Eide, Kjell, Planlegging og organisation, Universitetsforlaget, Olso, Norway, 1973.

[17] Elden, Max, Bank Employees Begin to Participate in Studying and Changing their Organization, conference on "Workers' Participation on the Shop Floor," Dubrovnik, Yugoslavia (working paper), 1976.

[18] Emery, Fred E. and Thorsrud, Einar, The Form and Content in Industrial Democracy, Tavistock Publications, London , England, 1969.

[19] Emery, Fred E. and Emery, Merrelyn, Participative Design: Work and Community Life, The Australian National University, Sidney, Australia (Occasional Papers in Continuing Education, No. 4), 1975.

[20] Glimell, Hans and Holmgren, Mette, Cognitive Style, Problem-Solving Preference, and Attitude to Computer Technology, University of Gothenburg, Sweden (working paper, Psychological Reports No. 21, Vol. 5), 1975.

[21] Hartman, W., Matthes, H., and Proeme, A., Information Systems Handbook, Philips Data Systems, The Hague, The Netherlands, 1968.

[22] Hedberg, Bo, "Computer Systems to Support Industrial Democracy," in Human Choice and Computers, Enid Mumford and Harold Sackman (eds.), North-Holland, Amsterdam, The Netherlands, 1975, pp. 211–230.

[23] Hedberg, Bo, "The Design and Impact of a Real-Time Computer System," in Systems Design, Work Structure, and Job Satisfaction, Niels Bjørn-Andersen, Bo Hedberg, Dorothy Mercer, and Andres Solé (eds.), Pergamon Press, London, England, 1977, forthcoming.

[24] Hedberg, Bo and Mumford, Enid, "The Design of Computer Systems: Man's Vision of Man as an Integral Part of the Systems Design Process," in Human Choice and Computers, Enid Mumford and Harold Sackman (eds.), North-Holland, Amsterdam, The Netherlands, 1975, pp. 31–59.

[25] Hedberg, Bo, Sjöberg, Sam, and Targama, Axel, Styrsystem och företagsdemokrati, BAS, Gothenburg, Sweden, 1971.

[26] IBM, Basic System Study Guide, International Business Machines, Armonk, N.Y. (technical report, Form F20-8150), 1963.

[27] Kilmann, Ralph H., "An Organic-Adaptive Organization: The *MAPS* Method," Personnel, Vol. 51 (May-June 1974), pp. 35–47.

[28] King, William R. and Cleland, David I., "The Design of Management Information Systems: An Information Analysis Approach," Management Science, Vol. 22 (November 1975), pp. 286–297.

[29] Lucas, Henry C., Jr., "Technological Consulting in a Grass Roots, Action Oriented Organization," Sloan Management Review, Vol. 14 (Fall 1972), pp. 17–36.

[30] Lucas, Henry C., Jr., Computer Based Information Systems in Organizations, Science Research Aasociates, Chicago, Ill., 1973.

[31] Mason, Richard O. and Mitroff, Ian I., "A Program for Research on Management Information Systems," Management Science, Vol. 19 (January 1973), pp. 475–487.

[32] McKinsey Company, Inc., "Unlocking the Computer's Profit Potential," Computers and Automation, Vol. 18 (April 1969), pp. 24–33.

[33] Mercer, Dorothy and Harris, Pauline, "A Case Study of an On- Line Computer System in a British Bank," in Systems Design, Work Structure, and Job Satisfaction, Niels Bjørn-Andersen, Bo Hedberg, Dorothy Mercer, and Andres Solé (eds.), Pergamon Press, London, England, 1977, forthcoming.

[34] Mitroff, Ian I. and Betz, Frederick, "Dialectical Decision Theory; A Meta-Theory of Decision-Making," Management Science, Vol. 19 (September 1972), pp. 11–24.

[35] Mumford, Enid, Systems Design for People, The National Computing Centre, Manchester, England, 1971.

[36] Mumford, Enid, Job Satisfaction: A Study of Computer Specialists, Longmans, London, England, 1972.

[37] Mumford, Enid and Pettigrew, Andrew, Implementing Strategic Planning, Longmans, London, England, 1975.

[38] Mumford, Enid and Ward, Tom B., "Computer Technologists: Dilemmas of a New Role," Journal of Management Studies, Vol. 3 (Oct. 1966), pp. 244–255.

[39] Mumford, Enid and Ward, Tom B., Computers: Planning for People, Batsford, London, England, 1968.

[40] Nordby, Trygve, "Strategier for bedre systemer," in Over til edb, Rolf Hoyer, (ed.), Tanum, Oslo, Norway, 1974, pp. 174–190.

[41] Nygaard, Kristen and Bergo, Olav Terje, "The Trade Unions-New Users of Research," Personnel Review, Vol. 4 (Spring 1975), pp. 5–10.

[42] Nygaard, Kristen and Bergo, Olav Terje, Planleggning, styrning og databehandling, (Vols. I and II), Tidens Forlag, Oslo, Norway, 1973.

[43] Nystrom, Paul C., Hedberg, Bo L.T., and Starbuck, William H., "Interacting Processes as Organization Designs," in The Management of Organization Design: Volume I: Strategies and Implementation, Ralph H. Kilmann, Louis R. Pondy, and Dennis P. Slevin (eds.), Elsevier North-Holland, New York, N.Y., 1976, pp. 209–230.

[44] Pettigrew, Andrew, "Information Control as a Power Resource," Sociology, Vol. 6 (May 1972), pp. 187–204.

[45] Pettigrew, Andrew, The Politics of Organizational Decision-Making, Tavistock Publications, London, England, 1973.
[46] Starbuck, William H., "Systems Optimization with Unknown Criteria," Proceedings of the 1974 International Conference on Systems, Man and Cybernetics, Institute of Electrical and Electronics Engineers, New York, N.Y., 1974, pp. 67–76.
[47] St. Pierre, William, Classification of Computer Periodicals, University of Wisconsin-Milwaukee, Milwaukee, Wis. (working paper), 1975.

North-Holland/TIMS Studies in the Management Sciences 5 (1977) 143–155
© North-Holland Publishing Company

ASSESSING ORGANIZATIONAL CHANGE STRATEGIES *

JOHN R. KIMBERLY

Yale University

and

WARREN R. NIELSEN †

University of Nebraska, Lincoln

It is relatively common to apply change strategies based on the behavioral sciences to problems of management, yet results are rarely assessed systematically. This paper provides some guidelines for assessment which are based on the authors' experiences in two large-scale change projects and which incorporate some central principles or organizational development. The lessons learned in assessing these two projects illustrate the pitfalls and opportunities that accompany assessment. Long-term, process-oriented, flexible designs developed in conjunction with organizational members can facilitate adaptation and can help organizations become self-designing and self-evaluating.

The behavioral sciences have been applied to organizational design and management increasingly over the past 25 years. Although most common in business and industrial settings, applications have also occurred in educational, governmental and other nonprofit organizations. Generally, the change efforts based on the behavioral sciences have sought to enhance organizational effectiveness by changing the social settings in which work takes place. Some recent efforts have changed the technological dimension of work as well.

In the past ten years, many of these efforts have fallen under the rubric of organizational development. The growth of organizational development has had three important characteristics. First, the literature on organizational change has exploded with descriptions and exhortations about what organizational development can do to improve organizational effectiveness. A 1973 bibliography [8] listed some 200 documents, and a 1974 review article [10] cited more than 170 articles and books. Over 20 books have appeared in the past five years alone. A second characteristic is the lack of systematic assessments of organizational

* Received April 1975; revised January 1976, March 1976.

† The authors would like to acknowledge the extensive comments of Paul Nystrom, William Starbuck and three anonymous referees on earlier versions of this paper. The present version owes much to their pointed criticisms. Preparation of this version was supported, in part, by the Centre de Recherche en Gestion, Ecole Polytechnique, Paris.

development projects. Does it really work? When is it likely to work and when is it not? With a few exceptions [3,4,6,11], such questions have been answered with anecdotes and personal testimonies rather than carefully developed evidence. Kahn [14], for example, noted that only about 25 percent of the publications have presented quantitative data and that serious methodological and conceptual questions can be raised about most of those. Thus, much of the literature neither provides a satisfactory basis for evaluating investments in this change strategy nor enhances understanding of organizational changes that result. Finally, the term, organizational development, has become less and less informative as more and more people have adopted it. Kahn called it "a new label for a conglomerate of things an increasing number of consultants do and write about" [14, p. 485]. Weisbord asked, "What is OD anyway? The longer I do it, and the more I read about it, the less I understand it" [18, p. 476]. Organizational development is often old wine in new bottles, and much of what currently passes for organizational development bore a different label ten years ago.

The point is not semantic, but merely that diverse behavioral science techniques are being used to guide organizational changes. Organizational development currently designates most, although not all, of this activity. Thus, the lack of systematic assessments characterizes change strategies in general, yet such assessments are needed by both managers and scientists. Assessment faces obstacles, but the payoffs can be high. This paper outlines an approach to the design and implementation of assessment based on the lessons learned from two large-scale assessment efforts. It begins by pointing out the advantages of assessment for managers and scientists and then describes the two projects in which the authors were involved. After a discussion of the lessons learned, some practical guidelines for assessment are presented along with some potential problems of implementation.

Why worry about assessment?

Organizations continuously review the results of resource expenditure and plan for subsequent utilization. Nearly every organization has its own performance measures, such as share of the market, profit, number of students educated, or number of clients rehabilitated. Decisions regarding future activities are made partly on the basis of feedback received about the results of resource expenditures, and in this sense, organizations are rational. Decisions continuously evoke evaluations that affect future decisions. Assessment is thus ubiquitous.

Though assessment is ubiquitous it does not mean that it is always carefully planned. Assessments of behavioral science-based organizational change strategies in particular tend to be cursory, unsystematic and impressionistic, and thus relatively ineffective as inputs to decision-making. In this sense, organizations are not as rational as they might be, for by helping organizations become self-evaluating, more systematic assessments of change strategies can play an important adaptive role for them. If carefully undertaken, they can provide the feedback needed to help determine two kinds of future activities. First, assessments provide bases for altering current change strategies. Is the organization being responsive to the change effort in a way that appears to justify its costs? If not, a decision may be made to abandon the strategy and perhaps to explore alternatives. Most change efforts, however, do not produce immediate and observable change in desired directions. The initial reactions normally include undesirable side effects, and, for this reason, strategies should not be abandoned too soon. By helping to identify unanticipated effects, assessments can suggest areas in which change strategies need to be modified rather than abandoned. Change efforts rarely unfold without developing problems that could not have been predicted, and they need to be responsive to changing conditions. With careful assessment, organizations need not rely on chance or revolution for cues.

Second, assessments can increase understanding of the change process which can, in turn, assist in developing better models of that process. As change strategies based on the behavioral sciences become more widely used, better models will be needed. Careful assessment can provide the empirical basis for developing such models.

If careful assessments of organizational change efforts offer such high potential, why are they so rare? One reason is that the results of changes in the social system of an organization are more difficult to measure than those in the production system [15]. These changes are often only indirectly linked to performance measures [16], and are not susceptible to straightforward quantitative analysis. Organizational assessment tends to be centered on activities which can be more easily measured regardless of the validity of the measures themselves as indicators of performance. Secondly, even where feasible, assessments of change efforts may be opposed because they raise the visibility of both success and failure. Third, they can be time-consuming and expensive, particularly from a short-run, narrowly focused, cost-benefit perspective. Finally, organizations may not have the professional capabilities necessary to undertake systematic assessments.

When outsiders are involved in the change effort, as they often are, there are additional factors which may mitigate against assessment. Some authors [10] have contended that the social context of the researcher/consultant/client relationship has built-in tensions which tend to lead either to action — consulting — or to research — development of organization theory — but not to both. Can the researcher's interest in measurement and rigor be accomodated simultaneously with an active, diagnostic, problem-oriented approach? To these authors, the answer to this question is "no." Others [2,19], however, have contended that the researcher/consultant is by definition part of the social system in which the change effort is being undertaken and that research and action cannot be separated. Attempts to separate them lead to an artificial perspective. There is support for both positions among researchers and consultants. It is the lack of a ready answer that mitigates against more frequent assessment when outsiders are involved. Beyond this debate is the variable duration of the outsiders' relationship with the client. Often the consultants are not involved long enough to undertake the kind of assessment needed, and in their absence, the skills and/or the motivation to do what is necessary may be lacking.

Lessons from the firing line

How can these difficulties be overcome? What are the basic ingredients of effective assessments of behavioral science-based organizational change efforts? Answers to these questions are based on the authors' experiences with two large-scale change projects. These experiences, described in the paragraphs that follow, indicated much about what should not be done as well as what should. The two projects took place in very different settings, but precisely because the settings were so different, the experiences taken together provide some general guidelines for assessing organizational change efforts.

Both the content and the setting of the first project were typical of those in which many applied behavioral science consultants work. The authors were called in to work with the top management team in one plant of a large multi-plant, multi-national corporation on a large-scale organizational development project. They were directly involved in this project for eighteen months. Only after the project was well underway did the consultants decide to take advantage of the research opportunities it offered, and at that point, the interest was primarily academic. Management was content with largely anecdotal evidence of the project's success, and what systematic data they did feel was important was collected in attitude surveys. Neither management nor the consultants saw the potential utility of more systematic assessment of the change effort. As a result, the consultants were able to evaluate the outcome of the project only in terms of (1) changes in employee attitudes measured before and immediately after the various phases of the project took place and (2) changes in productivity, quality and performance-to-budget based on data taken from company records for a period of 42 months before, during, and after the consultants' direct involvement. Positive change in each of these measures was expected on the basis of hypotheses derived from the literature on organizational change. Significant positive change was observed in all of the variables save one — productivity [16]. Although the variance in productivity decreased as expected, its absolute level, instead of increasing, actually decreased during the project, regaining its previous level only in the twelve month period immediately following the change effort. The data on quality, however, behaved in the predicted fashion. The variance in quality decreased significantly and its level improved significantly, as expected. These findings were initially puzzling. Why did the anticipated effects occur with quality but not with productivity?

As an answer to this question was sought, the concept of control seemed to offer a potential explanation. Management, the target group for the project, might in fact have had more direct control over quality than over productivity. The latter, it was reasoned, might have been influenced more by corporate policy and market constraints than by management behavior within this single plant. This hypothesis could not be directly tested. However, assuming that industry productivity rates reflected both the vagaries of corporate policy and market fluctuations, and if the control arguement was correct, then plant and industry productivity should be highly correlated.

In the ensuing analysis, the correlation between the two rates was found to be 0.90, and the importance of target group control thus became belatedly apparent. As outsiders, the authors had anticipated results from the change project *a priori* which, in retrospect, proved to have been partly unrealistic. Their expectations had been based on an incomplete view of the client system, and they had imposed their own definitions of both objectives and measures on the situation.

This experience with assessment led to two conclusions. First, and perhaps most important, the gains from building target group definitions of both objectives and measures into the assessment process were illustrated. When the organizational members themselves help define the outcomes to be expected from a change effort, the assessment made is more likely to fit the needs and objectives of the organization realistically. Second, the results demonstrated the need to be concerned with assessment from a project's inception. Absence of such concern in the case of this plant meant that potentially valuable information was unavailable, either to the consultant/researchers or to management.

The second project — an analysis of the development of a new medical school — differed from the first in three important ways. First, it was carried out in a large public university, a very different organizational setting. The profit criterion was absent and other factors such as the budget-making process of state government impinged on the client organization. Second, it involved the development of an entirely new organization, rather than the modification of an existing one. Most change efforts are apt to be carried out in on-going organizations with existing sets of norms, values and role relationships. Finally, the authors initially entered the setting as researchers rather than as consultants. They were contacted by the Dean of the new medical school because he was interested in having a behavioral science-oriented evaluation of his program. The specifics of the evaluation, however, were left to them.

The main features of the assessment design that was developed have been described in detail [17], as have some early indicators of the likely success of the change effort. The basic concerns in assessing this effort, concerns that resulted in part from experiences in the first project, were (1) that the assessment be longitudinal, monitoring the change effort over a period of years; (2) that it be process-oriented, focusing on the dynamics of the change effort; (3) that it be system-wide, encompassing the patterns of behavior and responses of all parties directly involved in the change effort, both internal and external to the organization itself; (4) that it be behavior-focused, monitoring not simply the attitudes of relevant parties but, more important, their behavioral responses to the change effort; and (5) that feedback be provided to the various parties in a manner which would permit its use as a basis for future action if so desired. Certain features of the design resembled what some have called action research [9,19].

The assessment undertaken reflected these concerns in that it (1) obtained the commitment of top management — the Dean and his immediate staff — to a long-term design; (2) involved periodic data collection to insure that basic aspects of organizational processes would be captured; (3) included data collection from all parties — administrators, students, community physicians and faculty — with whom the success or failure of the change effort primarily rested; (4) included a number of behavioral measures of process — patterns of sociometric contact, attendance in class, participation in faculty meetings — as well as various outcome measures — student performance, budgetary growth, faculty publication, and physician continuing education; and (5) provided for data feedback in many forms — regular monthly discussions for the Dean and his staff, periodic presentations at local medical society meetings for community physicians, twice yearly data summaries as well as frequent informal discussions for students, and seminar-type presentations of the results for faculty.

A key difference between the assessments developed for these two change efforts is that in the case of the medical school, assessment was planned from the very start and, thus, did not have to rely on retrospective attempts to generate potentially useful information. Its implementation, however, was hardly straightforward, and illustrates many of the problems as well as the opportunities of comprehensive assessment. First, the original design called for too many student interviews during the school year. Feedback from the students indicated that three interviews during the year intervened much too obtrusively in their lives and that by the third interview some were giving perfunctory responses. In addition, it was expensive to interview that often. Thus, the number of interviews was reduced from three to two per year. Second, it was found that some of the structured instruments developed during the first year of the effort had to be modified during subsequent years because of changes in the nature of the organization itself. These changes were vexing from the perspective of pure research, because it would have been desirable to have identical measures over time. From the perspective of informational quality, however, such changes were absolutely mandatory. Failure to have made the changes would have significantly impaired both the data quality and the ability of the system members to use it as a basis for further action. Third, the researchers' capacity to remain neutral did not last long, precisely because of the commitment to provide regular data feedback to the various parties involved in the change effort. The researchers realized after the initial feedback sessions that by controlling what data were fed back, they could influence the decision-making process. For this reason, they elected to ask the various parties themselves to define their own needs and to choose the data that were to be fed back. Very early in the project, then, the authors' role changed from pure researchers to researcher/consultants. Finally, as the change effort unfolded and the new medical school started to grow rapidly, members of its staff became aware of the research potential inherent in the assessment project, and conflict emerged between the researcher/consultants, who were outsiders, and some of the more research-oriented members of the school's staff over the issue of who should be able to collect what data from what parties for what purposes. This conflict was never completely resolved, but was partially dealt with by the creation of a Research Committee of insiders and outsiders to define jointly the assessment objectives and to engage in joint data collection where possible. All data collected were made available to everyone to use for whatever projects met with the Committee's approval.

A number of conclusions about assessment resulted from this experience. First, flexibility in design is extremely important. What may make sense on paper may not make quite as much sense in practice, and any design should be sufficiently flexible to permit changes to be made on the basis of feedback about its own strengths and weaknesses. Second, organizations do not hold still. Particularly where a long-term assessment effort is undertaken, researchers/consultants/clients must be prepared to modify the design where changes in what is being evaluated occur. Third, neutral, objective assessment does not exist, particularly where there is a serious attempt made to feed data back to parties involved in the change effort. Rather than attempting to create the illusion of objectivity, designs might better attempt to anticipate the inevitably political context of assessment and to capitalize on it. And fourth, questions about data ownership should be expected and confronted in the initial stages of project development. These questions can jeopardize the success of assessment efforts, and a great deal of time can be spent trying to resolve them if they are not explicitly recognized from the very start.

The final lesson comes in part from each project and concerns the inevitable gap between the theory and practice of assessment. To maximize their effectiveness in helping organizations become more adaptive, ideally assessment efforts would meet certain criteria. Among these, the most important are: (1) that the information needed for assessment be both known and available; (2) that the information be appropriately interpreted; (3) that precisely what is being assessed be clear; (4) that valid measures of the results of the change effort exist; (5) that the data collection strategy be compatible with the nature of the actual changes being assessed; and (6) that assumptions about cause and effect relationships in the change effort be made explicit. These conditions were not met completely in either of the assessment efforts described earlier. In the first project, for example, not all of the information that was needed was available because the assessment was initiated after the change effort. Not all of the information that was available was appropriately interpreted. It was only after the fact, for example, that the lack of control of the target system over productivity rates was recognized. And a before-after, or pre-post test, data collection design [5] was used for the attitudinal data, a design which was not entirely compatible with the process-oriented nature of the change effort itself. The second assessment effort profited from many of the lessons of the first, and approximated the ideal more closely. Nevertheless, there were some problems, particularly concerning the validity of the outcome measures used. Is the score obtained on a standard year-end examination a valid indicator either of how well the students performed or of how well the organization taught them? Is the number of publications a valid indicator of faculty performance?

The final conclusion, therefore, was that although the practice of assessment may never completely achieve the theoretical ideal, awareness of what the ideal would consist of permits the design of assessment efforts which more closely approximate it. The assessment design developed for the medical school conformed more closely to this ideal than that in the plant, and indicates the importance of careful planning based on an explicit set of criteria. The quality of designs can vary, as the differences between these two efforts suggest.

Some general guidelines for assessment design

As noted in the previous discussion, the design of the second assessment effort profited from many of the lessons learned from the first, and was, hence, more effective. It yielded more information of better quality which was more useful to the organization. A more general conclusion was also drawn from the experience with the two projects, a conclusion which suggests guidelines for the design of assessments in other settings. Stated briefly, application of certain principles adapted from the theory and practice of organizational development can greatly enhance the effectiveness of assessment efforts. Certain principles of behavioral science-based change strategies, in other words, can be applied to assessment of their results.

The principles and values of organizational development have been described in detail in a number of publications [9,10,13], and need not be repeated here. Because they are based on an optimistic view of human nature and its relation to the world of work, they have been criticized by some as being idealistic and unworkable. They have their passionate advocates and their dedicated critics. However, it is not necessary to endorse organizational development as a change strategy in order to recognize the potential applicability of certain of its principles to assessment. Four principles are particularly relevant in this regard: (1) organizational development is a process which has no finite end point; the process of improving organizational effectiveness is one of becoming as opposed to arriving; (2) the needs and objectives of every organization are in some ways unique because of both environmental and internal factors; change strategies therefore should be tailored to these needs and objectives; (3) organizations are complex, internally interdependent and continuously in flux; change strategies therefore should be process-oriented, long-term and adaptable; and (4) the individuals most directly affected by the change effort will have the greatest impact on its outcome; they should be involved, therefore, in determining its content and the conditions of its implementation.

Although these four principles are central to organizational development as a change strategy, they can be fruitfully adapted and applied to the design of assessment. Assessments incorporating adaptations of these principles would have the following characteristics: First, they would be process-oriented and based on multiple measures over time. The logic of before-after assessment is not compatible with the nature of most organizational changes. Although before measures are certainly needed to establish baselines against which the progress of the organization can be gauged, use of the before-after paradigm owes more to the language and techniques of experimental research than to an appreciation of the realities of organizational change processes. Process-oriented assessment begins at a particular point in time but has no specific end point. The timing of data collection is based on the characteristics of the focal system — certain particularly important activities, for example, may take place at certain times in the year — and data collection continues as long as the system finds the feedback useful.

Second, assessment designs would be based on the objectives and meet the needs of the focal system. Because these are unique in some respects, it is highly unlikely that canned, pre-programmed assessment packages will be as effective as ones which are tailor-made. This is not to say that there are no general classes of problems that organizations face, or that general theories of organization are impossible. Rather, the emphasis is on making the assessment effort as relevant as possible for the focal system, and this means taking unique as well as general aspects of the system into account.

Third, those organizational members who are the target of the change effort would be actively involved in determining both what gets assessed and how. The importance of including them in the process of planning organizational change efforts has been pointed out in the literature [1,2]; it is equally important that they be included in efforts to assess the results of those changes. The authors' experience strongly suggests that unless all parties are aware of what assessment involves, cognizant of its advantages and limitations, and reasonably committed to its importance, there is a substantial chance that the usefulness of the results will be compromised. Their input can be most useful if they are aware of the kinds of things that might be assessed, including the kinds of behaviors that they feel to be central in achieving the system's objectives. If they are encouraged to make their models of cause and effect — their practice theories — explicit, answers to the question of what should be assessed will come more easily. In addition, the process of defining their models of cause of effect will help to shape their expectations for the change effort as a whole, most likely in the direction of greater realism, thus reducing the often troublesome and discouraging gap between euphoric expectations and the realities of the change process. The overall goal should be to design assessments in which the parties involved feel a sense of ownership. Data from efforts conducted solely by outsiders or from efforts which are mandated by fiat from above are too easily dismissed as frivolous, false or irrelevant. Under certain conditions, of course, such efforts may be both appropriate and desirable. They obviously represent very different strategies, based on quite different values and needs than those of the approach to assessment advocated here.

Finally, designs would make provision for feedback to those involved. It is on the basis of such feedback that the full potential of assessment as an adaptive mechanism can be realized, and that movement in the direction of a self-evaluating organization can occur. Information collected can be used as a basis for continuing diagnosis, and once the internal environment of the organization encourages active and continuing diagnosis on the part of members, the organization has started to become self-evaluating. In the absence of such feedback, the long-term success of the change effort may be in some cases jeopardized [7].

Potential problems in implementation

Application of certain principles adapted from organizational development to the design of assessments of organizational change efforts has considerable promise. Organizational receptivity to the idea of comprehensive assessment and good assessment designs, however, do not *per se* guarantee success. There are a number of potential problems in the implementation of these strategies that can jeopardize their success. What does the authors' experience suggest these problems are, and how can they be avoided?

The first potential problem concerns the role of the consultants. It is not essential that outside consultants be involved either in a behavioral science-based change effort or in assessment. Many organizations have specialized staffs for this sort of activity, and some even have internal consulting personnel who function as initiators of change efforts. In general, however, either external or internal consultants — or some combination of the two — are involved, and the role that they play is extremely important. This role should be catalytic rather than deterministic insofar as possible. For example, the consultants should help to make the client aware of the range of measurement options available without determining which option is chosen. They should insure that the client is aware of what is involved in opting for a particular model of cause and effect without evaluating the choice that is made. They should point out alternative ways of interpreting the feedback that is received from the assessment process without placing an interpretation on it themselves. The role of the consultants, then, should be to facilitate the process whereby the organizational members decide what kind of assessment design they want. Doing this will help to minimize the possibility of rejection of the feedback and will help to develop an active orientation toward exploring its implications. This role is not easy, and the consultants will find that they are frequently tempted to intervene directly in the process. Serious questions will sometimes arise about the tenability of the catalytic role. The consultants will on occasion be asked by the client to intervene directly. On other occasions, the consultants may feel a sense of obligation to do so, particularly if they feel that feedback is being inappropriately interpreted or a faulty decision is being made about what should be assessed. These are admittedly difficult situations, but the assessment effort will be more effective in the long run if the actual decisions about its form and content are made by the parties involved, not by the consultants.

A second potential problem concerns the frequency of data collection. Depending on the objectives of the change effort, assessment may be focused on the decision-making process, on patterns of contact among various parties, on the characteristics of role relationships or any number of other possibilities. Interest will be in determining whether and to what extent change has actually taken place, and such a determination will necessitate periodic data collection. It is difficult to specify *a priori,* however, just how frequently this should occur. If collected too frequently, as was the case in the medical school project, there is a danger that participant responses will become perfunctory. On the other hand, if collected too infrequently, there is a danger that the data will not reflect important aspects of the change process. Development of a workable strategy is partly a process of trial-and-error. It also is aided by awareness of and commitment to the assessment goals by those involved. If they help to determine the implementation strategy with the knowledge that they will subsequently have to live with its behavioral demands, the potential for this to become a problem can be minimized.

Third, the tendency for behavior to adapt to evaluation criteria must be recognized and taken into account. This tendency is not mysterious; to the extent that organizational rewards are based on performance, it should not be surprising that energies will be directed toward those measures of performance that are perceived as leading to more positive rewards. These measures can be quantitative or qualitative. Their existence can be formally specified or informally communicated as a part of the local culture. Regardless, they will help to determine the behavior of organizational members in major ways. The problem, then, is insuring that the kinds of outcomes that are measured by the assessment activity are congruent with the overall objectives of the focal system or subsystem. Members will be well aware of the assessment criteria, and will most likely want the data to reflect positively on them. Many of them will therefore tend to adjust their behavior, if necessary, in ways which will result in positive personal assessments. In the extreme, lack of congruence could result in counter-productive behavior. This is a potential problem which should be confronted in the very early stages of a project. One of the benefits of bringing it out into the open is that the parties involved are forced to define clearly both their own objectives and the means of obtaining them.

A final potential problem in implementation is the fact that assessment is inevitably a highly political undertaking. Because it raises the visibility of various aspects of an organization's activities, there will be resistance and in some cases violent opposition to its implementation. Strategies for circumventing it or for undermining its effectiveness will no doubt develop as the organization adjusts to the fact of its existence and its implications. It is for this reason that the involvement of organizational members in its design and implementation is critical. Complete consensus, of course, will never be achieved and is probably not desirable. Were consensus to exist, it might indicate simply that the issues at hand were relatively trivial and that the most crucial aspects of the change effort were not being considered. Pockets of resistance should be expected. Opposition should, wherever possible, be brought out into the open and its roots should be explored. Assessment is likely to be most effective in the long run where the system norms encourage continuing diagnosis and where the political implications of process-oriented assessment are continuously examined.

Conclusions

The advantages of flexible, long-term, process-oriented designs for the assessment of organizational change efforts have not been widely explored in the theory and practice of applied behavioral science. The major advantage is adaptability. Comprehensive designs and careful implementation can provide organizations with important feedback about how well the change effort is faring, thus creating the possibility for data-based decisions about future courses of action. Should the change effort be continued as is, modified or abandoned? Given that organizations have limited resources, the capacity to respond realistically to this question is important. The type of assessment described in this paper enables an organization to make this kind of evaluation and to begin to become a self-designing, self-evaluating system [12,20]. This cannot be achieved without certain costs and risks. The approach outlined here requires much of the parties involved and includes risks in the process of design and implementation. It does not promise immediate, dramatic cures for organizational problems, most of which have probably developed over a long period of time. The authors' own experiences with assessment have provided most of the data on which the approach is based, and it is hoped that the approach will be further developed by others. As the results of their efforts become known, the effectiveness of various techniques of organizational change may be improved and the models underlying them may become more firmly anchored in the realities of the change process.

References

[1] Alderfer, Clayton P., "Change Processes in Organizations," in Handbook of Industrial and Organizational Psychology, Marvin D. Dunette (ed.), Rand McNally, Chicago, Ill., 1976, pp. 1591–1638.

[2] Argyris, Chris, Intervention Theory and Method: A Behavioral Science View, Addison-Wesley, Reading, Mass. 1970.

[3] Blake, Robert R., Barnes, Louis B., Greiner, Larry E., and Mouton, Jane S., "Breakthrough in Organizational Development," Harvard Business Review, Vol. 42 (November-December 1964), pp. 133–155.

[4] Bowers, David G., "OD Techniques and Their Results in 23 Organizations: The Michigan ICL Study," Journal of Applied Behavioral Science, Vol. 9 (January 1973), pp. 21–43.

[5] Campbell, Donald T. and Stanley, Julian C., Experimental and Quasi-Experimental Designs for Research, Rand McNally, Chicago, Ill., 1966.

[6] Dowling, W.F., "System 4 Builds Performance and Profits," Organizational Dynamics, Vol. 4 (Winter 1975), pp. 23–38.

[7] Frank, Linda L. and Hackman, J. Richard, "A Failure of Job Enrichment: The Case of the Change That Wasn't," Journal of Applied Behavioral Science, Vol. 11 (October 1975), pp. 413–436.

[8] Franklin, J.L., Organizational Development: An Annotated Bibliography, Center for Research on the Utilization of Scientific Knowledge, Institute for Social Research, University of Michigan, Ann Arbor, Mich. 1973.

[9] French, Wendell L. and Bell, Cecil H., Jr., Organization Development, Prentice-Hall, Englewood Cliffs, N.J., 1973.

[10] Friedlander, Frank and Brown, L.D., "Organization Development," Annual Review of Psychology, Vol. 25 (1974), pp. 313–340.

[11] Golembiewski, Robert T., Hilles, Rick and Kagno, Munro S., "A Longitudinal Study of Flexi-Time Effects: Some Consequences of *OD* Structural Intervention," Journal of Applied Behavioral Science, Vol. 10 (October 1974), pp. 503–532.

[12] Hedberg, Bo L.T., Nystrom, Paul C., and Starbuck, William H., "Camping on Seesaws: Prescriptions for a Self-Designing Organization," Administrative Science Quarterly, Vol. 21 (March 1976), pp. 41–65.

[13] Huse, Edgar F., Organization Development and Change, West, New York, N.Y., 1975.

[14] Kahn, Robert L., "Organizational Development: Some Problems and Proposals," Journal of Applied Behavioral Science, Vol. 10 (October 1974), pp. 485–502.

[15] Kimberly, John R., "Managerial Innovation," in Handbook of Organizational Design, Paul C. Nystrom and William H. Starbuck (eds.), Elsevier North-Holland, New York, N.Y., forthcoming.

[16] Kimberly, John R. and Nielsen, Warren R., "Organization Development and Change in Organizational Performance," Administrative Science Quarterly, Vol. 20 (June 1975), pp. 191–206.

[17] Kimberly, John R., Counte, M.A., and Dickinson, R.O., "Design for Process Research on Change in Medical Education," Proceedings: Eleventh Annual Conference on Research in Medical Education, Association of American Medical Colleges, (November 1972), pp. 26–31.

[18] Weisbord, Marvin R., "The Gap Between OD Practice and Theory – and Publication," Journal of Applied Behavioral Science, Vol. 10 (October 1974), pp. 476–484.

[19] Whyte, William F., Organizational Behavior: Theory and Practice, Irwin-Dorsey, Homewood, Ill., 1970.

[20] Wildavsky, Aaron, "The Self-Evaluating Organization," Public Administration Review, Vol. 32 (September 1972), pp. 509–520.

North-Holland/TIMS Studies in the Management Sciences 5 (1977) 157–170

MYTHS AND WISHFUL THINKING AS MANAGEMENT TOOLS *

STEN A. JÖNSSON and ROLF A. LUNDIN

University of Gothenburg

This paper discusses the role of crises in policy formation processes of organizations. After describing the development of Swedish Investment Development Companies as an empirical base, a tentative theory on the roles of myths is developed. It appears useful to think about organizational behavior, over time, in terms of a wave pattern of enthusiasm – each wave connected with a particular myth. Crises mark both the beginning and the end of a myth wave. Given that the tentative notions are empirical facts, some equally tentative prescriptions are suggested regarding how managers should exploit these patterns.

"Man lives by his imagination" is the opening sentence of an article written by Mason [14, p. B-409], analyzing the critical role of the planner's assumptions in the planning process. Shackle [19] refers to economics – the essence of planning – as formal imagination, indicating that it deals with speculations under *ceteris paribus* conditions. But what happens when the planner's imagination fails, when the planner only knows that something is wrong and that something else has to be done? What should the planner do when he or she realizes that the assumptions on which present plans are based simply prove to be inappropriate? Sociologists have studied effects of sudden disasters such as earthquakes and tornado touchdowns [1,5], when the crisis is visible to everybody, and people easily agree on the necessity for action. In contrast, this paper discusses cases where the crisis creeps up slowly. What, then, are the mechanisms for change in an organizational setting?

The research reported here is based on a firm belief that theory generation should be empirically grounded. During the last few years, the research program has evolved in accordance with the Glaser and Strauss model [6], getting its direction from inductive analysis of empirical observations. Despite the fact that the research still is in a theory generation phase, the empirical evidence available allows for some confidence in the generality of the findings. This is in opposition to Popper [18], who maintains that theory generation is just conjectures not to be taken seriously until refutation has failed. The authors believe that the scientific study of organizations is a process of knowledge production, where theory generation creating tentative knowledge from observations is a distinct and important step preceding theory tests.

* Received June 1975; revised January 1976, April 1976.

In generating theory concerning processes, coverage of these processes is more important than statistical precision of data. Data collection techniques and instruments were not standardized. In some cases, a cash flow analysis was used as background information for interviews. Sometimes a market decline was analyzed prior to a case study. In other instances, it was the work flow or technical progress that constituted the problem area of the firm studied. The empirical evidence has the form of historical accounts for processes where a wide spectrum of factors are important. Thus, the material concerns concrete events, actions taken and decisions, not general opinions.

A historical perspective appears necessary if one is generating explanatory hypotheses. However, this creates a serious problem of presenting the empirical evidence on which the assertions are based. The data cannot easily be aggregated into tables. Instead, this article presents some essential features of one set of cases, concerning the development of Investment Development Companies, as a base for descriptive and prescriptive conclusions.

The cases

The research program emerged from a study of Swedish Investment Development Companies (IDC). The IDC's are closely related to banks; their business idea is to buy successful small and medium-sized family businesses, finance their further development, supply know-how in different forms, then sell them or introduce them on the stock market. IDC's are organized as conglomerates with a very small staff at the head office. Ten IDC's were established in the early sixties – note that the U.S. conglomerates were very successful at that time, and they all ran into severe problems during the recession of 1966-68. The research question of the pilot study was: what kind of planning principles could be expected in such a company that has to coordinate resources in the development of 10-20 subsidiaries that were recently independent and successful units, and what went wrong in 1966-68?

Disturbed system policy

In the pilot study made by Jönsson [10], using participant observation, interviews, and annual reports as data sources in one IDC, a hypothesis was stated that one would expect an IDC to apply a disturbed system policy as a coordination principle. The idea was that an IDC would further its subsidiaries' development by deliberately creating imbalances between the available resource combination in a subsidiary and its aspiration level; these imbalances should be coordinated over time so that the IDC as a whole followed a balanced development path. The pilot study revealed that the crisis of 1966-68 led to a reinterpretation of the IDC's mission; this reinterpretation demanded a more detailed study.

In order to develop and refine the hypotheses further, an extensive field study covering all 10 IDC's was undertaken [11,12]. General managers and financial directors of both head offices and subsidiaries were interviewed, and all planning documents available were collected. In each interview, the respondent was asked to tell the story of how the policy formation process unfolded over the crisis period. Not until the whole story had been given — always encompassing the entire life of the IDC — did the interviewer challenge the respondent about some actions taken by the IDC. The stories were checked against planning documents and other interviews, and if necessary, additional interview sessions were held. Challenging the story appears a useful technique for gaining processual information, especially about crisis situations, when disagreements and differences in opinions lead the respondents to argue for their positions and against those of their adversaries.

Strategic development in a critical period

In the field study of the IDC's, very few indications of a disturbed system policy were found. Instead, the main findings relate to management's behavior patterns during the critical period. In the first phase of the crisis, when heavy losses were reported from the subsidiaries, the established control system seemed to break down as a planning vehicle. Then came a period of strategic indecision combined with a high priority on cost-cutting and with the development of a new management information system (MIS). Finally, a major policy change was implemented.

Five companies of the 10 studied went out of business one way or the other, two others reorganized and survived to become ordinary firms. The three remaining IDC's came out of the crisis with a new idea about the essential characteristics of their business or mission. The previous notion that financing expansion was the main problem was replaced by the idea that the scarce resource was management know-how. The lack of reliable information to evaluate different activities for ameliorating the crisis situation strengthened mistrust from the head office towards the leadership of the subsidiaries. Experiences embodied in the established MIS were largely disregarded as irrelevant when the new policy was developed. Instead, the new strategic orientation seemed to stem from an informal analysis of possible explanations of why things went wrong during the downswing.

Parallel to reinterpreting the company mission, efforts were put into improving and implementing the MIS in accordance with the new interpretation. The three organizations that continued as IDC's all designed new MIS to facilitate financial planning at the head office. Therefore, subsidiaries had to develop long-term budgets based on strategic analyses of markets, products, and competitors, for the next three to five years. These were followed up in monthly reports, which meant that new cost control systems were introduced in most subsidiaries. The field study was done while the new policy and MIS were implemented. The change in strategy was manifested in the subsidiaries as a more adequate and tight control system. Implementation often constituted a considerable intervention, and it was quite a painful process. There are cases where teams of key personnel resigned in protest, but in the same subsidiaries a couple of years later, employees were enthusiastic about the system that they believed would get things going again.

Recurring enthusiasm

The change in attitudes towards the future prospects of the IDC concept was most obvious in one of the IDC's, and the authors had the opportunity to examine that company more thoroughly. What happened was the following. A new top management team was installed in 1967 at the head office. Then new managing directors were hired in several subsidiaries. Almost without exception, they proposed a major research and development effort to modernize the product lines as a way out of the crisis. By then the head office had arrived at the conclusion that MIS development should have priority. One effect of implementing an MIS principally designed by the head office was greater influence of the comptroller function throughout the IDC. In addition to demands for frequent reporting, the new MIS was built around the notion that the base for communication between subsidiaries and the head office should be an analysis of the subsidiary's strengths and weaknesses. A continuous discussion of such issues would point to strategic problems for the subsidiary and lead to strategic flexibility and creativeness in the long-term plans, which were the basis for the subsidiary's yearly budget.

The new MIS was received enthusiastically in the subsidiaries. Stressing reporting and cost control, the new MIS also had an inherent strategic philosophy, which was used in selling the system to the subsidiaries' managing directors. Being technicians and preoccupied with new products, the directors were lukewarm to the new MIS initially. They felt that working with economic reports was a waste of time, especially in the crisis situation at hand, but the strategic prospects of the new system persuaded them and made them enthusiastic.

The following experiences of one building industry subsidiary were typical. Due to inadequate quality of the input data a tremendous effort was necessary to meet the demands of the new MIS. In 1970 the subsidiary went through a year cycle of planning and reporting with the new system. During that year, there was a rather mild recession for the building industry and some of the bold plans were shattered. When the time came to start a new cycle, several key people resigned from the comptroller department. A new team was hired, and a number of projects were started to improve inventory control and to standardize components in the product line. Again, there was a surge of enthusiasm, focusing this time on the input to the MIS. At the same time, aspirations concerning full-scale use of the MIS potential were lowered. As the projects began to give results, business conditions improved, reinforcing beliefs in the new system. The improved profits also gave the managing director the resources necessary to start an R & D program to improve the product line. By the time the R & D program produced a more competitive product line for market introduction, the MIS projects were completed and the new system was in full-scale use — after five years.

But then, due largely to the oil crisis, the European market declined to about 50% of its level a couple of years earlier. This was a final test of the MIS, and the system worked. The situation was analyzed and a number of adaptive measures taken. The management acted with confidence, because the MIS made it possible to see the consequences of the market decline. The crisis was real for everyone, but the uncertainty about what to do was much less than before. The situation created the opportunity for the comptroller to introduce de novo his strategic idea. For a number of years he had argued that the firm was too dependent on ups and downs of the building industry and that a new division should be acquired. This new division became the project that aroused enthusiasm and, maybe, wishful thinking.

Similar patterns were found in several other subsidiaries of the same IDC and in other IDC's. There apparently is a sequence of the following type: crisis; rally around a possible solution; enthusiasm and wishful thinking; vigorous action; decline in enthusiasm if not reinforced by positive feedback; crisis; new cycle.

Learning and tidal waves

One conclusion drawn from the extensive material on IDC's is that things happen in crisis situations that give new insights into change and development mechanisms in organizations. Tidal waves of enthusiasm and depression occur around leading ideas or myths about what is essential for the organization in its present situation (Figure 1).

In each phase of this cyclical process some elements of know-how or some procedures seem to be retained, whereby the organization over time forms its identity and historical heritage. Reasonably good residues from each myth period are saved,

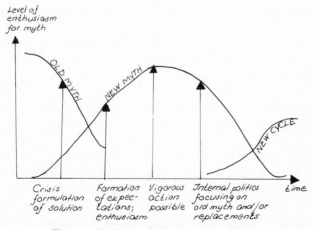

Figure 1. Typical organizational wave pattern.

and the sequence of myths and cycles can be traced by studying the different layers of these sediments [4].

New myths are born and gain adherents in the internal politics initiated by the genuine uncertainty in crisis situations. Power relations are changed and new actors appear on stage. The initial phase of the policy formation is unstable. Good ideas may be abandoned inexplicably but the process may also initiate new organizational structures, procedures and systems.

By applying this explanatory sketch [13] some substantive notions on the IDC's behaviors can be developed as well as a tentative formal model of organizational behavior in crisis situations.

Substantive notions on the IDC's

The following facts seem essential for understanding the development process of the IDC's:

1. The IDC's are young organizations. They were started during the early sixties in a general upswing of the Swedish economy. Modelled after the big U.S. conglomerates, they were very well received by the stock market. In fact, the stock market provided a sounding board that reinforced a world image that was detrimental to early and swift adaptation to the 1966-68 recession.

2. The business idea and world image of IDC's prior to the recession were acquisitions and financing of expansions. Around 1968 it changed to managing developmental processes in a decentralized system. This meant that central management previously using the role of bankers switched to being managers in a more direct sense. When the managers took charge in the new role, they discovered that the management tools were inadequate. MIS development got top priority, sometimes at the cost of strategic stagnation.

3. When a new control system was implemented, it focused attention on certain product-market dimensions — recall that five of the 10 IDC's did not take this step and two were overcome by strategic stagnation — and there was a tendency for some time to allocate scarce resources to these dimensions. The control system thus narrowed the scope of alternatives perceived. It was also apparent that later new ventures largely provided growth along the given dimensions. Every phase in a crisis leaves its print in the organization's memory.

4. Parallel to this development of strategic and administrative behavior, there had been a continuous change in power relations between head office and subsidiaries, between functions in subsidiaries and, of course, between persons. During their first years of existence, the dominating idea was that subsidiaries should lead the way and the head office should give adequate support, when needed. Power based on initiatives and control of information rested with the managing directors of the subsidiaries. During the 1966-68 crisis, when head office intervention resulted in high priority for MIS development, there was a shift of power to a coalition of comptroller people — head office and subsidiaries — and a growth of these departments.

This created conflicts in the subsidiaries and some key personnel in subsidiaries left. They were replaced by people mostly chosen by the head office comptroller. When the new control system and improved market conditions started to generate new resources, there was a new shift to R & D efforts and the comptrollor departments declined to a more normal power role. Finally, when a new market decline occurred, power again shifted toward the person or department that proposed a politically viable solution.

Tentative formal theory

The widespread notion that only individuals can have goals, aspirations, feelings, and perceptions is acknowledged. Thus, a model of the individual will be central to the concepts presented.

The individual

Every individual in an organization is normally fed with information from sources inside and outside the organization. At the same time, he is probably also an active information seeker. However, the information is filtered through his selective perception mechanisms. One reaction to anomalous, negative information about some vital processes involving the individual might be avoiding contact with that type of information again, or actively searching for supporting, positive information. General managers in subsidiaries showed a tendency to avoid and dislike the new MIS when it was installed. They felt that their job was to look out for new products and new markets — a policy they had always followed — and did not enjoy the idea that they might be evaluated or might have the possibilities to evaluate themselves, using data collected for the new MIS.

Evaluating incoming information might lead to redefined goals or aspiration levels [3]. Still another reaction is to focus attention excessively on environmental factors believed to be causing problems. The lengthy reorientation of the IDC's to the 1966-68 crisis can be partially explained in that way.

The prevailing myth is the one that presently guides the behavior of individuals at the same time that it justifies their behavior to themselves. Doubts as to the appropriateness of reasoning and actions foster the emergence of ghost myths. A ghost myth represents a different cognitive perspective on reality, and presents a partial alternative to the prevailing myth's answers to the what, why and how questions. In other words, a ghost myth is a possible explanation to why something is wrong.

If negative information prevails, individuals might become convinced that a ghost myth is more appropriate than the prevailing one. If and when this change occurs depends on how well established the prevailing myth is in the mind of individuals, what kind of experiences and expectations individuals have and what groups they belong to.

The delearning phase stems from tangible anomalies connected with the prevailing myth. The relearning phase is initiated by emotion and the will to reduce genuine uncertainty. Competing ghost myths offer different points of departure.

It should be noted that the use of myth as a metaphor does not imply that there is inherently anything bad or good with the myth or that it is true or false. It is simply a set of beliefs.

Figure 2 presents a simplified model of the process.

Perhaps one might conceive the process of the individual in terms of Bayesian decision theory.

The prevailing myth can be thought of as a structure of parameters and variables estimated by the individual. These parameters and variables are reestimated in the light of new information. Under normal conditions the prevailing myth provides the individual with a theory for understanding the world and a defense network against disturbing information. The individual thus estimates conditionally – given the prevailing myth.

If a new piece of information is far off from expectations and breaks the normal pattern, this might strengthen a ghost myth or lead to efforts of individuals to con-

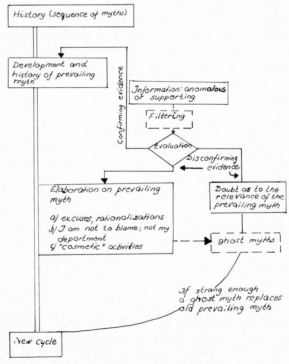

Figure 2. Myths and the individual.

ceal anomalous information to themselves. If disturbing signals are perceived sufficiently strong, so strong as to dominate the perceptual pattern, the prevailing myth can no longer provide a reliable structure of parameters and relationships. Then the Bayesian procedure breaks down and there will be a need for a fresh start with a new set-up of variables and relations to be estimated.

From individual to group

A necessary but insufficient condition for acceptance of a competing ghost myth is that individuals experience doubts whether their cognitive structures contain a reasonably good representation of the factors relevant for the situation. Tangible indicators of a crisis are needed to create a common feeling among members of the group that something is wrong. In this phase, the role of a sensor pointing to anomalies is important for development of doubts.

A crisis situation, almost by definition, opens up the organizaton for political processes. Proposers show up with their alternative myths and try to convince others and themselves of the appropriateness of their solution. The example of a proposed new division illustrates a presumptive candidate for a company-wide myth. Of course, not all proposers are successful in their attempts to gain impetus for their ideas. Managing directors of IDC subsidiaries tried, in vain, to receive acceptance for the idea that R & D efforts were crucial as the 1968 recession ended. Nevertheless, it is through these interactive processes within groups that the necessary shifts of myths take place. Through these processes, where enthusiasm replaces uncertainty, a dominant coalition is formed, approaching a unity of membership and opinion. In the group's discussion of the problem at hand, the authors assume that:

— an argument for a certain approach or opinion is sharpened when directed towards a dissident;

— if someone in the group assumes such a role of obstinacy, that person will serve an integrating function; other members of the group will overcome differences of opinion in their efforts to persuade that person that he or she is wrong.

It is hypothesized that when the group is approaching a solution, one can expect to find this constructive function of obstinacy at work. One reason why the groups at the IDC head offices acted so determined to implement a new MIS might be that they convinced themselves while opposing the subsidiary managers on the R & D issue.

From group to individual

The outcome of the group's deliberations is a solution in principle. This solution must be adapted to the organizational conditions and the situation at hand. It is assumed that political tactics like jockeying for position and power maintenance are evoked by the existence of a solution in principle, giving room for interpretation.

Acceptance is usually conditional on vagueness. It is when the organizational members see and understand a new pattern of tasks or a modified organization in the solution in principle, that their uncertainties begin to reduce and they generate expectations in relation to the perceived characteristics of the solution in principle. Initially, there will be a small number of proponents for the new policy. They are the ones that stand to lose if the policy is a failure. Then there will be a spectrum of early to late adopters.

The acceptance process is similar to a political process. As the new policy gains adherents, it gains political impetus and new social norms develop. The late adopters will play along, with reservations, making it possible for them to say sometime in the future, "Well, I told you that it would be a failure, didn't I?" They join in when they see that the new policy will survive, in which case their reservations are forgotten or referred to with the phrase, "Well, you shouldn't accept novelties until you are sure that they are good for the company. I wasn't sure."

One possible outcome of the political processes might be the emergence of competing new myths. That is, a dominant coalition may not form around one alternative; individuals might gather in antagonistic groups and discuss ends and means of the present situation. The temporary result is paralysis of action.

Myths and expectations

Conceptually, formation of expectations is often equated with forecasting, but using the term forecasting implies that questions of what and how are settled. In this schema, formation of expectations is different.

The imbalance that individuals feel by having the prevailing myth attacked by anomalous information, but with no alternative to use instead, is likely to compel them to work on a possible replacement – a ghost myth. Part of this elaboration can be described as expectation formation, but these expectations are influenced by hopes, desires and goals of the individuals involved rather than based on neutral facts as in ordinary forecasting. The function of expectation formation is for individuals to convince themselves that the ghost myth is in some sense a suitable replacement for the prevailing myth, a way to augment the enthusiasm for whatever is new in the situation. Then, they are open to influence from their reference group; they may even seek it actively.

This intertwining of hopes and expectations is probably even more important in groups than for the individual. In one way or other, the prevailing myth is accepted by members of the group. Due to differential exposure to information, or to personality traits, any change is likely to be initiated by one or two persons of the group. These persons will transmit crisis feelings to the group if that activity is a part of their roles or if they conceive of the possibility to enhance their own status in the group. Their activity produces a clash between the prevailing myth and any ghost myth that is evoked. The general consensus is broken and a feeling of uncertainty seizes members of the group if an acceptable alternative does not present itself immediately. This might happen when there is a consensus that something is wrong, but when there is no strong ghost myth. The general uncertainty of the situation produces diverse and conflicting expectations. Cognitive structures of individuals have not yet adapted to the new situation. Inconsistencies in cognitions have not been discovered.

For a crisis to be resolved, a new prevailing myth has to appear from among the alternative ghost myths. Group members must form some type of unity around one possible alternative solution to the pressing problem. Unity can be formed by inspiring the group members with enthusiasm for the alternative. People must be enthusiastic in order for an alternative to be viable. The initiators of change are dependent on a sounding board for their ideas to penetrate. The group is apt to listen if the problem is evident and the ideas are easy to grasp. Expectations formed at this stage help to build enthusiasm. They are derived from the emerging myth and serve to support it. They have the character of wishful thinking because there is no experience on which to build expectations.

Once a new prevailing myth is established, new rules of the game create a different structure, and the organization is again resistant to anomalous information for the time being. Expectation formation has both functional and dysfunctional aspects. Things happen because people get enthusiastic, sometimes overenthusiastic. But the more people expect, the more likely people are to become disappointed in the future, setting the stage for a new cycle.

Diverging expectations are normal and mark the beginning of a crisis at the group or organizational level. An emerging consensus marks the beginning of the end of a crisis.

An organization design principle

The study of IDC's revealed a wave pattern, where each wave was connected with a particular myth. Pettigrew [16,17] observed a similar phenomenon on the group level. The wave's rise is characterized by enthusiasm, bold initiatives in line with the myth — be it better control, MIS design, going international — and a great belief in the myth's appropriateness. The wave's apex marks the maximum in these respects, but it also marks the first recognized slip. The environment may have changed or the organization may have overdone something. Early in the downswing, hesitancy gives opportunities for ghost myths to develop. Ghost myths stem from possible explanations why anomalies appeared. Dissension and internal politics follow, leading to a new myth. In almost all observed cases, a good myth emerged — a sensible and well reasoned perception of what was important in the situation.

Some implications follow from these dynamics of strategy formation. Obviously a planning system based on a myth will be irrelevant, or at least partially irrelevant, when the prevalent myth is abandoned. Now, it seems virtually impossible to foresee the life span of any particular myth, but knowing about the ultimate decay of any myth is still useful.

Rather than designing a planning system that is in some sense perfect in relation to a new myth, one should design a system that satisfies minimum needs. "One should set up a tent rather than build a palace" is a principle advocated by information system designers. Some people argue that by the time the foundations for a MIS palace are laid, the problems have changed [7], while others emphasize difficulties in forecasting environmental shifts [9]. The organization may move even if the environment does not change. However, this is only a matter of stress. It all amounts to the insight that residence never is permanent; temporary shelter is what is needed.

One question this raises is whether a minimal planning system would not lower organization rationality. The answer is no, provided that the myth supporting the system is developed continuously. To develop a myth is to specify it, to differentiate it, to provide it with causal and explanatory factors. When the myth develops into a domain definition, it performs important control functions. Wildavsky [20, p. 511] discusses a model of control, "the internalized gyroscope.' By recruitment and training, forest rangers are socialized into central values which can be applied in all situations. Without apparent effort or innumerable detailed instructions, central control can still be achieved. In the same fashion, a myth serves as a coordinating factor during the wave's upswing [15].

Prescriptions for using myths

If organizations develop in wave patterns around consecutive myths, then what should be done about it? The wave pattern is a natural consequence of interactions between basic postulates set up by organizations and their environments. One should not tinker with it, but one should seek ways of getting past the troughs without much delay and arriving a little wiser. Organizations should prepare for troughs by increasing their ability to produce new solutions in principle when the time comes. Timing of efforts is important. This conclusion was also drawn by Clark [2] in his work on the development of colleges' missions and organizational sagas. Working on a counterplan as proposed by Mason [14] or using a devil's advocate in the upswing appears dysfunctional, because this kills the enthusiasm and team spirit. The importance of these factors is illustrated in a case presented by Guest [8], where a vicious circle of declining performance, tight control and defensiveness was broken by a new management style. On the other hand, dissension in the downswing may develop into a stalemate if no solution in principle is presented when needed.

When the prevailing myth is stabilized, when everything seems to be functioning well, and the trust in the appropriateness of the prevailing myth is firm, the organization should set up an ad hoc committee to investigate whether something is wrong and why. What comes out of such an inquiry is one or several ghost myths that could provide a solution in principle.

A new business idea is most likely to be accepted if it is introduced in a crisis situation, when the prevailing myth has been proven wrong, or when doubts appear in the downswing. It should, then, preferably be preceded by the devil's advocacy against the prevailing myth, setting the stage for the ghost myth to become a solution in principle and later a new myth that will inspire the organization with enthusiasm.

A solution in principle should be a solution in principle; that is, it should be vague enough to allow for imagination, but still innovative and open to individual interpretation to procure organizational members with a different vision of the future. This advances the chances for initial acceptance of the new myth at the same time that room is left for elaborating on and specifying the solution in principle. [1] At a late stage of a crisis, when a new myth is emerging from the solution in principle, any proposition not supporting the emerging myth will probably be swept away by the new enthusiasm.

A major problem is diagnosing where the organization is in the life cycle of the prevailing myth. A good diagnostic instrument is to develop the myth by elaborating on its causal and explanatory relations. Thereby, it becomes natural to substitute forecasting for the wishful thinking that goes with the enthusiasm.When one forecasts, the deviations from the expected outcome must be explained, and then one begins to doubt whether the assumptions behind the forecasts are wrong. Another advantage with an elaborated myth is learning from mistakes. If the real outcome cannot be explained using the elaborated myth, this indicates that it has to be changed, and since the myth is elaborated, it is possible to see what is wrong.

The whole belief system of organizational members is not totally shattered by crises. Neither are the formal and informal systems. Built up during the old myth's reign, some are kept and sink like sediments to the bottom of the organization. Therefore, a historical perspective is crucial for those seeking to understand organizations' developments.

References

[1] Baker, George W. and Chapman, Dwight, W. (eds.), Man and Society in Disaster, Basic Books, New York, N.Y., 1962.
[2] Clark, Burton, R., The Distinctive College: Antioch, Reed and Swarthmore, Aldine, Chicago, Ill., 1970.
[3] Cyert, Richard M. and March, James G., A Behavioral Theory of the Firm, Prentice-Hall, Englewood Cliffs, N.J., 1963.

[1] An anonymous referee, who "enjoyed the author's own myth about the role of myths," actually acknowledged the solution-in-principle idea.

[4] Danielson, Albert, Företagsekonomi – en översikt, (Business Administration – An Overview), Studentlitteratur, Lund, Sweden, 1975.

[5] Dynes, Russel R., Organized Behavior in Disaster, Lexington Books, Lexington, Mass., 1970.

[6] Glaser, Barney G. and Strauss, Anselm L., Discovery of Grounded Theory; Strategies for Qualitative Research, Aldine,Chicago, Ill., 1967.

[7] Glimell, Hans R., Designing Interactive Systems for Organizational Change, Business Administration Studies (BAS), Göteborg, Sweden (No. 24), 1975.

[8] Guest, Robert H., Organizational Change: The Effect of Successful Leadership, Irwin, Homewood, Ill., 1962.

[9] Hedberg, Bo L.T., Nystrom, Paul C. and Starbuck, William H., "Camping on Seesaws: Prescriptions for a Self-Designing Organization," Administrative Science Quarterly, Vol. 21 (March 1976), pp. 41–65.

[10] Jönsson, Sten A., Om utvecklingsbolagens planeringsproblem, (On the Planning Problem of Investment Development Companies), Business Administration Studies (BAS), Göteborg, Sweden (No. 11), 1971.

[11] Jönsson, Sten A., An Approach to the Study of Planning for Development in Investment Development Companies, (dupl.) University of Gothenburg, Göteborg, Sweden, 1972.

[12] Jönsson, Sten A., Decentralisering och utveckling, (Decentralization and Development), Business Administration Studies (BAS), Göteborg, Sweden (No. 21), 1973.

[13] Jönsson, Sten A., Lundin, Rolf A., and Sjöberg, Lennart, "Procesy Decyzyjne w Warunkach Kryzysu Organizacji," (Organizational Decision Processes in Crisis Situations), Przeglad Organizacji, (Organizational Review), Warsaw, Poland (No. 10), 1975.

[14] Mason, Richard O., "A Dialectical Approach to Strategic Planning," Management Science, Vol. 15 (April 1969), pp. B403-B414.

[15] Mitroff, Ian I., Nelson, John and Mason, Richard O., "On Management Myth-Information Systems," Management Science, Vol. 21 (Dec. 1974), pp. 371–382.

[16] Pettigrew, Andrew M., The Politics of Organizational Decision-Making, Tavistock, London, England, 1973.

[17] Pettigrew, Andrew M., Internal Politics and the Emergence and Decline of Departmental Groups, London Graduate School of Business Studies, London, England (Working paper), 1974.

[18] Popper, Karl R., The Logic of Scientific Discovery, Hutchinson & Co., London, England, 1968.

[19] Shackle, George L., Epistemics & Economics: A Critique of Economic Doctrine, Cambridge University Press, Cambridge, England, 1972.

[20] Wildavsky, Aaron, "The Self-Evaluating Organization," Public Administration Review, Vol. 32 (September-October 1972), pp. 509–520.

North-Holland/TIMS Studies in the Management Sciences 5 (1977) 171–181
© North-Holland Publishing Company

DESIGNING ORGANIZATIONS TO MATCH TOMORROW *

BO L.T. HEDBERG
University of Gothenburg

PAUL C. NYSTROM and WILLIAM H. STARBUCK
University of Wisconsin-Milwaukee

Many decades of economic growth have induced organizations to ignore environmental happenings and to act inertially, but future demands of the world's ecology will accelerate social and technological change. Policy makers can respond to change by facilitating organizational births and by mitigating the stresses caused by organizational deaths. However, the more effective policies are ones that help organizations persist adaptively: the goal should be to create self-designing organizations that continually appraise and revise their behaviors and that invent their futures as well as survive them. To foster self-designing organizations, policy makers and managers ought to modify the ways organizations evaluate their performances, and they ought to stimulate incremental experiments in organizations' strategies and in people's careers.

Organizations might be matched to tomorrow's world on the basis of accurate forecasts. But who knows which forecasts, if any, will turn out to have been accurate? Some forecasts have said that energy shortages, famines, and ecological decay will occur unless limits are placed on resource consumption [6,17,25]; these limits would require that nonindustrialized societies consume more resources while industrialized societies consume less. Other forecasts have stated that different societies will grow at different rates, with the important constraints on consumption arising from social and political decisions rather than from ecology [18]. Still other forecasts have asserted that consumption can rise indefinitely because vast potentials remain for using solar energy, new agricultural methods, pollution controls, and innovations that are still to be discovered [4,13]. The diverse forecasts even outnumber the forecasters.

However, the most effective designs for tomorrow's organizations vary little from forecast to forecast, because all of the forecasts imply that there will be rapid social and technological change. Equilibrium in resource consumption would not

* Received November 1975; revised April 1976, July 1976.

eliminate change. Quite the contrary. A fixed resource pool means some activities must be deleted whenever new activities are undertaken, and hence means an increased proportion of activities that are in decline. Since most forms of social and technological change are insuppressible, equilibrium in resource consumption would bring more rapid change between and within societies. Moreover, if organizations continue to behave inertially, consumption in the industrialized societies would exceed the long-run equilibrium levels; cutting back consumption would cause distress that might be avoided through gradual transitions.

Organizational inertia also impedes the creation and use of technological innovations. If technological innovations escalate consumption per capita while allowing populations to multiply, the world's saturating ecology would likely impose more and more constraints. Ecologically destructive or inefficient methods would have to be nonbenevolently forced out of use as soon as better methods appear. Either organizations would have to be made less inertial or traditionally inertial organizations would have to be replaced more frequently.

Because social and technological change appear likely to accelerate, social institutions ought to be designed to accommodate rapid change and to extract the benefits from it. Today's institutions find rapid change stressful largely because of networks of private and public organizations that lack adaptiveness. This article discusses ways to increase organizations' adaptiveness so that societies can respond creatively to ecological constraints and technological innovations. The next section explains how organizations in benevolent environments accumulate inertia and become less capable of handling transitions into new, perhaps nonbenevolent, environments. Then follows a statement of the basic alternatives open to policy makers who want to steer populations of organizations. It is advocated that top managers and policy makers stimulate the evolution of self-designing organizations — organizations that continuously diagnose their important problems, explore their future options, and invent new solutions as they develop. Some key properties of self-designing organizations are spelled out in the final sections: participatory information systems that transmit diverse messages, strategic experiments that disrupt complacency and stimulate curiosity, and jobs and careers that provide satisfying lives despite rapidly changing work environments.

Growing inflexible because of benevolence

The mental characteristics of people are important determinants of how organizations act. Human brains can analyze the implications of only a few simultaneous influences, and they bog down in the difficulties of weighing numerous future uncertainties. Therefore, organizations have to keep activities simple — by breaking big tasks down into small ones, by ignoring contingencies and potential options, by grouping stimuli and responding to them with standardized routines. For example, accountants and internal revenue agents compare tax returns with various rules of thumb: careful investigations are not wasted on returns that conform to ordinary patterns.

Whether standardized routines produce good solutions depends on an environment's constancy and benevolence. Environments that change slowly provide time in which to create new methods and to refine old ones. However, organizations are unlikely to try to improve methods that appear to work, and familiar results are usually assumed to be nearly optimal. Benevolent environments rarely make enough threats to keep organizations alert: lost opportunities are less visible than are customers' complaints, law suits, or financial losses.

Decades of almost continuous economic growth have encouraged the organizations in industrialized societies to depend on standardized routines. Signals that routines are failing are rare; resource margins are adequate to absorb the errors from slightly inappropriate responses to slightly misperceived stimuli; responses can be invented gradually. Organizational failures are typically attributed to managerial inexperience and to deviations from conventional practices rather than to stresses originating in environments.

Furthermore, standardized routines have been tailored to gradually expanding economies. Budgets are thought of as minimum aspirations rather than as upper limits to expansion; financial plans focus on maximizing growth while retaining small buffers against temporary setbacks. Long-term commitments, such as purchase contracts, assume that productivities will rise through learning and through returns to scale as well as through technological innovations. Forecasts of demands for products or services reflect managers' ambitions more than external realities [5,26,27].

Consistently benevolent environments undermine organizations' readiness to act and their sensitivity to environmental events. Fewer resources are expended monitoring environmental happenings. Plans replace messages as the media for intra-organizational coordination. Redundancies and irrationalities are shifted out of job assignments and authority domains. Organizational ideologies grow up about standardized routines, and conformity to tradition becomes a primary criterion for accomplishment [3,10,20,24].

Steering the population of organizations

If the future is going to expose organizations to rapid change and possibly to less benevolent environments, policy makers will have two basic options. Substantial increases in organizational death rates can be accepted, with resources being transferred from dying to newly born organizations. Alternatively, organizations can be made more adapttive so that they can survive to explore and to develop in altered environments.

These two options are not mutually exclusive, and policy makers are likely to use both. However, improving organizations' adaptiveness wastes fewer resources and promises more benefits than does stimulating higher turnovers in the population of organizations. Small, incremental changes cause less difficulties for organizations and their members than do abrupt, revolutionary shifts. Organizational death nearly always causes psychological stress and consumes human and material resources. Policies to increase organizations' deaths and births require effective systems for transferring resources from dying to newborn organizations. At present, efficient transfer systems exist mainly for financial resources: transfers of people, knowledge, and equipment are handled poorly. Unless the new organizations are more congruent with long-term environmental constraints than were the former organizations, replacing one organization with another brings only the temporary benefits of change as such. It is doubtful that anyone knows enough about the future to say reliably which organizations are the most appropriate ones to die or what kinds of organizations ought to be created.

Traditional strategies for designing organizations start with forecasts of what stresses tomorrow's organizations will face, and then attempt to design organizations that meet the envisioned needs. Although these forecast-oriented designs are common, both their realism and effectiveness must be questioned.

Some liabilities of forecast-oriented designs derive from the difficulty of taking the future into account. To the extent that the future can be predicted, it is easier to specify some of its constraints than to imagine opportunities that might be realized within these constraints. Consequently, forecast-oriented designs tend to be conservative solutions that fail to reap full advantage from their environments.

Forecast-oriented designs readily become self-fulfilling prophesies: they can create the situations they were designed to meet. For example, if forecasts predict considerable technological innovation, organizations will incorporate large research departments that generate technological innovations. Similarly, if public agencies expect aggressive animosity from their clients, they will use physical barriers and rigid rules to protect employees from clients and will use esoteric jargon and impersonal procedures to keep clients at a disadvantage; frustration and bewilderment then breed ill will and noncompliance. In many instances, the major contribution of forecasts is to foster social change in one direction instead of another.

If policy makers are going to facilitate particular kinds of social change, they certainly ought to acknowledge the value premises underlying their social policies, and they should choose their social policies overtly after comparing alternative futures. But it is far from clear that top managers and policy makers ought to control social change directly.

The alternative way to design organizations to match the future is to adopt a metastrategy in which the top managers and policy makers define their role as similar to that of arithmetic teachers, whose effectiveness is measured by their students' ability to solve arithmetic problems rather than by their own ability to solve such problems. Within this metastrategy, the goal shifts from solutions invented by policy makers to combinations of hardware, software and people which continually invent, revise, adapt, generate and modify their own solutions [11].

Self-designing organizations are more promising vehicles for approaching the uncertain future than are organizations that rely on forecasts. Self-designing organizations would evaluate their own defects and strong points; they would develop opportunities instead of defending past actions; they would adapt to surprises; and they would resist the accumulating of inertia.

The main prerequisite for self-designing organizations is probably an ideological commitment to impermanence. Organizations should be seen as means, not ends. Members should avoid basing their personal satisfactions on the roles and methods that characterize the present, and they should seek satisfactions in the activities and skills that are creating the future. Current methods and policies should be questioned continuously, and strategies should be chains of experiments; even apparently adequate methods should be discarded in order to make way for new trials [15,31,32].

Self-designing organizations will encounter at least three groups of technical problems. Firstly, self-designing organizations need timely information about changes in their environments and their performances, so that they will have enough time to invent appropriate methods. Secondly, means are needed to counteract organizational inertia and to keep organizations exploring alternative futures. Thirdly, self-designing organizations have implications for their members' jobs and reward systems; they are likely to require new attitudes toward work and new job systems. The ensuing sections of this article discuss these problem areas in sequence, and point out actions that policy makers and managers can take in order to foster self-designing organizations.

Transmitting change signals

Self-designing organizations depend on efficient information systems that can trigger timely adjustments to changing internal and external conditions. The important characteristics of information systems include input signals from diverse sources and rapid perceptions of change. For example, one study found that hospitals with information systems that highlight both expenses and medical performances can better achieve high-quality treatments at low cost and better match their internal structures to environmental requirements than can hospitals with information systems that focus primarily on monetary measures [8]. Another study found that the more profitable business firms are those that use diverse criteria to evaluate themselves [9].

Although new computer technologies can improve information processing, crucial improvements are needed in the information being processed. Most organizations currently rely on accounting systems and formal reports to measure their performances, but these measures are at best partial. Organizations that suddenly find themselves in trouble evidently are ones that have relied on routine, formal reports too heavily [24]. Because accounting systems mainly reflect material and financial resources — neglecting such resources as skilled personnel, know-how, or investments in future markets — organizations can accumulate hidden resources and dissipate them without recognizing these trends or measuring most of the trends' effects [12].

When there are no generally accepted performance measures, organizations can respond to observed deficiencies by shifting to new performance measures that portray their activities favorably [22]. Even when performance measures are generally accepted ones, evaluation and adaptation suffer from insufficient upward communication; messages are often distorted or blocked while traveling from lower organizational levels toward decision centers.

Participation in organizational governance can improve organizational self-evaluations by bringing in outside expertise and by making better use of inside expertise. Representatives of workers, customers, clients, suppliers, patients, governments, interest groups, and citizens can supply additional information about opportunities and threats in organizations' environments or expose obscure difficulties within organizations, thereby improving organizations' reaction times and their decision bases. Participation in organizational governance may also reinforce members' loyalty and increase organizations' cohesion in the face of rapid change. Organizations with informal, nonhierarchical communication links react faster and more easily to changes in their environments.

Widespread participation in organizational governance will require information systems that keep each participant adequately informed. Although, so far, electronic information technology has been used mainly to increase control by top-level personnel, it could help to decentralize decisions and to distribute decision aids and accurate information to lower-level personnel, customers, clients, or community members [21,28].

How should managers and policy makers improve performance measurements? Rather than allocating resources to elaborate performance evalutions, policy makers should foster informal communications and should encourage managers to elicit brief performance appraisals from diverse groups. Policy makers and managers also should combat reliance on formal accounting systems, and they should reject misleading precision in statements about past performances and future expectations. Top managers ought to monitor environments more and internal methods less. Time and effort ought to be invested searching for new measures of organizational success that include ecological consequences.

Stimulating organizational curiosity

Management theories have long prescribed skill specialization, systematic coordination, clear objectives, and unambiguous authority structures. These widely accepted prescriptions say an organization should be internally differentiated and yet harmonious, should use explicit communication channels and explicit decision criteria, and should act decisively and consistently. Such properties can enhance the performances of organizations that inhabit slowly changing environments: ad hoc analyses can be replaced by standardized routines; routines can be multiplied, reduced to their essential elements, and then preserved in capital equipment and training programs; communications can be compressed with efficient codes; and responsibilities can be delineated precisely [7,14,30]. Because they are designed for benevolent and relatively slowly changing environments, today's organizations avoid debates and conflicts, and they impose rationality on activities.

Rapid change will require increased risk-taking and experimentation by organizations that seek to survive. Competition in a stabilized population of organizations or pressures from technological innovations will favor organizations that can seize opportunities and create unique niches of competence. Increased risk-taking will raise organizational death rates, but will also improve the adaptiveness of the surviving organizations.

Self-designing organizations will need planning systems that expect the unexpected and that stimulate curiosity; such systems will differ from the systems currently advocated for long-range planning. In fact, a study of British firms found no evidence that consensus about objectives, clearly defined roles, or formal planning correlated positively with financial performance or innovativeness. Instead, financial performance correlated positively with reliance on informal, unofficial communication channels and with the number of different kinds of information used during reviews of company policies. Organizations with elaborate long-range planning systems seemed less able to explore their futures than organizations with less programmatic ways of forming strategies [9].

Organizations' searches for new modes of behavior are motivated by dissatisfaction and triggered by signs of failure, and intervals of doubt and reappraisal precede genuine efforts to reorient strategies. Reappraisals are not fostered by the organizational practices that clarify goals and that allocate tasks logically and unambiguously. Consequently, self-designing organizations ought to use logical contradictions, ambiguities, and overlaps to counteract complacency and to stimulate innovations.

The essence of all efforts to reduce organizational inertia is to induce organizations to act as if optimal is an impossible state. Links between current methods and current goals should be seen as transient. Behaviors should be planned as sequences of experiments to test the stability of environmental phenomena and to discover better ways of behaving in the future, and the experiments should continue even after optimal behaviors appear to have been found. Because shifting environments and uncertain futures give organizations the task of optimizing unknown criteria, continuous experimenting along a trial-and-error trajectory makes better sense than does attempting once-and-for-all solutions to problems that will change [1,2,16,29].

Experiments can be stimulated by making organizations pursue different goals at different times, by letting separate departments pursue incompatible goals simultaneously, and by undertaking iterative improvements instead of attempting to find overall optima immediately [32]. All of these strategies remind organizations' members that goals and criteria are erroneous approximations that can be corrected and improved.

The key design challenge is to balance the levels of discretionary, uncommitted resources. Discretionary resources must be available if organizations are to try experiments, to develop new capabilities, to take risks, and to survive transitions to new environments. But when discretionary resources grow too large, there are not enough warnings of change, and so adaptive capabilities wither.

If policy makers and managers want to encourage adaptiveness, they should think thrice before punishing entrepreneurial ventures. Promotions and incentives ought to reward people who deviate from familiar methods, who take risks, and who ask imaginative questions. Occasional failure ought to be every manager's right, and policies and educational programs ought to foster ideological commitments to exploring unknowns rather than to mastering the known. Instead of criticizing organizational subunits for having unclear and contradictory goals or for duplicating the activities of other subunits, policy makers and top managers should interpret conflict and ambiguity as generators of healthy changes. Investment policies and tax incentives ought to favor flexible assets that convert to diverse uses and ought to nurture efforts to recycle existing assets. Hiring criteria should place high values on people's versatility and their preparedness to learn, and organizations ought to set up programs to help their personnel unlearn outdated traditions and standardized routines. Contracts and commitments should shirk the long term and focus on the short term.

Living in self-designing organizations

An orientation toward flexibility will mean that most interpersonal relationships are temporary ones, that job assignments will change frequently, and that hierarchical statuses and prerogatives will shift. There may be high job turnover as people depart who dislike newly adopted task arrangements, and as people arrive who possess needed abilities. Departments, work groups, and individuals require latitude in which to evaluate and to reorient themselves, and this in turn means latitude in which to err and to harm themselves.

There are real reasons for wondering how satisfying such jobs can be. How much pride can people take in rapidly vanishing accomplishments and in solutions which are automatically assumed to be faulty? Can the people who prefer clear, stable assignments learn to be happy with endless sequences of experiments and reorientations? will inconsistencies and ambiguities induce apathy and alienation in people, as they did in Pavlov's dogs? Little is known about such issues. Unstable, experimental situations may make today's people uncomfortable mainly because today's organizations promote stability, consistency, and permanence. Perhaps people can draw as much satisfaction from the activities that keep organizations viable as they now draw from repeated routines and familiar structures [32]. Perhaps people can take pride in creating new methods rather than in reusing elegant methods, and people can enjoy partially answering important questions instead of precisely answering inaccurate questions [19]. Perhaps careers that aggregate similar jobs in different organizations can be more satisfying than careers that aggregate different jobs in the same organizations [23].

What actions should policy makers and managers take to improve jobs and employment systems? People should be encouraged to try out alternative jobs, and transfer systems should be developed that reduce the difficulties and expenses of discovering new employment opportunities, of moving into new organizations, or of changing occupations. A person's long-term financial security should not depend on continued employment with the same organization. Information about job openings and available people should be widely disseminated, perhaps through publicly supported information systems. Educational curricula ought to deemphasize narrow specialization, and educational policies ought to treat learning as a lifetime activity. Opportunities should be created for people to distribute through time the costs of mid-career reorientations. There should be as much freedom for individual people — to innovate, to experiment, and to adapt — as there is for the organizations people can and will create.

Starting to begin

Because no one can accurately forecast the future, no one can design organizations that match tomorrow's challenges. However, self-designing organizations would reduce the costs of forecast errors by rapidly adapting to what really occurs. Self-designing organizations redesign themselves to match tomorrow.

Individual organizations can strive to become self-designing and to remain so, and some organizations may succeed. But today's social environments seriously impede the redesign efforts of isolated, individual organizations, and self-designing organizations will not grow prevalent unless they receive support from compatible social institutions and appreciative ideologies. People will have to face up to the deficiencies in systematic methods, rational analyses, and consistent behaviors; and people will have to acknowledge the virtues of impermanence, dissension, bare adequacy, uncertainty, and ambiguity. Societies will have to follow new policies and put new social technologies into operation — technologies that encourage flows of people and of information, and policies that foster continuous experiments and strategic versatility by people and by organizations. Policy makers and managers as well as everyone else will have to honor the complementarities among actions by individuals, by organizations, and by societies, because the social institutions needed to support self-designing organizations must themselves be supported from below.

It is far from obvious what steps can take the world from where it is to where it ought to be. Yet this ignorance is itself an informative guide to action: it implies that steps will have to be discovered progressively through incremental experiments in pursuit of ambiguous, shifting goals. Ignorance of what steps to take is also reassuring, for it means that experiments still lie ahead. The excitement and fun come from designing, not from having designed.

References

[1] Box, George E.P. and Draper, Norman R., Evolutionary Operation, Wiley, New York, N.Y., 1969.

[2] Campbell, Donald T., "Reforms as Experiments," American Psychologist, Vol. 24 (April 1969), pp. 409—429.

[3] Clark, Burton R., "The Organizational Saga in Higher Education," Administrative Science Quarterly, Vol. 17 (June 1972), pp. 178—184.

[4] Cole, H.S.D., Freeman, Christopher, Jahoda, Marie, and Pavitt, K.L.R., (eds.), Models of Doom: A Critique of The Limits to Growth, Universe, New York, N.Y., 1973.

[5] Crecine, John P., Governmental Problem Solving, Rand McNally, Chicago, Ill., 1969.

[6] Forrester, Jay W., World Dynamics, Wright-Allen, Cambridge, Mass., 1971.

[7] Galbraith, Jay R., Designing Complex Organizations, Addison-Wesley, Reading, Mass., 1973.

[8] Gordon, Gerald, Tanon, Christian, and Morse, Edward V., Hospital Structure, Costs, and Innovation, Cornell University, Ithaca, N.Y. (working paper), 1974.

[9] Grinyer, Peter H. and Norburn, David, "Planning for Existing Markets: Perceptions of Executives and Financial Performance," Journal of the Royal Statistical Society, (Series A), Vol. 138 (Part 1, 1975), pp. 70—97.

[10] Hedberg, Bo L.T., Organizational Stagnation and Choice of Strategy, International Institute of Management, Berlin, Germany (working paper), 1973.

[11] Hedberg, Bo L.T., Nystrom, Paul C. and Starbuck, William H., "Camping on Seesaws: Prescriptions for a Self-Designing organization," Administrative Science Quarterly, Vol. 21 (March 1976), pp. 41—65.

[12] Hopwood, Anthony G., "Problems with Using Accounting Information in Performance Evaluation," Management International Review, Vol. 13 (2-3, 1973), pp. 83—98.

[13] Kahn, Herman, Brown, William, and Martel, Leon, The Next 200 Years: A Scenario for America and the World, Morrow, New York, N.Y., 1976.

[14] Khandwalla, Pradip N., "Mass Output Orientation of Operations Technology and Organizational Structure," Administrative Science Quarterly, Vol. 19 (March 1974), pp. 74—97.

[15] Landau, Martin, "On the Concept of a Self-correcting Organization," Public Administration Review, Vol. 33 (November-December 1973), pp. 533—542.

[16] Lindblom, Charles E., "The Science of Muddling Through," Public Administration Review, Vol. 19 (Spring 1959), pp. 79—88.

[17] Meadows, Donella H., Meadows, Dennis L., Randers, Jørgen, and Behrens, William W., III, The Limits to Growth: A Report for The Club of Rome's Project on the Predicament of Mankind, Universe, New York, N.Y., 1972.

[18] Mesarovic, Mihajlo and Pestel, Eduard, Mankind at the Turning Point: The Second Report of The Club of Rome, Dutton, New York, N.Y., 1974.

[19] Mitroff, Ian I. and Featheringham, Tom R., "On Systematic Problem Solving and the Error of the Third Kind," Behavioral Science, Vol. 19 (November 1974), pp. 383—393.

[20] Mitroff, Ian I. and Kilmann, Ralph H., "On Organization Stories: An Approach to the Design and Analysis of Organizations Through Myths and Stories," in The Management of Organization Design: Volume I, Strategies and Implementation, Ralph H. Kilmann, Louis R. Pondy and Dennis P. Slevin (eds.), Elsevier North-Holland, New York, N.Y., 1976, pp. 189–207.

[21] Mumford, Enid and Sackman, Harold, (eds.), Human Choice and Computers, North-Holland, Amsterdam, The Netherlands, 1975.

[22] Nystrom, Paul C., "Input-Output Processes of the Federal Trade Commission," Administrative Science Quarterly, Vol. 20 (March 1975), pp. 104–113.

[23] Nystrom, Paul C., "Designing Jobs and Personnel Assignments," in Handbook of Organizational Design, Paul C. Nystrom and William H. Starbuck (eds.), Elsevier North-Holland, New York, N.Y., forthcoming.

[24] Nystrom, Paul C., Hedberg, Bo L.T., and Starbuck, William H., "Interacting Processes as Organization Designs," in The Management of Organization Design: Volume I, Strategies and Implementation, Ralph H. Kilmann, Louis R. Pondy, and Dennis P. Slevin (eds.), Elsevier North-Holland, New York, N.Y., 1976, pp. 209–230.

[25] Oltmans, Willem L., On Growth, Putnam's, New York, N.Y., 1974.

[26] Pondy, Louis R., "Effects of Size, Complexity, and Ownership on Administrative Intensity," Administrative Science Quarterly, Vol. 14 (March 1969), pp. 47–60.

[27] Schumacher, Ernst Friedrich, Small is Beautiful: A Study of Economics as if People Mattered, Blond and Briggs, London, England, 1973.

[28] Simon, Herbert A., "Applying Information Technology to Organizational Design," Public Administration Review, Vol. 33 (May-June 1973), pp. 268–278.

[29] Starbuck, William H., "Systems Optimization with Unknown Criteria," Proceedings of the 1974 International Conference on Systems, Man and Cybernetics, Institute of Electrical and Electronics Engineers, New York, N.Y., 1974, pp. 67–76.

[30] Starbuck, William H. and Dutton, John M., "Designing Adaptive Organizations," Journal of Business Policy, Vol. 3 (Summer 1973), pp. 21–28.

[31] White, Orion F., Jr., "The Dialectical Organization – An Alternative to Bureaucracy," Public Administration Review, Vol. 29 (January-February 1969), pp. 32–42.

[32] Wildavsky, Aaron B., "The Self-Evaluating Organization," Public Administration Review, Vol. 32 (September-October 1972), pp. 509–520.

NOTES ABOUT AUTHORS

Niels Bjørn-Andersen ("Designing Information Systems in an Organizational Perspective") is Associate Professor at Copenhagen School of Economics and Business Administration, where he was formerly Director of The Institute of Organization and Industrial Sociology. He has been a Research Fellow at the Manchester Business School, and has written several monographs and articles concerning the design of management information systems and the behavioral effects of information systems.

Stefan D. Bloomfield ("A Goal Approach to Organizational Design") is Associate Professor of Management Science and Assistant Director of Planning and Institutional Research at Oregon State University. He holds a B.E.S. in engineering science from Johns Hopkins University, and an M.S. and Ph.D., both in operations research, from Stanford University. His principal interest is in the application of management science to the administration of higher education. He is past Chairman of the Northwest Chapter of TIMS, and is a member of TIMS, ORSA, and the Association for Institutional Research.

E. Eugene Carter ("Designing the Capital Butgeting Process") is Professor and Head, Department of Finance at the University of Illinois – Chicago Circle. He holds a B.S. from Northwestern University and an M.S. and Ph.D. from the Graduate School of Industrial Administration, Carnegie-Mellon University. He has published articles in the areas of finance and organizational decision making in a variety of academic and management journals, is author of *Portfolio Aspects of Corporate Capital Budgeting,* and co-author of a new text, *International Financial Management.*

Martin P. Charns ("Organizing Multiple-Function Professionals in Academic Medical Centers") is Assistant Professor of Organizational Behavior at the Graduate School of Industrial Administration, Carnegie-Mellon University. He earned a B.S. in mathematics from Case Institute of Technology and an M.B.A. and D.B.A. from Harvard University. He is interested in organizational theory, and organization and management of health-related organizations. He is a member of the American Sociological Association and the ACM.

Patrick E. Connor ("A Goal Approach to Organizational Design") in Associate Professor of Management at Oregon State University. He received a B.S. in electrical engineering from the University of Washington, an M.S. in industrial administration from the Krannert School at Purdue University, and a Ph.D. in organization theory from the University of Washington. He is the editor of *Dimensions in Modern Management* (Houghton Mifflin, 1974) and the author of a number of journal articles. Professor Connor's research interests include interrelationships among structural, administrative, and organizational outcome variables, professionals in organizations, and values as an organizational variable. He is a member of the Academy of Management, American Sociological Association, and Pacific Sociological Association.

Bo L. T. Hedberg ("Designing Information Systems in an Organizational Perspective"; "Designing Organizations to Match Tomorrow") is Associate Professor of Business Administration at the University of Gothenburg, Sweden, and a member of TIMS and IFIP. He has been a

Research Fellow at the International Institute of Management, Berlin, and Visiting Associate Professor at the University of Wisconsin-Milwaukee and at the London School of Economics and Political Science. He has written several monographs and published articles on management information systems and organizational design.

Sten A. Jönsson ("Myths and Wishful Thinking as Management Tools") is Professor of Accounting and Finance, University of Gothenburg, Sweden. He was associated with the International Institute of Management, Berlin, while this paper was written. He holds a Pol. Mag. and Fil. Lic. from the University of Gothenburg. His present research interests are strategy formulation in crisis situations and planning in local government.

Steven Kerr ("Professionals in Bureaucracies: A Structural Alternative") is an Associate Professor of Organizational Behavior at The Ohio State University. He is the co-author of *Managerial Process and Organizational Behavior,* and has authored or co-authored approximately twenty-five journal articles. He is chairman of the Organization and Management Theory division of the Academy of Management, consulting editor in management to Grid Publishing Co., and on the editorial review board of the *Academy of Management Journal.* His research interests include evaluation and reward systems, leadership, and professionalism.

John R. Kimberly ("Assessing Organizational Change Strategies") is a Visiting Assitant Professor in the School of Organization and Management at Yale University. He received a B.A. in sociology from Yale University and an M.S. and Ph.D. in organizational behavior from Cornell University. He was an Assistant Professor of Sociology at the University of Illinois and a Visiting Fellow in the Centre de Recherche en Gestion at the Ecole Polytechnique, Paris. He is the author of several papers on problems of organizational change and technological innovation, and is currently doing studies of cross-national technological innovation, social policy in health, education and corrections, and organizational design and effectiveness. Professor Kimberly is a member of the AAAS, the American Sociological Association, and Phi Kappa Phi.

Paul R. Lawrence ("Organizing Multiple-Function Professionals in Academic Medical Centers") is Wallace Brett Donham Professor of Organizational Behavior at Harvard University. His current research is in organizational structures and environmental influences. He has authored numerous books and articles and is a member of the American Sociological Association and the Association of Applied Social Scientists.

Rolf A. Lundin ("Myths and Wishful Thinking as Management Tools") is Associate Professor of Business Administration at the University of Gothenburg, Sweden. He holds an Ekon. Lic. from the University of Gothenburg and a Ph.D. in management science from the University of Chicago. His principal interest is in policy formation in various types of organizations. Presently, he is conducting research on local government problems such as crises and organizational development. Professor Lundin is a member of TIMS and ORSA.

Morgan W. McCall, Jr. ("Making Sense with Nonsense: Helping Frames of Reference Clash") is Research Psychologist at the Center for Creative Leadership and an adjunct member of the graduate faculty at the University of North Carolina–Greensboro. He holds a B.S. in administrative sciences from Yale University and received a Ph.D. in organizational behavior from Cornell University. His current research interests focus on how organizational leaders interact with the systems in which they are embedded.

Will McQuillan ("Managing Turbulence") is a Senior Research Officer at the London Business School, working in organizational behavior in the public sector. He was formerly with the University of Aston's Industrial Administration Research Unit.

Les Metcalfe ("Managing Turbulence") is a Senior Research Officer in Organizational Behavior and Public Sector Management at the London Business School. He received a B.A. in government and economics from Manchester University, and an M.S. in public administration from the London School of Economics. Since 1969 he has worked at the London Business School on an interorganizational study of the effectiveness of Economic Development Committees in integrating the activities of government, management and trade unions and guiding development at the industry level.

Warren R. Nielsen ("Assessing Organizational Change Strategies") is Assistant Professor of Management, College of Business Administration, University of Nebraska, Lincoln. He received a B.A. in psychology from the University of Utah and an A.M. and Ph.D. in labor and industrial relations from the University of Illinois, Urbana. Professor Nielsen, a consultant to several organizations in the public and private sectors, is the author of a number of papers on the application of behavioral science techniques to problems of organizational health and effectiveness. He is currently studying organizational decision making and models, patterns of resource allocation and worker satisfaction, and the effectiveness of planned organizational change. Professor Nielsen is a member of the Academy of Management, the OD Network and the Industrial Relations Research Association, and is President of Nielsen and Associates, a management consulting firm specializing in organizational diagnosis and development.

Paul C. Nystrom ("Why Prescription is Prescribed"; "Designing Organizations to Match Tomorrow") is an Associate Professor in the School of Business Administration, University of Wisconsin-Milwaukee. He earned a B.S. in economics, an M.A. in public administration, and a Ph.D. in industrial relations from the University of Minnesota. His research publications are in the areas of organizational design and manpower planning. His memberships include the Academy of Management, the American Psychological Association, the American Sociological Association, the Society for General Systems Research, and TIMS. Professor Nystrom is an associate editor of *Management Science,* a past chairman of TIMS College on Organization, and is co-editing the forthcoming, three-volume *Handbook of Organizational Design* (Elsevier North-Holland).

Janet Schriesheim ("Professionals in Bureaucracies: A Structural Alternative") is Assistant Professor of Administrative Sciences and Public Administration in the Graduate School of Business Administration, Kent State University. She has presented papers at regional and national meetings of the Academy of Management and the American Psychological Association, and has published theoretical and methodological articles in such journals as *Organizational Behavior and Human Performance* and *Educational and Psychological Measurement.* Her research interests include professionals in organizations, leadership, motivation, attitude scaling, and philosophy of science.

Val Silbey ("Diagnosing Latent Relationships for Coordination") is an Assistant Professor of Management at Florida International University. He holds a B.S. in business administration and an M.B.A. from the University of South Carolina and earned a Ph.D. in organizational systems at the University of Pennsylvania. A member of ACM, Professor Silbey is interested in the structure and behavior of systems.

William H. Starbuck ("Why Prescription is Prescribed"; "Designing Organizations to Match Tomorrow") is the Evan and Marion Helfaer Professor of Business Administration at the University of Wisconsin-Milwaukee. He earned an A.B. in physics at Harvard University and an M.S. and a Ph.D. in industrial administration at Carnegie-Mellon University. He has served on the faculties of Purdue, Johns Hopkins, Cornell, and London Graduate School of Business Studies, and he was a senior research fellow at the International Institute of Management, Berlin. He has published in the areas of organizational design, decision making, computer simulation, and organizational growth. His memberships include the American Sociological Association, TIMS, and Sigma Xi, and he is a fellow in the American Psychological Association. Professor Starbuck is on the editorial board of the *Journal of Applied Social Psychology,* is a former editor of *Administrative Science Quarterly,* a past chairman of TIMS College on Organization, and is co-editing the forthcoming, three-volume *Handbook of Organizational Design* (Elsevier North-Holland).

Richard F. Vancil ("Designing Organizational Responses to an Inflationary Environment") is Professor of Business Administration and Chairman of the control area faculty at Harvard Business School. He received a B.S. from Northwestern University and an M.B.A. and D.B.A. from Harvard University. His interests are in the broad field of management systems, focusing particularly on resource allocation systems and measurement systems. He is a co-author of *Managerial Economics* (Irwin, 1973) and *Management Control Systems* (Irwin, 1972), as well as numerous other articles and books. He is also active as a corporate director and management consultant.

Mary Ann Von Glinow ("Professionals in Bureaucracies: A Structural Alternative") is a Ph.D. candidate in organizational behavior at The Ohio State University. Ms. Von Glinow has presented and published manuscripts in proceedings of the Eastern, Midwestern, Southwestern and National Academy of Management, and at national AIDS, and an article co-authored by her is scheduled to appear in *Organizational Behavior and Human Performance.* She also co-authored "Human Information Processing and Problem Solving," in *Managerial Accounting: The Behavioral Foundations* (L. Livingstone, editor, 1975). Her research interests include professionalism, organizational climate, and problems of measurement in the social sciences.

Marvin R. Weisbord ("Organizing Multiple-Function Professionals in Academic Medical Centers") is Director of Organization Research and Development, health care consulting division of Block-Petrella Associates, Inc. He has consulted and done research with several health care, education and research organizations. He teaches organizational diagnosis and consultation skills in the NTL Institutes Professional Development Program, is an associate editor of *The Journal of Applied Behavioral Science,* and is a member of the International Association of Applied Social Scientists.

Steven C. Wheelwright ("Designing Organizational Responses to an Inflationary Environment") is an Associate Professor at the Harvard Business School. He earned a B.S. in mathematics from the University of Utah (magma cum laude) and an M.B.A. and Ph.D. from the Graduate School of Business, Stanford University. He is the author of numerous cases and articles in the fields of corporate strategy, forecasting and production planning. He authored or co-authored the books *Computer-Aided Modeling for Managers, Forecasting Methods for Management, Interactive Forecasting,* and *Quantitative and Technological Methods of Forecasting.* His consulting involves the application of computers and management science techniques to today's business strategy and operating problems.

REFEREES FOR THIS ISSUE

The College on Organization thanks the following referees for their contributions:

PETER ABELL, Imperial College of Science and Technology
HOWARD ALDRICH, Cornell University
THOMAS J. ALLEN, M.I.T.
IGOR ANSOFF, Vanderbilt University
CHRIS ARGYRIS, Harvard University
BERNARD BASS, University of Rochester
JOHN V. BAUMLER, Ohio State University
VICTOR BERLIN, U.S. National Bureau of Standards
FREDERICK BETZ, U.S. National Science Foundation
HAROLD BIERMAN, JR., Cornell University
L. VAUGHN BLANKENSHIP, U.S. National Science Foundation
RICHARD G. BRANDENBURG, SUNY at Buffalo
DANIEL N. BRAUNSTEIN, Oakland University
DON BRYANT, Tavistock Institute of Human Relations
CHARLES P. BONINI, Stanford University
ELMER H. BURACK, Illinois Institute of Technology
E. EUGENE CARTER, University of Illinois-Chicago Circle
T.J. CARTWRIGHT, York University
MARTIN P. CHARNS, Carnegie-Mellon University
THEODORE CHIAO, Joseph Schlitz Brewing Co., Milwaukee
JOHN CHILD, University of Aston in Birmingham
C. WEST CHURCHMAN, University of California, Berkeley
WILLIAM S. COMANOR, University of California, Santa Barbara
DAVID W. CONRATH, University of Waterloo
WILLIAM W. COOPER, Carnegie-Mellon University
PATRICK CRECINE, Carnegie-Mellon University
LARRY L. CUMMINGS, University of Wisconsin-Madison
RICHARD M. CYERT, Carnegie-Mellon University
JAMES H. DAVIS, United Methodist Church, New York
RICHARD H. DAY, University of Wisconsin-Madison
WILLIAM R. DILL, New York University
ROBERT DODDS, Hickling-Johnston, Ltd., Toronto
ROGER L.M. DUNBAR, International Institute of Management
ROBERT DUNCAN, Northwestern University
JOHN M. DUTTON, New York University
RICHARD E. ERICSON, George Washington University
JAMES E. FRANK, Florida State University
JOHN H. FREEMAN, University of California, Berkeley
THEODORE FRIED, J.C. Penney Co., New York
THOMAS S. FRIEDLAND, University of Illinois

JAY R. GALBRAITH, University of Pennsylvania
DENNIS GENSCH, University of Wisconsin-Milwaukee
DONALD GERWIN, University of Wisconsin-Milwaukee
TERRY GLEASON, University of Pennsylvania
ROBERT T. GOLEMBIEWSKI, University of Georgia
GERALD GORDON, Cornell University
SUE M. GORDON, Ithaca College
CHADWICK HABERSTROH, University of Wisconsin-Milwaukee
DOUGLAS T. HALL, Northwestern University
RICHARD H. HALL, University of Minnesota
BO L.T. HEDBERG, University of Gothenburg
FRANK A. HELLER, Tavistock Institute of Human Relations
PAUL HIRSCH, University of Chicago
PHILLIP L. HUNSAKER, University of Wisconsin-Milwaukee
E. GERALD HURST, JR., University of Pennsylvania
EDGAR F. HUSE, Boston College
HARVEY KAHALAS, Virginia Polytechnic Institute and State University
JOHN D. KASARDA, University of North Carolina
RALPH KILMANN, University of Pittsburgh
DONALD C. KING, Purdue University
LAWRENCE W. KOZIMOR, David M. Dornbusch & Co., San Francisco
RAYMOND P. LAUER, St. Charles Boys Home, Milwaukee
SANG M. LEE, Virginia Polytechnic Institute and State University
KAREN LEGGE, University of Sheffield
ARIE Y. LEWIN, Duke University
THOMAS A. MAHONEY, University of Minnesota
SPYROS G. MAKRIDAKIS, INSEAD
ROGER MANSFIELD, Imperial College of Science and Technology
RICHARD O. MASON, U.S. National Science Foundation
ROBERT MASON, Georgia Institute of Technology
CHARLES J. McMILLAN, York University
ARLYN J. MELCHER, Kent State University
GEORGE MILKOVICH, University of Minnesota
HENRY MINTZBERG, McGill University
IAN MITROFF, University of Pittsburgh
LAWRENCE B. MOHR, University of Michigan
RICHARD R. NELSON, Yale University
RICHARD NORMANN, Scandinavian Institutes for Administrative Research, Lund
GREG R. OLDHAM, University of Illinois
ROY PAYNE, University of Sheffield
JOHANNES M. PENNINGS, Carnegie-Mellon University
CHARLES PERROW, SUNY at Stony Brook
ANDREW M. PETTIGREW, London Graduate School of Business Studies
JEFFREY PFEFFER, University of California, Berkeley
LOUIS PONDY, University of Illinois
W.L. PRICE, University of Ottawa
ERIC RHENMAN, Scandinavian Institutes for Administrative Research, Stockholm
KENDRITH M. ROWLAND, University of Illinois
DAVID P. RUTENBERG, Carnegie-Mellon University
HENRY SCHMANDT, University of Wisconsin-Milwaukee
STANLEY E. SEASHORE, University of Michigan